LESS THAN GLORY

Also by Norman Gelb

THE BRITISH
THE IRRESISTIBLE IMPULSE
ENEMY IN THE SHADOWS

LESS THAN GLORY

NORMAN GELB

G. P. Putnam's Sons / New York

 Published on the same day in Canada by General Publishing Co. Limited, Toronto.

Library of Congress Cataloging in Publication Data

Gelb, Norman.
Less than glory.

Includes index.
1. United States—History—Revolution, 1775–1783.
I. Title.
E208.G44 1984 973.3 83-17694
ISBN 0-399-12902-2

Printed in the United States of America

For Cecile

CONTENTS

Historians relate, not so much what is done, as what they would have believed.

—Benjamin Franklin

1

LESS THAN GLORY

Could I have foreseen what I have and am likely to experience, no consideration on earth should have induced me to accept this command.

—GEORGE WASHINGTON

The American Revolution—the most celebrated event in the history of the United States—is habitually made out to be something it never was. More than a score of decades have passed since the birth of the American nation, but the circumstances attending that explosive genesis are still regularly misrepresented and misunderstood. Embellishment and fabrication still distort popular impressions of what happened then and why.

The American Revolution was, for example, not a glorious upheaval only occasionally marked by bouts of anguish and suffering. It was plagued from beginning to end by misery, hardship and devastation.

The Revolution was not greeted with jubilation throughout the fledgling nation. It was a personal catastrophe for tens of thousands of Americans, many of whom were tormented by their countrymen in ways Americans would today consider cruel and barbaric.

The Revolution was not buoyed along by unshakable confidence in the ultimate triumph of the cause of liberty. Premonitions of disaster relentlessly stalked the American rebel leadership. Fearing defeat, capture and the gallows, most signers of the Declaration of Independence prudently kept their identities secret for a long time after independence was formally proclaimed.

Though many people bitterly objected to the imposition of British taxes, for most Americans the liberty and justice for which the Revolution was fought were no more than slogans. They had been just as free to speak, worship and move about before the war as they were to be afterwards—and they still would have to pay taxes, much steeper than any with which they had ever been saddled before.

In fact, the American Revolution was a muddled, sometimes chaotic, frequently tragic event which has the distinction of having been both inevitable and a fluke. There are solid reasons why it had to happen and strong evidence to show that it needn't have taken place.

The rebels ultimately gained a convincing victory. But Americans paid for it with fatalities far greater than any government of the people would today consider politically tolerable, and the revolutionary army was plagued so ceaselessly with troop shortages, discipline breakdowns, supply scarcities and mass desertions that the Revolution might have been crushed had the British enemy been less timid in the field at the beginning or if the French had not come, painfully slowly, to the rescue toward the end.

The meagerness of civilian support for the army was scandalous. "I despise my countrymen," snarled Continental Army Colonel Ebenezer Huntington, appalled at civilian indifference to the plight of his starving, half-naked troops. "I wish I could say I was not born in America."[1]

Had the Revolution not occurred, America would, of course, be a different country today. For better or worse, it probably woud be richer and bigger, embracing not only Canada but maybe even—as Benjamin Franklin once forecast—the smallish offshore kingdom known as Great Britain.

Most popular accounts of the Revolution have been cozily laundered or tidied up. They describe how men died at Bunker Hill, suffered at Valley Forge and endured against the odds elsewhere in their heroic struggle. But they also manage to concoct an overall landscape of historic splendor when, in fact, most of the component elements were heavily laced with wretchedness and grief. They transform minor successes which had only marginal impact on the course of the war into epic triumphs and turn strong-minded visionaries who were groping their way in the dark into infallible demigods.

It is understandable. Patriotism may in some cases be the last refuge of scoundrels; it is nevertheless an exhilarating, reassuring, agreeable emotion, best cultivated by magnifying the grandeur of a nation's achievements and neglecting its questionable deeds and experiences.

Not that the American Revolution can be dismissed as merely a questionable deed. It was of immense, enduring significance. It changed the course of history. In addition to being the forge on which the American nation was originally fashioned, it inspired recognition of democracy as the proper form of government for people everywhere, even for those who are still denied it. Once it had succeeded, rule by kings and tyrants, long considered natural, unavoidable and appropriate in most parts of the world, could never again be deemed respectable among people of goodwill, or tolerable by people capable of doing something about it.

By making liberty and the pursuit of happiness plausible goals, the Revolution inaugurated an era in which all individuals might aspire to, and strive for, things never before conceded to be within the grasp of ordinary folk. For that reason, it justifiably remains an exalted, illustrious occurrence in the popular imagination, particularly when flags fly and orators declaim, when drums roll and fireworks burst, at parades, parties and clambakes each Fourth of July.

Those are joyous events, bubbling with national self-esteem. There is no reason why they should not be. After all, whatever the pluses and minuses of the American Revolution, its end product was the American nation, a land which, whatever its shortcomings (which sometimes are formidable) and might-have-beens (ditto), was and is a land of hope, imagination, diversity, enterprise, freedom and opportunity.

There is, however, much more to the American Revolution than its ultimate results, its place in history and the admiration it still arouses. Whatever else it was, the Revolution was a time of agony for Americans. Like all revolutions, it brought out the worst in people as well as the best. Its countless moments of heroism, virtue and sacrifice were accompanied by equally countless acts of cruelty, selfishness, venality, small-mindedness and oppression. It was beset by political trivialities, territorial jealousies and military confusions. Like all wars, it was a shambles.

The residue of misunderstanding, neglect and even falsification of so many revolutionary matters is sustained as much by limited awareness of what actually transpired as by patriotic license. It is, for example, not commonly appreciated that while striving desperately to create, practically out of thin air, a fighting force capable of challenging the might of the British Empire, George Washington was badgered, interfered with, unsupported, and plotted against by members of Congress, fellow officers and others as devoutly revolutionary as himself, and that he regularly succumbed to bouts of blackest despair.

Though it is not widely acknowledged, Congress—much given to bickering and dickering—frequently had trouble raising a quorum to get on with the job of running the Revolution. At one stage, it was unable to reprimand one of its members because he was needed for the quorum that would do the reprimanding. "I was never so sick of anything in my life," moaned congressional delegate John Mathews of South Carolina.[2]

Patrick Henry's stirring choice of "liberty or death" in his support for the Revolution is one of the most memorable pronouncements in American history. It is, however, less often recalled that Patrick Henry's son, like thousands of other Americans, chose a third option. Scanning the bodies of the dead strewn across the battlefield after a victorious but bloody encounter with the British, Captain John Henry broke his sword into pieces, resigned his commission and retired from the war.

Tales of how the troops went hungry and barefoot as they soldiered on in the name of liberty rarely also record that it was common practice for their commissary officers to use army funds to buy provisions which they then resold to the army at inflated prices. Not a few patriots emerged from the war richer than when they went in.

For help in their struggle for liberty and justice, rebel leaders turned to the king of France, a tyrant far more despotic than the English monarch they so persuasively castigated. At one stage, they even permitted themselves to refer to Louis XVI, who was soon to be beheaded by his own enraged revolutionaries, as the "protector of the rights of mankind." That it was only a diplomatic nicety made it no less shabby for men who sent others into battle to protect those rights.

Most telling of all, despite the inspiring oratory of America's earliest patriots, the cause of independence did not even come close to having the support of an undivided people. In fact, only once in their history—during the Civil War eight-five years later which was partly the consequence of a tragic failure on the part of the revolutionaries—would differences between Americans be as widespread, profound and bitter as they were at the birth of their nation. The fiercest, cruelest battles of the war were not between Americans and British troops. They were between American rebels and Americans loyal to the British motherland. "If a stop cannot be put to these massacres," General Nathanael Greene warned, "the country will be depopulated."[3]

No hard and fast statistics are available, but support for the Revolution was very far from unanimous. The evidence indicates that at the start just as many Americans opposed the Revolution as supported it, and just as many again didn't care one way or the other—not enough to want to take sides. That they themselves were so irreversibly taking sides came almost as a surprise to leaders of the Revolution—men like Thomas Jefferson, Benjamin Franklin, George Washington and John Adams.

Only months before the Declaration of Independence, the men who would become the Founding Fathers of the United Sates of America firmly rejected suggestions that their goal was an independent nation—and they meant it. They swore undying loyalty to the British crown which was soon to be the target of their invective—and they earnestly meant that too. They wanted merely to assert and protect the rights and liberties of British Americans, which they and all other inhabitants of the colonies then were.

Even on the day the first shots of the rebellion were fired, it would have been hard to find a confessed rebel in any of the thirteen colonies which constituted the original nucleus of the American nation. They were British—an identity which they did not find objectionable—and the king of England was their king. Yet little more than a year later, the Revolution was officially proclaimed and the War of Independence was well and truly joined. It remains the most remarkable turnabout in American history.

* * *

There were convincing reasons for Britain's American colonies to seek their own way in the world. Americans were increasingly looking westward toward the immense, inviting wilderness they were already beginning to colonize and transform, rather than across the Atlantic to the motherland. Any attempt by a far-off, arrogant nation, set in its ways, to impose its will on a young, irreverent, thrusting land was bound to be futile—revolution or not.

But the issues which divided Americans into rebels, loyalists, don't-knows and don't-cares were diverse and complex. They included law-and-order, taxes for defense, religious affiliation and national identity. Some issues raised at the time probably would arouse greater controversy today.

People, for example, of the kind now committed to the peace movement would probably have sided vigorously (better redcoat than dead!) with those Americans who opposed the Revolution, seeing nothing but bloodshed and destruction in the challenge laid down to Britain's formidable military might. As the struggle wore on, more and more people had doubts about it. The famous Spirit of '76 was really the Spirit of '75. In 1775, Americans rushed to take arms against the British; by the end of 1776, the harsh realities of war had made many of them apprehensive and despondent. And the war still had seven more years to run.

People who were, at the time, conservative by inclination and who reflexively distrusted radicals—or liberals, as we call them today—generally opposed the rebellion, or finally supported it only with great reluctance. Transported back in time, their present-day conservative ideological heirs would probably react the same way. The conservative–radical divide that has been threaded through the fabric of American history had its roots in the Revolution. Conservative policies were ultimately influential in mapping out the structure of the country, but launching the War of Independence was a radical triumph to which patriots of other political persuasions grudgingly had to reconcile themselves, a fact which American conservatives today prefer to forget.

People who deplore the desecration of the environment today would undoubtedly have supported the British who, for their own reasons, sought to limit the expansion of colonial settlement and thus curb the relentless encroachment on Indian territory. This outraged American speculators—including some leading patriots—who had their eye on western real estate.

American Catholics, more secure today than they were then, would be offended by the bigotry of many revolutionary firebrands who labeled British efforts to guarantee Catholics the right to worship as they pleased a papist conspiracy and one more reason to throw off the British yoke.[4]

People who worry today about social strife would, at the time, have dreaded the consequences of a war, no matter what its goal, in which the attitudes of Americans were so sharply divided. Reverend Nicholas Collin of Philadelphia looked about him as the Revolution gathered steam and was appalled: "Everywhere distrust, fear, hatred and abominable selfishness were met with. Parents and children, brothers and sisters, wife and husband, were enemies to one another."[5] It was an exaggeration surely, by a man pained and astonished by the temper of the times, but it was not a complete fabrication.

All revolutions are minority events at first, and, as with all revolutions, a lot of people affected by the American Revolution questioned its wisdom. But whatever its subsequent significance for America and the world, some of their doubts can be seen today to have been well grounded. In fact, given a straightforward account of the circumstances which prevailed and the issues at play, a great many people living today would wonder whether the Revolution should really have taken place. Most Americans, had they lived then, like most Americans who did live then, probably would not have supported it.

The complete truth about the Revolution did not sit comfortably at the time even with many of its leaders. Charles Thomson, first secretary of the first American Congress and a dedicated revolutionary, declined to write a history of the revolutionary period. "I could not tell the truth," he explained, "without giving great offense. Let the world admire our patriots and heroes. Their supposed talents and virtues . . . , by commanding imitation, will serve the cause of patriotism and our country."[6]

Their *supposed* talents and virtues?

Was it all propaganda?
Of course it wasn't.
What was it, then?

2

THE ROOTS OF REBELLION

We are contending with the State from whence we spring, with those who were once our fathers, our guardians, our brethren, with those fleets and armies which were lately our protection . . . from tyranny and oppression.[1]

—JAMES DUANE, member of the Continental Congress

To be an American had little political significance before the Revolution. Americans then had only one national identity in common: they were British.

Some Americans were proud to be British. Most simply considered it a fact of life, of little importance except when they were challenged by foreigners—the French up in Canada and out West or the Spanish down in Florida. Until the very eve of the Declaration of Independence, there was nothing to indicate that any Americans considered being British an onerous or disagreeable imposition. For many, being part of the British Empire was a source of considerable satisfaction and reassurance.

The Virginia House of Burgesses called the dependence of the American colonies on Britain "our greatest happiness and only security." Benjamin Franklin maintained he had never "heard in any conversation from any person, drunk or sober, the least expression of a wish for a separation, or a hint that such a thing would be advantageous to America."[2] Francis Hopkinson, who was to be a signer of the Declaration of Independence (and who was, incidentally, the first American songwriter), declared, "We in America are in all respects Englishmen, notwithstanding that the Atlantic rolls her waves between us and the throne to which we all owe allegiance."

Before it gained independence, America was a geographic rather than a political entity, a name rather than a nation. There certainly was no serious suggestion that the thirteen colonies which were about to disconnect suddenly and violently from the motherland might unite. The idea was farfetched. People from Maryland were Marylanders. It set them apart from other Americans. People from Georgia were Georgians. There were Yorkers and Jerseymen and Rhode Islanders. There were Carolinians and Connecticuters. Thomas Jefferson was known to refer to Virginia as "my country." Benjamin Rush lyrically asked, "O! Pennsylvania, can the world boast of such happiness as thy sons enjoy?" And they all were British, displaying all the trappings of subjects of the king.

English was the language most of them spoke. They prayed in English. One in every four of them had been born in Britain or their parents had been born there. Most of the others were descendants of people who had earlier emigrated from Britain. English law was their law. It guaranteed them immunity from arbitrary arrest, the protection of habeas corpus, and trial by jury if charged with a crime. As their unrestrained pre-revolutionary outcry against British government misdeeds demonstrated, it also guaranteed them freedom of speech. Members of nonconformist European sects had fled to British America to escape religious persecution in their native lands and to practice their beliefs in one corner of the colonies or another. A ruling in a British American court in the colony of New York had laid the foundation of freedom of the press.

These were no trifling benefits in a world where absolute autocrats ruled just about everywhere else and where people born poor could at no time in their lives expect to attain anything but lowly status. Americans knew that. Recording his impression of

New Englanders who were loudest in their denunciation of British oppression, Johann Kalb, the Bavarian who became one of George Washington's most valued generals, said the liberties they enjoyed "swelled their pride and presumption" so much that they had become more English than the English themselves.

Americans were freer, less subject to authority, than any other people in the known world at the time. Until immediately before the Revolution, there was no more talk of British tyranny in the colonies than there was in Britain. The British—amongst whom Americans were numbered—would no more have blamed Britain for wrongs commited against them than Americans today would blame America rather than an American government for policies of which they disapproved. When complaints were made, the king's erring ministers were held responsible, not the king himself, not Britain.

The earliest defenders of American liberties against British transgressions confined themselves to charging the British government with violating English law and English practice in its dealings with the colonies. As law-abiding British Americans, they found this not only wrong but distinctly distasteful as well. Even liberty-taking, pugnacious Sons of Liberty, when they first began forcing reluctant merchants to boycott English goods until American rights were fully honored, claimed to be acting in defense of British law. They suggested that George III, "one of the best of earthly kings," owed them his thanks for their efforts to defend the British constitution against unlawful abuses by His Majesty's blundering government.

In many ways, the colonies remained clearly recognizable offshoots of the home country. English visitors to Boston were struck by how much that city, with its wharfs and warehouses, winding streets and neat rows of houses, resembled their own Bristol. Philadelphia was, after London, the second city of the British Empire. Many New England villages were not unlike villages in old England.

The inns and taverns of America were much like those dotting the English landscape. Taverns in Pennsylvania and elsewhere featured boxing, bull-baiting and similar English diversions to amuse their clientele. The old English game of quoits, from which horseshoe pitching would evolve, was popular among Americans. Like those in England, young men and boys in America played cricket and a form of rugby, which was later to be transformed into football. American clergymen regularly denounced gambling on horseraces, a popular pastime on both sides of the Atlantic.

The American gentry went fox hunting in Virginia much as the British gentry did in the English shires. Like merchants in Britain, American merchants up and down the coast systematically smuggled goods past His Majesty's locally recruited customs inspectors and tax collectors. The very names of American places evoked English imagery: Plymouth, Richmond, New London, New Hampshire, New York and, of course, New England.

American political thinkers reflected long and hard on the principles propounded by David Hume, John Locke (the ideological father of the American Revolution) and other British philosophers. American scholars thought of Shakespeare as part of their own literary heritage. Political controversy in London was studiously monitored in the cities of America, where people took sides in purely English disputations.

Leading American scientists—including botanist Alexander Garden, who gave his name to the gardenia, physicist William Wells and polymath Cadwallader Colden—were British-trained, as were many of the most prominent American doctors and lawyers. Young businessmen, like future revolutionary firebrand John Hancock, spent time in England to perfect their entrepreneurial skills. Richard Henry Lee, who was to be one of the more determined advocates of rebellion, sent his two young sons to be educated in England. Many well-to-do Americans did the same. While living in England before the war, Benjamin Franklin considered buying a home and settling down there.

Many Americans had fought as British soldiers in the French and Indian War, which ended a little more than a decade before the Revolution, and, despite the snootiness of British officers they served under, some, like George Washington, had contemplated a career in the British Army. Eleven of the twelve generals who were originally chosen to lead America's revolutionary forces had served in uniform under the king. Three of them had been born in Britain.

The uninterrupted immigration of Britons to America, where they immediately became British Americans, maintained the close links between the colonies and the motherland. There were no formalities to be undertaken to affect the transformation. Englishman Thomas Paine became one of the most forceful and effective American revolutionaries barely a year after he arrived in Pennsylvania from London. Americans went the other way too, settling in England equally without formality or ceremony, including Henry Cruger of New York, who became a member of Parliament and who survived an attempt by opponents to have him disqualified from taking his seat in the House of Commons because he was an American.

All the colonies maintained agents in London, emissaries who represented them in the British capital. Their job was to further the commercial interests of Pennsylvania or Virginia or whichever colony had commissioned them to argue its case in matters of business, law and boundary disputes with other colonies, and generally to cultivate contacts in the British government on behalf of their clients. The more skilled they were at making their way through the corridors of power in London, the better they were appreciated by their employers. They were often called upon by prominent individuals in the colonies they represented to undertake private commercial or legal assignments in England.

The fact that many of these colonial agents—mostly lawyers or merchants—thought of England as their home (some were, in fact, Englishmen) did not affect their standing with their colonial employers. Nor did it influence the way they did their jobs. It was much like a California company today retaining a Washington lobbyist to represent it with American government agencies.

Each of the colonies had closer links with England than it had with its colonial neighbors in America. Several were locked in bitter rivalries which made the prospect of union between them improbable. When settlers in remote corners of Massachusetts were plagued by a rash of Indian attacks, that colony's appeals to other colonies for assistance went unanswered. It had to rely on its own militia and the British garrison. Maryland charged import taxes on ships' cargoes arriving for delivery in neighboring Pennsylvania. New York taxed goods passing through its port bound for New Jersey.

Boundary disputes between colonies were bitter and sometimes resembled disputes between nations. When Connecticut laid claim to a part of Pennsylvania, fighting broke out between settlers from the two colonies, with the governor of Pennsylvania calling the Connecticut people worse than Indians in their ruthlessness. New York speculators tried to oust New Hampshiremen from disputed territory in what was to become Vermont, while Massachusetts had an eye on the same patch of land. The militias of Virginia and Pennsylvania were often brought by territorial squabbles to the verge of armed confrontation. Playing it safe, Virginia laid claim to western land reaching up as far as the Canadian border, crossing the claims of three other colonies. Rhode Island's boundaries, in continual dispute, were so indistinct it was suggested that the people who marked them off had decided the colony "was bounded on the north by a bramble bush, on the south by a blue jay, on the west by a hive of bees at swarming time, and on the east by five hundred foxes with firebrands tied to their tails."

When a ban on the import of British goods was implemented during the buildup to rebellion, colonies accused each other of secretly breaking the boycott. South Carolina merchants protested that shameless entrepreneurs in Georgia still smuggled in British goods and then sold them at inflated prices to colonies which had stayed true to the ban. New York was said to be trading with British merchants across the border in Canada, rather than across the Atlantic, to evade detection of the ignominious boycott-busting practices of its merchants. Others were similarly accused—not without justification.

Even within colonies, antagonisms could be intense and violent, especially—as in Pennsylvania and North Carolina—between back-country folk and residents of the fertile low-lying coastal plain where the cities and the plantations were. James Otis, one of the most forceful critics of British encroachment on American liberties, said in 1765, "Were these colonies left to themselves tomorrow, America would be a mere shambles of blood and confusion."

The prospects for harmonious union among the colonies were seen as equally remote by foreign observers. Reverend Andrew Burnaby, an English traveler, was certain there could be neither unity nor independence for America:

> Fire and water are not more heterogeneous than the different colonies. . . . Nothing can exceed the jealousy . . . which they possess in regard to each other. . . . Were they left to

> themselves, there would soon be civil war . . . while the Indians and Negroes would, with better reason, impatiently watch the opportunity of exterminating them all together.[3]

Even Thomas Jefferson had once forecast that if separated from Britain, the colonies would be at each other's throats: "One will call in France to her assistance, another Great Britain, and so we shall have all the wars of Europe brought to our own doors."[4]

As the First Continental Congress convened in Philadelphia in 1774, less than a year before the savage encounter with the redcoats at Bunker Hill, there was no suggestion of either dissolving the British connection or splicing the thirteen colonies together into one nation. The link with the motherland was unquestioned, noncontroversial, firm.

The French and Russian revolutions, when they took place, were the turbulent products of long-accumulated, irrepressible gripes and grievances, vast historical crescendoes finally reaching breaking point. The American Revolution, however, seemed an unlikely explosion, a surprise which not even its leaders could forecast or, indeed, advocate until practically the last minute.

The seeds from which both the American Revolution and the American nation sprouted were planted in American soil by two very different sorts of people: adventurers and saints. They arrived from England more than 150 years before independence, the adventurers to get rich, the saints in search of God's country. The former were risk-taking treasure-seekers; the latter, fire-eating moralists. As such, these pioneer settlers bequeathed to the American people the two most distinctive strains of what was to be the national character.

The fortune hunters arrived first. They sailed up the James River into Virginia in 1607, dropped anchor, stepped ashore and settled in. A few years later, the saints, pious Pilgrims one and all, also aiming for Virginia, reached dry land and praised the Lord at Cape Cod instead. For neither did America at first appear to be the promised land.

The one hundred twenty men of the Virginia contingent, having been lured across the Atlantic by tales of New World riches, found death instead. After six months, only fifty-three of their number had survived the ravages of disease, hunger and hostile

Indians. Despite new arrivals from England, so demoralized did the settlement become that strict military discipline had to be imposed. Like convicts, these early Americans were marched off to their chores and to church each day to the sound of a beating drum. Sir Thomas Dale, governor of the Virginia colony, dryly confessed, "Every man allmost laments himself of being here."

The introduction to America was dismal for the Pilgrims as well. Only half their number lived through the unfamiliar severity of the first Massachusetts winter. Having come from a more dreary but more moderate climate, one of them unhappily noted that the weather was "sharp and violent and subject to cruel and fierce storms." They had come to a "hideous and desolate wilderness full of wild beasts and wild men."

Nevertheless, both those British American colonies endured, recovered and ultimately prospered. Before long, the Virginia people had a charter from the king in London officially entitling them to "all Liberties, Franchises and Immunities . . . as if they had been abiding and born within this our realm of England." They thus knew their rights virtually from the beginning and no doubt would have claimed them without royal dispensation.

As for the Pilgrim Fathers, they had always been obedient only to God and their own consciences. It was defiant conviction and self-assurance that had led them across the ocean and had seen them through to the first Thanksgiving.

There was, for both, much settling down to do, studying of the terrain, coming to terms with the environment, taking root and fanning out. But the legacies of liberty and defiance handed down by the adventurers and the saints—and the questing impulses of subsequent, mostly British immigrants to the colonies in the following decades—were destined to fashion collision with authority as an unquenchable feature of the New World experience. These legacies ultimately helped transform the undisputed allegiance of British Americans to their motherland into bitter reproach, then outright rebellion.

Outbursts of greater or lesser intensity against local powers—whether elected or appointed by the king—recurred with obstinate regularity in colonial America. Not for nothing did Americans acquire a reputation in the motherland for being undisciplined, insubordinate and troublesome. Their unruliness ranged from insurrection in Virginia, where small planters rose in fury against the governor because of high taxes, low prices for their tobacco and special privileges for well-connected plantation owners, to the more subtle conspiracies of Long Island townships seeking merely to be shifted to the jurisdiction of the Connecticut colony whose ruling body was less high-and-mighty then the New York authority under whose writ they fell.

Boston was particularly susceptible to angry public demonstrations, including violent protests against the early existence of thriving houses of ill-repute in that fair city. There and in other colonial seaports, mobs formed to obstruct the off-the-street draft of merchant seamen into the British fleet. (Impressment was little more than kidnapping for slave labor at sea, and was commonly perpetrated in British ports as well.)

In New York, German immigrant Jacob Leisler led an insurrection against local authorities whom he and his followers believed to be engaged in a "popish plot" against the predominantly Protestant inhabitants of that city. When western-Pennsylvania frontiersmen, angered by the failure of Pennsylvania authorities to protect them against hostile Indians, marched on Philadelphia, even Quakers there armed themselves against these enraged backwoodsmen. In prerevolutionary North Carolina, hardly a decade passed without some group or other resorting to violence to underscore or redress a grievance. Just a few years before the Revolution, bands of back-country Carolina farmers and frontiersmen called Regulators (they aimed to "regulate" legal improprieties out of existence) rebelled against corrupt local sheriffs, tax collectors and court officials.

These incidents were never specifically anti-British in character or intention. Indeed, many of the Regulators, for example, later fought on the side of the British against the Revolution. Nevertheless, as displays of restlessness and license, they undermined the control and authority that were part and parcel of Pax Britannica. Only the most deluded popinjay at the royal court in London could think of Americans, of whatever colony, as submissive colonials.

There were, however, more fundamental factors in the process of disconnection. After all, disobeying authority was not a practice altogether remote from the English experience. The English had even beheaded their own king in the seventeenth century, long before the French thought of so spectacular a gesture. But Britain's American offspring had developed a personality of their own. In the process of making America their home, the colonists had compiled an extensive catalogue of distinctive ways and attitudes.

Class divisions did persist in the cities of the North and the plantation domains of the South. As elsewhere, there were rich and poor, with the former enjoying privileges denied the latter, and doing what they could to perpetuate them. There were recurring suggestions that a hereditary American aristocracy be established to distinguish between people of quality and those of a meaner sort. The Continental Congress would later consider (and spurn) a proposal that officers' commissions be marketable to guarantee that the army would be officered by "gentlemen," which meant those who could afford to buy officers' ranks. But class divisions in colonial America were far less rigid and far less effective than those which plagued the British and still do.

Even though it did not usually signify wealth and comfort, widespread ownership of land gave Americans a self-regard not duplicated by ordinary people in other places at the time. It was not easily shaken by the futile delusions of would-be American aristocrats. The pioneer mentality of the country, the leveling impact of life on the frontier, opportunities to alter personal circumstances, and the Pilgrim heritage of equality for all under God, kept Americans from being fixed immutably on different rungs of the ladder of society.

Success stories were already common. Social mobility, for which America would one day become famous, was already a reality. Rich, well-connected families, like the Dulanys of Maryland, the Livingstons of New York and the Belchers of Massachusetts, had all stemmed from origins which were modest almost within living memory. Jacob Lamb, a wealthy merchant who was to be a general in the revolutionary army, was the son of a thief who had been banished from England. It would have been impossible in Britain for an Englishman of humble origins to reach as exalted a position in his own country as Benjamin Franklin, the son of a candle and soap maker, or Patrick Henry, who started his career at the age of fifteen as a clerk in a country store, did in America even before the Revolution. For the gifted, for the ambitious, for the determined, doors could open and things could happen in the colonies, regardless of what had gone before.

To foreign visitors, the unique geographical mobility of Americans was a constant wonder. They readily shifted about to seize new opportunities, tap new lands, build new homes or simply abandon disagreeable or unrewarding situations. An English visitor marveled, "It is scarcely possible in any part of the continent to find a man . . . who has not changed his farm and his residence many different times." Commenting on American restlessness, Lord Dunmore said, "Wandering about seems engrafted in their nature. . . . They . . . forever imagine that the lands further off are still better than those upon which they are already settled."[5]

The contrast with the attitudes, inclinations and possibilities of people back in Britain was glaring, particularly to those who had only recently crossed the ocean as immigrants. Americans were more daring, more questing than their cousins on the far side of the Atlantic. They radiated self-confidence and self-respect.

Back in Britain, just embarking on the industrial revolution that would change the world, there was an atmosphere of nervousness, anxiety and futility for ordinary folk, understandable when long-established ways are challenged by sweeping transformations. The drift of the population there was from the countryside where most people lived but where jobs were growing increasingly scarce to the factories and shipyards of the cities and to dismal mining towns. The grime, sweat and toil of the great Machine Age was becoming a feature of the life of the English workingman.

With countryside real estate long before parceled out between the self-perpetuating aristocracy and gentry, whatever opportunities there were for new wealth or achievement in England were in the swelling cities which Charles Dickens portrayed with such devastating grimness. In the American colonies, on the other hand, though opportunities also existed in the cities, where fortunes were indeed being made, the primary attraction for immigrants was the wide open spaces, the great inviting wilderness which imbued a person with a sense of his own worth and disinclined him to bow his head to anyone.

Preformed ideas and attitudes, imported from abroad, also

contributed significantly to molding the colonial imagination. Immigrants from Britain arrived attuned to the theory of equality before the law and the practice of individual liberty. The many who arrived from Ulster (commonly called the Scotch-Irish) were, then as now, proud and obstinate. A prayer of theirs is said to have beseeched God, "Grant that I may always be right, for Thou knowest I am hard to turn."*

Scottish Highlanders, many of them driven from their Scottish homes by aristocratic landlords claiming the land for sheep grazing, were sturdy upland folk who gravitated toward America's frontierland where they need not fear having to cope with would-be masters on their new home ground. Independent-minded, hardworking Welsh farm people also headed for the fringes of colonial settlement, while people from Ireland (still part of Great Britain) made for both town and country in the colonies.

The Germans, the largest non-British contingent, were mostly members of dissident religious sects like the Mennonites, the Moravian Brethren and the Schwenkenfelders who had fled for sanctuary in America because they were determined to do things and worship God their own nonconformist way. Among the German settlers there were also many who, like immigrants from France, Switzerland and other countries, had come to escape poverty, war and military service in their native lands. The half-million blacks in America at the time of the Revolution were almost all slaves and had, of course, not arrived voluntarily.

Hardy and self-reliant, resourceful and enterprising, colonial Americans no longer needed the guidance of the British motherland. But revolution had until then played no part in molding them into the distinctive people they had become. They had borrowed from the British whatever they had found useful and agreeable and had rejected whatever did not suit their tastes or aspirations.

If there had been variations in the events leading up to independence—if the more farseeing politicians who had recently been in control of the British government had still been in power, if the views of all British Americans could have been surveyed

---

* A foretaste of things to come: Many Protestant immigrants from Ulster who supported the Revolution at the beginning developed doubts about its merits when Catholic France came to the aid of the revolutionaries.

and brought to bear on the situation, if even dedicated rebels could have foreseen the wretchedness of the war, or if they could have anticipated how long it would last and how little Americans then living would gain from its consequences—there would have been no Revolution, not in 1776 and probably not for a long time afterward.

3

THE ROAD TO WAR

The government of England was, in the main, a gentle government, much as our fathers complained of it. Her yoke was easy and her burden was light.

—SENATOR GEORGE FRISBIE HOAR of Massachusetts, 1901[1]

The belief that the Revolution was an uprising of the American people against British tyranny is both gratifying and a fantasy. British encroachments on American rights were very real. They were also persistent enough to inspire rebel leaders to enduring insights into the meaning of freedom. But, in effect, those British misdeeds were vexations at worst, botherations, having only marginal impact on the way of life of Americans or on the prosperity of the American colonies in the decade before the Revolution.

No wholesale brutal suppression of freedom was involved; no arbitrary arrests or incarcerations; no grinding poverty imposed by a foreign power or a privileged elite. Indeed, it was only a privileged American elite which bore the brunt of British transgressions. Very few Americans were even remotely subjected to the heavy weight of tyranny about which advocates of rebellion expostulated so forcefully.

Immigrants continued to flow in from Europe to experience the wonders of freedom and opportunity available in British America as nowhere else. Despite commercial restrictions imposed by the British authorities, the economy of the colonies flourished. Despite claims that the liberties of Americans were being systematically extinguished, criticism of British perpetrations continued to be vociferous and unrestrained. Whatever changes were being called for, there was no feeling that the situation was sufficiently disagreeable to provoke a major upheaval.

Men who would later find themselves orchestrating the Revolution were genuinely riled by suggestions that when they objected to the policies of the British government, independence was what they really had in mind. Joseph Hewes of North Carolina was not pretending when, in the summer of 1775, he said, "We do not want to be independent. We want no revolution. . . . We are loyal subjects of our present most gracious Sovereign."[2] But within a year, he was one of the many Americans who thought differently. Within that year, the motherland was transformed into the enemy, and George III, so recently deemed "our most gracious Sovereign," had become a hated tyrant. It was a remarkable reversal. America was an impetuous place even then.

At first, the French rather than the British had been the enemy. French settlements in Canada and Louisiana had been linked by a chain of outposts—Fort Niagara, Detroit, Fort Duquesne (Pittsburgh), Kaskaskia in what is now Illinois, Vincennes in Indiana, Fort Rosalie (Natchez) and others. These wilderness sanctuaries had been hacked out of the forest not merely to establish a French presence in the heartland of the New World. They were also the vanguard of what France hoped to fashion into a North American empire of its own. That empire was to straddle the sprawling American West and, in due time, if circumstances permitted, was to control the thriving British colonies on the Atlantic coast.

These French projections were, of course, anathema to the British. Despite the rambunctiousness of their inhabitants, the American colonies were the most prized of Britain's overseas territories. Incalculable riches were to be extracted from America—

wheat, rice, tobacco, animal skins, timber, perhaps even gold. There was also the pride and glory of keeping the Union Jack flying in the New World over regions which, in all likelihood, would expand and grow increasingly lucrative with the passing of time. Not to meet and demolish the cross-ocean challenge from England's traditional cross-Channel rival was unthinkable to the king, his ministers and Parliament.

To Americans, French hopes and ambitions were equally unpalatable. They amounted to a threat laid down by a foreign culture, a strange language, a religion commonly despised, a genuinely tyrannical monarchy, and a people who retained working alliances with Indian tribes prone to savage assaults on American frontier settlements.

"What will become of us God only knows," moaned Reverend Jonathan Edwards of Massachusetts at the prospect of French success. What would become of their territorial ambitions was particularly worrying to Americans who hungered after land beyond the official western boundaries of their colonies. Virginia, for example, made claims to land ownership all the way to the Pacific, though no one even imagined how far away that "South Sea" might be. The only certainty was that the French had no right to stand in the way.

Americans, therefore, knew they had much at stake in the confrontation with the French in which, after first scoring impressive gains of the kind which so alarmed Reverend Edwards, France was decisively vanquished. But it was never a foregone conclusion. At times, the British and their British American auxiliaries seemed on their way to disaster and could well have been beaten—as twenty-two-year-old Colonel George Washington realized when he and the Virginia militia under his command were forced to surrender in 1754 to the French at Fort Necessity, in the wilds of western Pennsylvania near where Uniontown stands today. "New France" might well have survived and prospered clear across western America, with consequences for the British colonies, American lifestyles and world history which are intoxicating to contemplate.

But it didn't happen that way. The peace treaty of 1763—a mere thirteen years before the Declaration of Independence—ended the French and Indian War and, with it, the foreign challenge to British America. Britain's victory, enthusiastically celebrated in the cities and towns of America, brought much relief and comfort to the colonies. It also set the stage for the rebellion of Americans against their British protectors and against their king.

A people in a hurry even then, and already addicted to the sort of introspection and self-pulse-taking which obsesses them still, Americans wasted no time in seizing upon developments to reexamine their attitudes toward themselves and the world about them. They quickly concluded they no longer needed a British military presence in their midst.

The redcoats had done their job with admirable finality. Not only was the French threat eliminated once and for all, but the colonists were now confident they could manage without external backup in dealing with hostile Indians whom they had routed in many rough-and-tumble engagements during the conflict. The link with Britain, the protective Britannic embrace, was expendable. The colonies could survive without it. They had come of age.

Nevertheless, they displayed no desire to break the British connection. Loyalty to the crown had always been an undemanding and, in many ways, a rewarding aspect of the American heritage. It gave a calming sense of proportion to antipathies and rivalries between colonies and regions. In this headstrong, buoyant, restless land, it gave colonists a sense of stability, continuity and national identity. Philadelphian John Dickenson said, "Torn from the body to which we are united by religion, liberty, laws, affections, relations, language and commerce, we must bleed at every vein."[3]

Preparations for that surgical break were, however, put in motion soon after the French challenge had been met and obliterated. Some among those who led the way would later repudiate the Revolution. Some would even do what they could to crush it. But the catalyst was the same for those who were going to draw back from the edge as for those who would advance step by unforeseen step toward open rebellion: the British government's folly and narrowness of perception which permitted rebels to contend that Americans were being oppressed when in fact they were only being badgered and pestered.

* * *

With, as the Declaration of Independence points out, liberty and the pursuit of happiness involved, it seems frivolous to trace the American Revolution back instead to bills of lading, legal documents, newspapers and such stuff. The "Stamp Tax" levied on those items a decade before the Revolution was the first major British tax in the colonies. The reaction to it, while itself falling short of revolution, was violent, bitter and contagious—not because the tax was effectively administered (it wasn't), or because it lasted long on the books (it didn't), or because Americans were seriously affected by it (they weren't). It was the very idea of the offending tax which touched off the storm that was the overture to out-and-out rebellion.

It had cost the Treasury in London a fortune to finance defense of the colonies against the French and to confront France's imperial gropings elsewhere in the world. Trying to balance their books, British ministers couldn't see why Americans shouldn't shoulder part of the expense of administering the British Empire, especially since they were beneficiaries of His Majesty's government's benevolent expenditures. It was, however, an obligation which few colonists were inclined to recognize, and fewer still prepared to honor, not when they had no say in the matter, and not with British merchants extracting substantial profits from colonial trade, thereby indirectly already taxing Americans.

The requirement that people in the colonies should nevertheless be subject to British taxes inflamed the American imagination, as the suspicions of Alexander Hamilton would soon indicate:

> Perhaps before long your tables, chairs and platters, and dishes, and knives and forks, and everything else would be taxed. Nay, I don't know but that they would find means to tax you for every child you got, and for every kiss your daughters received from their sweethearts; and God knows, that would soon ruin you.[4]

Most disconcerted by the Stamp Tax were lawyers, merchants, shipowners, newspaper publishers (a dangerous breed to antagonize) and others most directly affected by it. But throughout America in 1765 it became a focus of a much wider fury, unleashed by the insinuation that Parliament in London could tax the colonies any way it liked, anytime it wanted.

The rate of the tax was not the issue. Regular taxes levied by local authorities in the normal course of events were more of a burden to the average taxpaying British American. Just like today, people in the bigger cities—Philadelphia, New York, Boston—felt they were short-changed, not receiving as much feedback from local assessments as less densely populated up-country or down-country districts.

At the same time, people in outlying communities complained that, considering the risks they took to tame the hinterland, taxes squeezed out of them by their local governments were extortionate and corruptly assessed. Tavern keepers, artisans and others whose limited landholdings might have given them unfair advantages when property taxes were reckoned were, like self-employed people today, subject to specially formulated assessments which they considered prejudicial.

In comparison, proposed British taxes were modest for most Americans affected by them. Complaints about them were out of proportion to the damage they could do. Nevertheless, trying to compel Americans to stomach the tax on their legal documents, newspapers, etc., was to prove of enduring significance.

Complex arguments were devised by learned American jurists who pointed out in great detail how the tax was both improper and unsound under English law. Such a response was in keeping with British American traditions and practices but was unlikely to have much impact on the financially hard-pressed British government. However, the activities of the Sons of Liberty, new upon the scene but the wave of the future, should have taught the king and Parliament a lesson. They didn't, and because they didn't the British were ultimately sent packing.

The Sons of Liberty were informal fraternities which sprang spontaneously into existence at the time of the Stamp Tax to challenge British high-handedness—not because it was British, but because it was high-handed. There were Sons of Liberty protest meetings at which angry voices sometimes edged ominously close to treason against the motherland. There were menacing Sons of Liberty torchlight processions. There were Sons of Liberty houndings of government officials. Respected senior servants of the crown in America were made to scamper like frightened rabbits down side streets and alleyways to escape the less than respectful attentions of rampaging mobs. Some barely escaped serious beatings. Some didn't escape at all. Some had their homes wrecked and their property destroyed.

The men appointed to serve the crown as Stamp Tax officials were Americans. (The British generally tried to employ local personnel to help collect local revenue in colonial territories. It was safer.) Before the popular backlash against the tax was kindled, there had been a stampede in the colonies for appointments to the Stamp Tax service. These were well-paid, high-status, senior civil-service jobs, requiring little exertion.

Prominent colonials used their influence to secure positions for friends. Benjamin Franklin did not like the tax, but he put in a good word anyway for an old crony and political ally, John Hughes, for the post of Pennsylvania stamp master. The favor soon proved to be no act of kindness. Little subtlety was evident in the advice Hughes was publicly given to withdraw from the job. There were threats in abundance, mixed with imaginative curses. A handbill distributed in the streets of Philadelphia was explicit:

> *Grant heaven that he may never go without*
> *The Rheumatism, Itch, the Pox, or Gout.*
> *May he be hamper'd with some ugly Witch,*
> *And dye at last in some curst foulsome Ditch.*
> *Without the Benefit of Psalms or Hymnes,*
> *And Crowds of Crows devour his rotten Limbs.*[5]

Rather than risk such a fate, Hughes resigned his commission. In Maryland, chief stamp distributor Zachariah Hood took a quick look at himself hanged in effigy and hurried far out of reach of local Sons of Liberty. In Rhode Island, Governor Samuel Ward chose to leave town to avoid having to cope with Stamp Tax rioters. In Boston, Stamp Tax administrator Andrew Oliver resigned after he had both been hanged in effigy and had his house ransacked. New York's Lieutenant Governor Cadwallader Colden (the distinguished scientist referred to earlier) was driven by a mob to take refuge aboard a British warship when he sought to implement the tax. In many places, mob victims, peering around in panic for officers of the law to rescue them, spotted local sheriffs in the crowds cheering on their attackers.

Prevailing economic conditions helped fuel the bitter reaction to the Stamp Tax. At the time, the colonies were in trouble. The boom stimulated by the French and Indian War had fizzled out, and the prosperity which immediately preceded the Revolution had not yet materialized. During this demoralizing slump, bankruptcies abounded. Creditors squeezed debtors. Real-estate values collapsed. Things were bad enough without colonial taxpayers being required to bow to the insult and injury the British blithely sought to impose.

But also reacting forcefully to the tax were people who would never have been deprived of so much as a farthing by it. Among them were many "mechanics" (laborers) and artisans thrown out of work by the slump, as well as the poor and rootless of the cities, nursing grievances that had nothing to do with contracts or bills of lading. Their fury was easily aroused. But they were not necessarily the prime movers of violent antitax eruptions. Prominent in the crowds of angry protesters were men who ordinarily deplored mayhem and disorder and normally did what they could to prevent it. So said William Gordon, a contemporary chronicler:

> The mob consisted not of mere rabble, but were composed much of independent freemen and freeholders. . . . Merchants, assemblymen, magistrates, &c., united directly or indirectly in the riots, and without their influence and instigation the lower class of inhabitants would have been quiet; but great pains were taken to rouse them to action.[6]

Leading New York politician and landowner William Livingston was closely linked to the Sons of Liberty in his colony. William Allen, son of the chief justice of Pennsylvania, led an antitax mob in Philadelphia. In South Carolina, Henry Laurens, later to be president of the Continental Congress, recognized some of the most distinguished local citizens, poorly disguised, in a mob that had broken into a house in search of a Stamp Tax official. Elsewhere too, many among the well-to-do, law-abiding men of rank were not averse to direct action to make the tax unenforceable.

Even among those Americans who deplored the excesses of the

mobs, there were few who thought the Stamp Act justified. Pillars of the community, men of position and influence, spoke out strongly against it. They included many who were fundamentally submissive to British statute and law and who would later be driven by the Revolution to flee to England. They declined to join in labeling the tax the dirty work of malicious mischief makers in London, but they urged Parliament to reconsider this violation of the rights of British Americans.

So extensive and vehement was the reaction to the Stamp Tax that the British were compelled to conclude that it was a mistake. The tax simply could not be collected in the obstreperous colonies. Instead of pressing ahead with it, in a statesmanlike display of common sense Parliament withdrew it, a prudent act which gratified Americans profoundly. There was little gloating at this victory. Good had triumphed over evil, and people were prepared to let bygones be gone. In some places, repeal of the tax and King George's birthday were celebrated simultaneously. A wave of renewed affection for the motherland swept the colonies. Justice had been done. It was, after all, no bad thing to be British.

However, though it was not apparent at the time, historic precedents had been set. Some Americans had been violently abused and silenced by other Americans because they had been prepared to obey a British law. Nine colonies—including some which entertained bitter grievances against each other—had sent delegates to a Stamp Tax Congress in New York, a gathering called to defend the "rights and privileges of the British American colonists."

Most important of all was a lesson the Founding Fathers never fully appreciated: the British government had been forced to climb down by a vigorous display of American determination, *short of war.* There had been unpleasantness. But no towns had been put to the torch. No armies had been sent into battle. There had been no horrific massacres. No men froze, hungered and died in the ranks. It had created no widows, no orphans. No irreparable hatreds had been stirred between Americans. None had been driven into exile. It had been a historic, practically painless triumph for American independence—to soon forgotten.

When confronted with the determined, sustained resistance of the king's loyal American subjects, the British government had backed down. It couldn't afford not to. On the other hand, when later challenged by a full-scale armed rebellion, as an imperial power with a proud military tradition, Britain couldn't do otherwise than call out its army and navy.

The stillborn Stamp Tax was, of course, not the last bid by the British to assert control over the unruly colonies. In the years leading up to the Revolution, other impositions were conjured up in London by the king's ministers. Some were more provocative than others, but none had a critical bearing on the economy or way of life in the colonies. Organized reaction to them was sometimes strong, sometimes slight, depending on who had to pay a price for them or who was stirred to outrage in other ways. But verbal protest was invariably bitter. Unlike the mainland British, British Americans were not given to understatement. The objectives, the methods and even (horror of horrors!) the authority of the British government were regularly called into question. Hyperbole and howls of anguish filled the columns of the colonial press.

As a foretaste of the jingo compulsions that were to become embedded in American press practices,[7] the *Newport Mercury* wailed that British measures threatened to deprive Americans of their "rights and privileges, drain us suddenly of our cash, occasion an entire stagnation of trade and discourage every kind of industry, and involve us in the most abject slavery." The *New Hampshire Gazette* warned that British measures could be "fatal to almost all that is dear to us." Americans, it was said, were being made "absolutely dependent for the air we breathe and the water we drink" upon uncaring men living in luxury an ocean away. It was said the colonists were being allowed no more control over their own affairs than were their cattle. They were compared to the Israelites in Egypt, at the mercy of cruel taskmasters. Comparisons were always to ancient history; never to French peasants, Russian serfs, English factory drudges or any other people then living who, unlike Americans, were genuinely downtrodden.

While some people counseled against excessive passion and hasty conclusions, newspaper publishers in the colonies were quick to discover that excessive passion and hasty conclusions did wonders for paid circulation. The number of profitable newspapers in the colonies increased strikingly in the ten years leading up to the Revolution. The American hunger for sensationalized news coverage was evident even then.

The sequence of objectionable British decrees was meat and potatoes to an enterprising, imaginative editor. Americans had been instructed by Parliament on what they were forbidden to manufacture or export (in competition with British-made goods) and that they were required to buy most of their imported goods from British sources. That these restrictions had little effect on the economy of the colonies did little to tone down cries of outrage.* (James Madison was to complain that the British monopolized American trade two years after independence had been won far more than they did before the Revolution.)

A British tax on tea was dismissed by one loyal British American as insignificant, costing him the equivalent of "a bushel of flax seed once in thirty-three years. Ridiculous!" But that tax provoked vehement protests, as did the British ban on the scramble for Indian land west of the Appalachians. That ban was meant to discourage Indian uprisings which might require the costly deployment of redcoats for frontier duty. Like frustrated property developers blocked by zoning laws, land speculators were incensed, though the ban was only meant to be temporary. It was against British interests to block further colonial expansion westward. In any case, the prohibition was not enforceable. Americans were too irrepressible, too unsubmissive and too restless to be barred from the rest of America by a boundary line imposed on them in far-off London.

Disagreeable as all these irritations were, and no matter how persistent were the cries of protest they aroused, none generated fundamental disenchantment with the motherland. None provoked as vigorous or sustained an uproar as the abortive Stamp Tax. No matter what the British decreed, Americans continued to find ways to pursue their own interests rather than those of the British Empire.

Nevertheless, in their furious reaction to the Stamp Tax, the colonies had skated very close to the rim of rebellion. Without realizing the significance at the time, they had tasted British

* "If parliamentary regulations did sometimes tend to cramp American commercial opportunities, the colonists were apt to ignore the restrictions."—Arthur M. Schlesinger, *The Colonial Merchants and the American Revolution*, 17.

blood and some Americans had found it very palatable. They would be back for more.

The wrath of the rebels at Britain's fumbling attempts to dominate and control America was genuine and heartfelt. The bid to impose ordinances and edicts on the colonies seemed very much like what their history books and philosophical tracts portrayed as old-fashioned tyranny. From time to time, suggestions were floated that the colonies might right the balance by being represented in Parliament. But as a small minority in the House of Commons, Americans would at best have been curiosities, Yankee-Doodles-come-to-town. They would still have felt themselves to be at the mercy of British wants and whims. The time had come for a more basic change.

But in singling out the British as the butt of their campaign for democratic liberation, rebels were being sanctimoniously selective. Democratic practices in their own colonial assemblies, which were much more susceptible to their influence, could hardly have borne the close scrutiny of anyone genuinely determined to promote government by consent of the governed.

Southern legislatures were for the most part run for and by plantation owners and would continue to be their domain for some time to come. Only six percent of the white population of Virginia owned enough property to have the right to vote. In New York, a self-perpetuating cabal of lawyers, within which differences were mostly personal rather than political, had long contrived to run the assembly. An unchanged group of local dignitaries had been in control in New Hampshire for many years and showed no readiness to relinquish its commanding position. It was estimated that about two percent of the population of Philadelphia had the right to vote. Town meetings which ran Boston were setups for control by demagogues. Sixteen percent of the population had the right to vote in Massachusetts, but only one in four who were entitled to do so actually exercised that right. (Ironically, after the war, only three percent of the state's population voted, despite improved democratic procedures.) As the rebellion unfolded, patriotic local committees throughout the colonies, which took upon themselves the power to make and enforce rules and regulations, rarely allowed themselves to be distracted by having people vote for or against them in the communities over which they presided.

Such specifics did not overly concern rebel leaders as they started down the road to revolution. They did not intend to turn their world upside down. Their goal at that stage was merely to end British intrusions in American affairs. They wanted home rule for the colonies within the British Empire. And despite their exasperation at repeated British shenanigans, Americans had increasingly been achieving exactly that!

Colonial assemblies had long been chipping away at British rule. They had largely gained control over their own budgets and expenditures. In many of the colonies, they were well on their way toward totally muzzling the influence of the crown's official local representatives, reducing them to figureheads dependent on assembly votes even for their salaries. Parliament in London had been obliged by American noncompliance to eat humble pie and withdraw some of its impositions, or watch them waste away through neglect. Though the British were trying to claw back some of the authority they had shed, a relentless evolution of independent authority in America was taking place. Before long, it would have gained the colonies almost as much independence through obstinacy and persistent erosion as they gained through the martyrdom and suffering of tens of thousands of Americans.

The simple facts were that Britain was not a tyranny and Americans were not subjugated. The complicated fact was that Britain was burdened with a government of limited perception and subtlety at a time when the colonies had produced a corps of proud, defiant, determined, articulate leaders who spoke of justice and dreamed of a political paradise on earth, a nation of virtuous citizens governing themselves in peace and harmony by common consent.

The more cautious of the colonists warned of the hazards ahead if the challenge to British authority was overly rash. John Dickinson, neither a toady nor a coward, but distinctly worried, urged his fellow Americans to practice restraint: "Let us behave like dutiful children who have received unmerited blows from a beloved parent. Let our complaints speak . . . the language of affection and veneration."

Though the Revolution was then just a few short years away,

and though the mulishness of the British continued to arouse much resentment in the colonies, Americans generally did, in fact, draw back and relax. An improved economic climate helped spawn and sustain a softened mood. The bustle of reviving ports testified to American commercial enterprise which already accounted for trade equivalent to one third that of Britain, the greatest maritime nation on earth. American shipyards hummed with activity, ceaselessly churning out vessels for both British and American traders.

The colonies had already established one of the world's great fishing industries. The same British codes and practices which restricted aspects of American commerce offered American businessmen the substantial benefits of protected markets elsewhere in the empire. British intrusions into American affairs were unquestionably disagreeable. Had America at the time already developed a more sophisticated economy, and could those intrusions have been enforced, they would have caused much damage and disruption. As it was, they did not. Suggestions that Britain was strangling the economy of the colonies were hardly credible.

The Boston Massacre in 1770, traditionally judged to be the first violent act of the War of Independence, was nothing of the sort. It was a minor incident, not much different from other minor incidents between British troops and Americans in other places where redcoats were garrisoned.

Nursing a sentiment that would cause George Washington much grief, the colonists never felt comfortable in the presence of standing armies. Nevertheless, men who would later lead the Revolution were among those who condemned the ruffians who had baited a single British sentry in Boston and then provoked the troops who came to his rescue into firing by bombarding them with stones. Five men died, but John Adams successfully defended the British soldiers in court, getting murder charges against them reduced to manslaughter. Despite emotive accounts in the newspapers ("The blood of our brethren . . . ," "The groans of the dying . . . ," "The mangled bodies of the dead . . . "), Adams had few illusions about the men who had been victims of the "massacre" and who were transformed into martyrs by the press:

> We have been entertained with a great variety of phrases to avoid calling this sort of people a mob. Some called them shavers, some called them geniuses. The plain English is they were probably a motly rabble of saucy boys, Negroes, mullatoes, Irish teagues, and outlandish Jack-tars and why we should scruple to call such a set of people a mob, I cannot conceive, unless the name is too respectable for them.

A lot of Americans were uneasy about the implications of mob action in Boston. That "capital of sedition" was increasingly seen as a hotbed of irresponsible mayhem. Merchants and landowners were particularly worried. A New York newspaper reflected their concern: "It is high time a stop was put to mobbing, without which property will soon be very precarious."

The backlash went further than just talk. The leaky embargo on British imports, patched together by the colonies to force Britain to behave in its dealings with America, collapsed altogether amidst a welter of recriminations between the colonies, each of which feared the others were benefiting from its own increasingly pointless sacrifices. Efforts to sway the king's ministers to be more reasonable and more responsive to the wishes of Americans were commandeered by moderates who were convinced the English would be more amenable to sensible argument than to the excesses of hotheads, hooligans and rabble-rousers. After all, prominent Englishmen—Lord Chatham, for example, and Edmund Burke—were sternly lecturing their colleagues in Parliament on the iniquities and dangers of mistreating the colonies. Merchants in London and Bristol, fearing the collapse of transatlantic trade, warned against pushing Americans too far. Agents in England of the individual colonies did their best to impress upon influential Englishmen the danger of the course of action their government seemed bent on taking.

It was true that the king's ministers felt obliged not to appear timid in the face of American defiance. But governments and their policies came and went in England (pro-American Chatham had only recently been prime minister), and, despite the abuse soon to be heaped on him, the king was neither stupid nor wicked. It was true that he had no intention of bowing to American impudence. However, in the prelude to the Revolution, intentions rarely resembled what followed. At that stage, for example, not even Samuel Adams and his fellow conspirators in Boston, for all their defiant oratory, were yet thinking of independence. The charade in 1773 in which those conspirators, masquerading as Indians, chucked cargoes of British tea overboard into Boston Harbor was a protest against the Tea Tax rather than an act of Revolution.

That Boston Tea Party, now celebrated as a great patriotic event, aroused considerable disapproval in the colonies. George Washington feared that it would provoke severe British retaliation. Benjamin Franklin and others urged that the jettisoned tea be paid for. In some towns, adverse reaction to the Tea Party led patriotic Committees of Correspondence to dissolve themselves because it was said their activity might encourage similar acts of anarchy and confusion.

Though welcomed in England, such sentiments were not enough to calm the fury there over what was seen as unabashed vandalism. Boston had to be punished, and punishment was not long in coming. The Boston radicals were said to have gone too far; now it was the turn of the British to do the same. By decree of the government in London, the port of Boston was closed. The city was put under martial law and was, in effect, occupied by British troops. The British military commander was empowered to commandeer the homes of Bostonians. It was rash. It was excessive. It was, finally, undeniably an arbitrary, tyrannical act. (It was also a heavy drain on the British Treasury and not all to the liking of British merchants whose trade with Boston was abruptly discontinued.)

The British were convinced other Americans would agree that Boston got only what it deserved, and some did feel that way. But this blind act of suppression aroused intense alarm throughout British America, generating greater unity than the Boston conspirators could ever have hoped for. It seemed suddenly evident that if such extreme retribution could be meted out to Boston, it could be meted out to any of the other colonies as well when the British felt they were stepping out of line.

Indignation and bitterness, much toned down since the Stamp Tax turmoil, reawakened with a vengeance. Patriots mounted platforms in every American town and city to vow that Boston would not stand alone. A gathering of leading Philadelphians resolved that the closing of the port of Boston was "dangerous to the liberties of the British colonies." Moderates, still putting their trust in English law, rebuked the British government for transgressing against it. Freeholders in Albemarle County, Virginia, joined in declaring that "all such assumptions of unlawful power" were "dangerous to the right of the British empire in general." As an act of solidarity, food was donated everywhere to be shipped to Bostonians now that their normal sea supply routes had been severed and, if the newspapers were to be believed, now that they were subject to the heartless whims of the occupation army.

A major clash was now unavoidable. Deploying troops where they are unwelcome inevitably extends and intensifies any wrangle. The garrison based in Boston had to be protected from external threats in the surrounding countryside, which boiled in indignation at the British military presence. When word filtered back that rebel arms which might be used against the forces of the king were stored not far away, the British commander dispatched troops to search them out and render them useless. Thus, in April 1775, the detachment of redcoats sent to Concord on just such a mission tangled on the way with Massachusetts irregulars who had congregated at Lexington, without a clear idea of what they were meant to do. In fact, the first shots that day were fired in confusion by redcoats at the outnumbered Minutemen after they were already obeying a British command that they remove themselves from Lexington Green, where they had gathered to face the tough-looking British troopers.

The shock of actually being shot back at by an assortment of unmilitary rustics when they reached Concord down the road confused the redcoats still further. It also cost them casualties, as did the sniping at them by the Minutemen when they scrambled in unaccustomed disorder back toward Boston after partly fulfilling their Concord mission and after, without knowing it, having touched off the War of Independence.

Remarkably, there still was no call for independence. American irregulars had hounded the redcoats back to Boston. Stories of atrocities allegedly committed by the king's troops at Lexington and Concord circulated throughout the colonies. Thousands of furious New Englanders converged on Boston to lay siege to the thousands of British soldiers in the city and force them out.

But, though the actions of the British government and the British military commander were unreservedly condemned, reaffirmations of allegiance to the crown were sounded throughout the colonies. It was clear to Americans that something had gone dreadfully wrong and had to be put right. The British had to be made to back away once more—more convincingly than they had done earlier. But casting loose from the motherland was still not deemed a solution worthy of consideration.

The Continental Congress had been convened a few months earlier, in the autumn of 1774, to see what could be done to guarantee American liberties *and the harmony of the British Empire.* When, after Lexington and Concord, it chose George Washington to command the American forces, Washington still referred to the British troops with whom he was sent to tangle as the "ministerial army," thus absolving the king of any blame for the Boston foolishness. The first flag the Americans flew in the rebellion bore a Union Jack as well as stripes to indicate that the aggrieved colonies were still British. A chaplain of troops ready to take on the redcoats in mortal combat included the usual prayer for the well-being of the king in his daily service.

All that would soon change. Blindly, the British did nothing to sustain and encourage the underlying faith of the colonists in their British American identity. British government intransigence made a climb-down by the rebels brandishing their rage outside Boston, and by all Americans who sympathized with them, impossible. And a new factor, Thomas Paine's *Common Sense*, was introduced upon the scene.

Thomas Paine had not been successful at anything he had attempted at home in England. He had failed as a corset maker (his father's profession). He had failed as a teacher. He had been a tax collector and had been fired from that job. He had twice been unsuccessfully married. Nevertheless, he had met Benjamin Franklin in London and had sufficiently impressed him to be given a letter of introduction to Franklin's son-in-law in Philadelphia. It described Paine as someone who might well fit into a job as a "clerk or assistant tutor in a school, or assistant surveyor."

Instead, he crossed the Atlantic to take up the career for which he had been destined, the calling for which he proved himself eminently well suited. He became a stirring political journalist and a professional revolutionary. (He would subsequently move on to seek a role to play in the French Revolution, from whose jails years later President Thomas Jefferson would be called upon to rescue him.)

Arriving in Philadelphia, Paine, supporting himself by writing articles, proceeded to compose a detailed, incisive, lucid, unambiguous denunciation of monarchy (the "Popery of government"), of Britain ("shame upon her conduct") and of the king of England ("the Royal Brute"):

> In England a king hath little more to do than to make war and give away places; which in plain terms is to impoverish the nation. . . . A pretty business indeed for a man to be allowed eight hundred thousand sterling a year for, and worshipped into the bargain! Of more worth is one honest man to society, and in the sight of God, than all the crowned ruffians that ever lived. . . . Ye that tell us of harmony and reconciliation, can ye restore to us the time that is past? Can ye give to prostitution its former innocence? Neither can ye reconcile Britain and America. . . . There are injuries that nature cannot forgive. . . . As well can the lover forgive the ravisher of his mistress, as the continent forgive the murderer of Britain.

Applause for *Common Sense* when it appeared was not unanimous among patriots. John Adams, convinced that its author was dedicated to destruction on principle rather than to American liberties, dismissed it as being largely "ignorant and foolish."[8] Landon Carter of Virginia called it "rascally and nonsensical." But George Washington had no doubt that its castigation of monarchy contained "unanswerable reasoning," and Charles Lee, Washington's second in command, had never seen "such a masterly irresistible performance."

That Paine's pamphlet was a compelling tour de force could not be doubted. It convinced countless British Americans that his homeland had no justifiable claim to their allegiance and that the moment for independence had come. For the first time, they were persuaded that their king not only was an ordinary mortal but was a rogue and a scoundrel as well. Paine convinced them that the regal robes of George III were transparent, that underneath he was a man like any other, except that he presumed to rule others and commit injustices against them.

After *Common Sense*, many fewer Americans remained in awe of the throne or of the British constitution in which their leaders had until then always put their trust. It was no longer necessary for rebels to concoct unwieldly distinctions between their good and noble king and his wicked, mischievous advisers. Britain—the nation, the people, the king—could finally be drawn out of the shadows to become the enemy, without qualification, without restraint. It would be challenged to do its wicked worst against the champions of liberty.

There could no longer be calm consideration of alternatives. There would no longer be any grasp of the implications of the fact that it would have cost the British more than five years of the taxes they *hoped* to extract from the colonies to pay for stationing redcoats in America for only one year—a burden which the British Treasury would not have been able to sustain very long but which the British government would have felt obliged to carry if faced with a military showdown.

It was no longer a time for quibbling over details. British Americans had to choose to be one or the other, and they had to face the consequences of their choices. The British government and the American rebel leadership, now irreconcilable adversaries, had conspired to leave people in the colonies no other alternative. The possibility of compelling the British to give ground without exposing America to a protracted bout of death and destruction had been forfeited.

4

CONCLAVE OF PATRIOTS

The business of the Congress is tedious beyond expression. This assembly is like no other that ever existed. Every man in it is a great man, an orator, a critic, a statesman and therefore every man upon every question must show his oratory, his criticism, and his political abilities.

—JOHN ADAMS[1]

Different sorts came together to constitute America's first Congress: city lawyers and country squires, self-made men and heirs to great fortunes, radicals and conservatives, hotheads and mild-mannered sophisticates. Some were men of great scholarship, well versed in history and philosophy. Some were superbly articulate, bubbling with fiery righteousness or graced with subtle wit. All were committed to a noble cause.

It was seven months before the clash at Concord laid the groundwork for the war, and more than a year before Tom Paine's *Common Sense* made common sense of a break with Britain. The congressmen were not excessively ambitious. They had gathered only to reaffirm the liberties of British Americans in a way—they weren't sure how—that would impress His Gracious Majesty, King George III. They wanted only to divert him from the disagreeable path along which his bungling ministers were leading him.

In the House of Lords in London, Lord Chatham, chafing at his government's myopia in the face of the gathering American storm, termed their gathering in Philadelphia "the most honorable assembly of statesmen since those of ancient Greeks and Romans." Compared to the assortment of dunderheads, wastrels and popinjays who cluttered up the British Parliament, social standing and wealth being their primary qualifications for membership, America's first congressional conclave was indeed composed of an impressive group of men.

They had been baptized in early America's environment of self-sufficiency and distrust of authority. They had a profound sense of duty to the people, and to justice. To them, many of today's overprivileged congressmen and senators would have too closely resembled their image of self-indulgent, self-serving members of the British Parliament whose ill-considered decrees aroused American ire and transformed the world. Benjamin Franklin had looked frowningly on the games played in government circles in London, where "numberless and needless places, enormous salaries, pensions, perquisites, bribes and groundless quarrels, foolish expeditions, false accounts or no accounts, contracts and jobbs devour all revenue . . ."[2]

That such a description might one day be applicable to the American Congress they created would have horrified the first congressmen who converged on Philadelphia's Carpenters' Hall on September 5, 1774. It would have sent them scrambling helter-skelter homeward. These were men of principle, the cream of the colonies, probably the cream of the empire.

But as they congregated for the first time, they had absolutely no idea of the historic adventure upon which they were embarking. Not one of them could imagine the dimensions of anguish, misery, pride and glory they and their countrymen would experience over the next decade as a result of their own proceedings. They stumbled along a course they were unable to chart and ended up doing—and being celebrated for doing—what they had specifically said they did not want to do: they created a nation.

At least they inaugurated the process. Most of the men who succeeded these distinguished trail-blazers during the war and who were officially in charge of America's destiny at the height of the Revolution were less inspiring. Sometimes they were a shiftless aggregation, immersed in trivia while men died. Their private affairs often took precedence over their public responsibilities. They created an American army but repeatedly failed to provision the farmer-warrior-patriots they sent into battle. They floundered helplessly about as America's war economy rampaged out of control. They grew addicted to parliamentary posturing, endless speeches, callings of the previous question, submissions of trifling amendments and such stuff.

"We murder time," Charles Carroll of Maryland lamented, "and chat it away in idle, impertinent talk."[3] It was a complaint shared by John Mathews of South Carolina, who vowed, "I'll be damned if you ever catch me here again" if he could manage to be relieved of his congressional assignment.[4]

When British military threats forced Congress into exile, first to Baltimore, then to York, Pennsylvania, those down-market substitute venues for America's beleaguered revolutionary regime seemed so dreary after the seductive big-town pleasures of Philadelphia that many delegates chose not to go into exile with it. "What a lot of damned scoundrels we had in that Second Congress," confessed Gouverneur Morris, who served in it for a year.[5]

Before the British were finally forced out, some congressmen blatantly engaged in practices which their present-day successors would not be able to risk without being made to answer for it to the voters—and the the FBI.

When the Continental Congress (no one yet presumed to call it the *American* Congress) met, as the summer of '74 drew to a close, dissolving the British connection was not even a remote consideration. Most delegates had arrived with instructions very much like those of the Viriginia contingent: "to secure British America from the ravage and ruin of arbitrary taxes, and speedily as possible to procure the return of that harmony and union so beneficial to the whole Empire and so ardently desired by all British America."[6] No one suspected that less than two years later the term "British America" would widely be considered an abominable contradiction and those who still believed in it would be deemed villains and traitors.

For most of the fifty-six congressional delegates, Philadelphia was an exotic place. The second-largest city in the British Empire, it boasted a large population, estimated at 40,000. New York, the next-largest American city at the time, could claim only some 25,000 inhabitants, virtually all of them clustered on the southern tip of Manhattan Island. Gallant Boston numbered a mere

16,000 souls, while Charleston with 12,000 and Newport with 11,000 constituted the smallest two of the big five American cities. Most communities consisted of only a few hundred people. For American frontiersmen, the nearest neighbor might be many miles away.

Philadelphia was the height of modernity. It already had parallel streets, numbered or named. Hundreds of whale-oil street lamps made it the best-lit city in the British Empire. It had a hospital and salaried police constables. It even had regular garbage collection and easily accessible public water pumps. Carriages and horseback riders had to be careful of traffic while traversing town. There were elegant town houses set well back from the hubbub and outlying sleepy villages not far off. There was also the phenomenon of dwellings, shops and countinghouses crammed in among the city's dingy warehouses.

Peter Kalm, a much-traveled Swedish visitor, said that Philadelphia's "fine appearance, good regulations, agreeable situation, natural advantages, trade, riches and power" were "by no means inferior to those of any, even of the most ancient towns of Europe." This was high praise indeed at a time when many untutored European patricians still thought of America as a land of outcasts, ruffians and savages, despite the fact that vessels dispatched by enterprising Philadelphia merchants (some ignoring official British prohibitions) ventured out as far as the Mediterranean, and even farther, to buy and sell and to bring back, among other things, fine wines and lush carpets. There was nothing backward about the City of Brotherly Love. There were those among its rich who already vacationed in Newport and who speculated in local real estate, some particularly favoring land to the south of Philadelphia, in which direction knowledgeable investors expected the city to grow.

As they convened their first session, the congressional delegates, having settled in as best they could in this metropolis, went about the task of taking one another's measure. Many had arrived burdened down with legacies of the rivalries between their colonies. Those rivalries proved tenacious enough to prompt some delegates, once the break with Britain became unavoidable, to contemplate the emergence of not one but several independent American nations, perhaps an Atlantic tier of loosely linked commonwealths.

At the beginning, however, the emphasis was not on issues which divided the colonies. It was on the goal which had brought them together: to induce the bullheaded British government to see reason and behave. But it was already evident that different philosophies would be at play in Congress.

Radicals and conservatives were as much at loggerheads as todays liberals, who welcome change which they believe to be for the public good, and today's conservatives, who believe change is more likely to have damaging consequences—and for the same fundamental reason. Though they sometimes deviated from positions they might have been expected to assume, what divided radicals and conservatives in Congress when it first met was their approach to the form that the link between the colonies and Britain should take. Moderates in the middle sometimes favored one school of thought, sometimes the other, depending on circumstances.

Radicals like Patrick Henry and John Hancock insisted the British government and Parliament should no longer retain any authority over the internal affairs of the American colonies. They were prepared to swear allegiance to the king, but wanted it understood that in America he would be merely a figurehead, a symbol of unity in the empire, helping to sustain the cherished links with the motherland but shorn of any power to impose taxes or restrictions.

Though equally offended by the folly of British impositions, congressional conservatives were convinced that in the long run American liberties were more likely to be guaranteed within the framework of the existing British system, properly monitored, than if the colonies, in effect, cut themselves adrift. Parliament, the conservatives conceded, was far less than perfect. But to renounce it as a legislature of last resort and a watchdog against local abuses would be to jeopardize balance, cohesion and order in the America that was and the America that was to be. Unlike the radicals, they were certain that the quarrel with the motherland could be patched up without resorting to extreme measures (which might backfire), and that ground rules could be established to ensure that such trouble did not recur.

James Duane of New York declared, "A firm union between the parent state and her colonies ought to be the great object of Congress."[7] Pennsylvania Congressman Joseph Galloway told his fellow delegates, "I have looked for [the rights of Americans] in the constitution of the English government and there found them. We may draw them from this source securely."[8]

Some conservatives feared the British would get fed up with American impudence and leave the colonies to stew in their own turbulent juices. New Yorker Philip Livingston warned, "If England should turn us adrift, we should instantly go to civil wars among ourselves to determine which colony should govern the rest."[9]

Suspicion between conservatives and radicals was rife, as the Massachusetts contingent discovered when they lobbied their colleagues to support strong action to force the British out of Boston. John Adams felt obliged to indulge in conspiratorial congressional maneuverings of a kind not unknown in later times. He wrote his wife about it:

> We have numberless prejudices to remove here. We have been obliged to keep ourselves out of sight and to feel pulses and sound the depths; to insinuate our sentiments, designs and desires by means of other persons; sometimes of one province and sometimes of another."[10]

The strategy worked. Delegates John Dickinson of Pennsylvania, George Read of Delaware and other conservatives had arrived looking for ways out of the impasse with Britain but prepared to resist the harangues of New England radicals whom they considered intemperate, uncompromising and shrill. Edward Rutledge of South Carolina spoke of the "low cunning" of the New Englanders.

However, conservatives found themselves under pressure from an unexpected direction: from southern radicals like Richard Henry Lee of Virginia and Christopher Gadsden of South Carolina, men whose accents and mannerisms did not reflexively arouse their regional prejudices. Joseph Reed of Pennsylvania marveled that, contrary to what he had been led to expect, compared to some of the southerners "the Bostonians are mere milksops." Warned by an English friend that these milksops were bent on independence, moderate congressional delegate George Washington met privately with some New Englanders and then declared, "I am as well satisfied as I can be of my existence that no such thing is desired by any thinking man in all North America."[11]

Though exasperated by conservative reluctance to bring Congress alive with a quick, sharp, unceremonious response to British transgressions, the New Englanders knew enough to bide their time. They realized that their cause would be lost if they alienated the colonies represented by delegates with whom they did not see eye to eye. What was more, not even the most fiery of the radicals believed at that stage (1774) that there was any great longing in America for independence. Astonished by British bungling, Oliver Wolcott of Connecticut, later to be a signer of the Declaration of Independence, said the American attachment to Britain was so strong that it would have required only the abilities of a child to keep the colonies in the British Empire. The normally impulsive Samuel Adams held himself in check in Philadelphia. This was not Boston. No counterfeit Indians would make an impression here. "We must be content," he said, "to wait till the fruit is ripe before we gather it."

However, the radicals did not intend to twiddle their thumbs while waiting for their moment to arrive. While their less impassioned colleagues concocted arguments and petitions with which to sway the ham-fisted British, they called upon the evidence of British actions, and upon aversion to tyranny and oppression, to recruit wavering delegates to the hard line. William Livingston of New Jersey was later to say that, though improbable when they first met, the decision to opt for independence less than two years later was the product of radical-inspired congressional attitudes which neutralized whatever possibility existed in the colonies for reconciliation with Britain.

Step by step, outright rebellion was made inevitable. Step by step, those who believed that an open challenge to Britain could be avoided were outflanked. Robert Morris, John Jay and other conservatives were to play central roles in the Revolution. But it was launched despite their efforts to seek a less painful, less heroic way to guarantee American liberties.

Shortly after Congress convened for the first time, poignant details of civilian suffering in occupied Boston were whisked to Philadelphia by hard-riding radical courier Paul Revere. They were accompanied by a plea from other Massachusetts radicals for retaliatory measures by Congress against the British oppressors. Deeply moved by the much exaggerated plight of the Bostonians under the British thumb ("We are robbed of the means of life," "The streets of Boston throng with military executioners"), Congress was steamrolled into resorting for the first time to what has since become a recurring feature of American foreign policy: economic sanctions.

A ban was declared on the import of British goods into the colonies and on the export of goods the British normally bought. Conservatives felt obliged to go along for fear that otherwise Congress might proceed to even more drastic measures. Another precedent was established at the insistence of South Carolina conservatives. They made the sanctions selective by declining to agree to them, and even threatening to withdraw from Congress, unless a special dispensation excluded a ban on rice exports, important to South Carolina's economy.

Once the economic sanctions had been pushed through, there seemed to be little hope for congressional backing for a detailed plan designed to resolve the confrontation with Britain without further friction or strife. The plan, devised by Joseph Galloway, would have called for an American parliament to share responsibility with Britain for the American colonies. While not offering the colonies full independence, the plan proposed giving them a veto over measures affecting internal affairs. It would also have linked the colonies together on the road to lasting union.

Radicals were dismayed by the plan. They saw it as a threat to hard-won solidarity with beleaguered Boston and a ploy to isolate them from their moderate allies in Congress. It almost served that purpose.

Despite the economic sanctions sternly imposed against the British, despite the widely publicized plight of the Bostonians, the plan just narrowly missed receiving congressional backing. It was shelved by only one vote—an indication that radical dominance in Philadelphia was not yet complete. That one vote was, however, enough to sink the plan forever. To firm up their momentarily endangered congressional clout, radicals then succeeded in striking all record of the debate on the Galloway proposals, and the proposals themselves, from the minutes.

They were being very careful. There was no indication at that time (though there would be later) that the British might be receptive to a power-sharing scheme for the colonies. But there were to be no telltale signs that Americans were so lacking in determination as to be amenable to a face-saving compromise. As far as the radicals were concerned, such a solution would leave the British in a position to perpetuate their tyrannical grip on the colonies. Compromise was out of the question. The British would simply have to yield or find the colonies a source of expensive grief.

Congressional delegates who, just eight weeks earlier, had arrived in Philadelphia with no idea what authority they could wield in the campaign to protect American liberties, then proceeded to assume powers in dealing not only with the British adversary but with Americans as well. They authorized local committees publicly to name American "foes to the rights of British America," a move which left those "foes" exposed to harassment by their patriotic neighbors. Those committees were also empowered to enforce bans on English goods and even to examine the ledgers of local businessmen to make certain the ban was observed. Not all businessmen felt aggrieved by this crackdown on dealings with the British, and with good reason. In some places, it was decided that debts owed to English merchants did not have to be paid until the British withdrew from Boston and ended their suppression of American liberties.

Having accelerated the pace of events, Congress adjourned, the delegates agreeing to meet again the following spring (1775) unless the British saw reason and backed down before then. Conservative delegates went home apprehensive of what lay in store. Radicals left preparing for a showdown.

By the following May, when the Continental Congress reconvened, heavy-handed British behavior had turned grievance into insurrection. Shots had been fired. Men had been killed. The doings at Lexington and Concord had been seared into the consciousness of the American people. Newspapers told of "Bloody Butchery by British Troops," and of redcoat "cruelty and barbarity never equalled by the savages [Indians] of America." Reports of the defiance and determination of the heroic New England Minutemen, laying siege to the barbarous British in Boston, echoed through the colonies.

The situation was bounding out of control. To congressional

radicals that was as it should be. Control could only be to the advantage of the British tyrants. Mayhem could only contribute to belated recognition by His Majesty's advisers that their policies were misguided and counterproductive. Armed clashes might still be necessary to drive the point home, but things were falling into place.

To congressional conservatives, too many people seemed to have lost all sense of proportion. They agreed that the New Englanders were absolutely right to rally to arms in the face of British provocation. But the apparent impatience of so many patriots to go to war worried them. They had reason to believe that the British government was wearying of the confrontation. According to reports they received from London, if given a way out the British would take it.

> All our demands are on the point of being granted. Our great friends in Parliament . . . continually send us word that complete success is in sight . . . , that by persisting a little longer . . . we shall certainly win for ourselves every political advantage we have ever professed to desire, and shall become a group of great, free, self-governing colonies within the British empire.[12]

Disgusted with such signs of what he took to be foolish gullibility, and the danger it might pose to the implementation of effective congressional action, John Adams commented dryly, "The Congress is not yet so alarmed as it ought to be."

Alarmed or not, Congress had to do something about the swarm of patriots clustered around Boston, confronting the British with the greatest challenge they had yet encountered in the New World. New England farmers and townsfolk had grabbed their weapons and had scampered off to the fray without hesitation or misgivings. Israel Putnam, the old Indian fighter soon to be a general in the Continental Army, had rushed toward Boston straight from the Connecticut field he had been plowing when he heard of the clash at Concord. The Minutemen had no qualms about using force to defend American liberties. That sort of zeal made the foot-dragging by conservatives in Congress appear excessively timid and difficult to sustain.

Putting aside their qualms and anxieties, they joined their less cautious colleagues in an unqualified commitment to the campaign to liberate Boston. They agreed that Congress should formally adopt the irregulars besieging the redcoats in that city. They agreed, too, that units of riflemen be dispatched from other colonies to swell their ranks. Not a few congressmen still nursed doubts about what exactly their legal powers were or, in fact, whether they had any. But Congress now had a military wing. America, not yet a nation, had an army, and that army was deployed against the troops of the country to which all the colonies still pledged allegiance.

A shrewder government than Britain possessed would long before have tried to exploit regional rejudices in the colonies to isolate New England from the rest of British America. Many Americans were worried about the seemingly relentless drift toward war, and the British, through their spies in the colonies, knew it well. John Dickinson tried to convince "our brethren in Great Britain of the importance of . . . harmony between them and us, and of the danger of driving us to despair."

But instead of strengthening the hand of the American peace movement, the British, to the horror of congressional conservatives, took further steps to provoke American outrage. In February 1776, when radicals had finally gotten around to openly asserting that independence was the only solution, word reached the colonies that Parliament had approved a blockade which, in effect, would have barred the colonies from trading with one another! Even more infuriating, and more likely to cause material damage, the Royal Navy was instructed to seize American ships on the high seas. Such authorization of acts of piracy was too much to tolerate, and when North Carolina's Joseph Hewes said, "Nothing is left now but to fight it out,"[13] his fellow conservatives could only agree.

Within limits. A show of force was one thing. Cutting loose from the motherland once and for all was still something else altogether. It was a mistake to equate the two. A disgusted John Adams sourly remarked that some of his colleagues saw independence as "a hobgoblin of so frightful mien that it would throw a delicate person into fits to look it in the face."[14]

He was right. Trepidations about the consequences of independence were trotted out once more. Wouldn't British tyranny be replaced by an even greater tyranny once the protection of British law was removed? Wouldn't colonies go to war with each other over disputed territory once America no longer came under the calming influence of the empire? How could Americans win a war against the mighty British Army and Navy?

Radicals sneered at such trepidations and at conservative illusions about British justice and magnanimity. Not without reason, they suggested that some conservatives feared independence might give power to all the people rather than just the "better sort." In reply, conservatives condemned the radical inclination to think of hopes that war might still be avoided as high treason. They charged radicals with rejecting the possibility of reconciliation with Britain under any terms whatsoever.

Accusations, innuendoes, insults flowed back and forth. One congressman noted, "We do not treat each other with that decency and respect that was observed heretofore. Jealousies, ill-natured observations and recriminations take the place of reason and argument. Our tempers are soured."

Both radicals and conservatives had reason to be anxious about developments. The radicals were exasperated by requests from the delegates of New Jersey, Pennsylvania and New York for more determined efforts at reconciliation. Maryland's colonial convention expressed the hope for "a happy settlement [with Britain] and lasting amity." Many Americans were growing jaded by the woes of the Boston martyrs and alarmed at decay in local government and law enforcement because of the turmoil and uncertainty. So widespread were such feelings in 1775 and even in early 1776 that at virtually any point the crisis could have been defused, the radicals thwarted and colonies pacified by displays of British statesmanship.

After coming so far, radicals worried that all might still be lost. They suspected that given the slightest encouragement, conservative congressmen would hem and haw, tug their forelocks to the king's ministers and brake the momentum that was leading to independence and freedom.

As for congressional conservatives, though many Americans were faced with a crisis of loyalties, with few exceptions they had no doubt whose side they would be on if the worst could not be avoided. Some had already become intimately involved in preparing for the unwanted armed struggle as key figures on the congressional committee secretly formed to solicit foreign assistance for the army. Though they had not yet completely lost hope that the British would come to their senses, each passing day seemed to make a proclamation of independence, and the portentous consequences of such proclamation, more credible, more inevitable.

In March 1776, the redcoats were forced out of Boston by General Washington's men. As word spread of that magnificent achievement, a gung-ho spirit of militant patriotism coursed through the land. It was no longer a time for weak-kneed shilly-shallying. It was no longer a time for doubters and waverers. America could, America would, be independent!

The radicals had won their argument. Conservatives had, however, their own ideas about how to proceed—or rather about how not to proceed. On June 7, 1776, one month before the Declaration of Independence, a resolution was introduced in Congress declaring: ". . . these United Colonies are and of a right ought to be free and independent States." Conservatives shied away from it. Though they had been won over to the cause of independence, they believed that a *declaration* of independence was premature, that most Americans might not favor it and that, in any case, it was bad tactics.

It was easy enough to spout off about independence, but, in order for the colonies to attain it, they had to achieve unity of purpose and be prepared to coordinate their actions. Such harmony was hardly in evidence, the conservatives said. South Carolina's Edward Rutledge declared, "The inhabitants of every colony consider themselves at liberty to do as they please upon almost every occasion." To declare independence would give "our enemy notice of our intentions before we had taken steps to execute them."[15]

Such arguments, whether based on tactical considerations or on more fundamental objections, were enough to get the vote on the independence resolution put off until the beginning of July, by which time radicals were confident Congress could be whipped into line. But on July 1, delegates of only nine of the thirteen colonies were prepared to back the independence declaration, not enough for a convincing display of American unity, nor enough to guarantee that a rebellion against oppression would not crumble because of divisions among Americans.

However, congressmen who held back had to accept that the desire for independence was now overwhelming among most Americans who were willing to air their feelings, and that the British were not going to see reason and ease off. Aware that their hopes for peace were futile and that they were now only being obstructive, conservatives in Pennsylvania's delegation voluntarily absented themselves when the independence vote was retaken on July 2, permitting their colony's no to be reversed. Delaware's vote was swung in favor of independence when its divided two-man delegation was joined at the last minute by a third member, the radical Caesar Rodney, who had ridden his horse through a thunderstorm all through the night to reach Philadelphia in time to break his colony's deadlock. New York's reluctance to go along with the majority (its delegates had been instructed to press for reconciliation with Britain) was masked by granting its delegation permission not to vote until it could engage in further consultations back home. South Carolina, last of the nay-sayers, was persuaded to vote yes to keep America's independence decision from being marred by just a single dissenting voice. All in all, it was a skillful display of perseverance and political maneuvering by the radicals, aided by the bumbling, intransigent British.

Thus was the Declaration of Independence agreed to. It was formally proclaimed two days later, on July 4. As for the actual signing of that historic document, contrary to the evidence presented in John Trumbull's famous patriotic painting celebrating the event, many of the men who affixed their signatures were not in attendance on July 4. Some did not get around to signing for many weeks afterward. One of them—New Hampshire's Matthew Thorton—wasn't even a member of Congress until the following November. While the signers would forever be proud of having been associated with the birth of the American nation, they had committed acts of high treason against the British crown. If the Revolution had been crushed and if they had been caught, they would have faced serious punishment.* Most, therefore, discreetly concealed their identities until overdue Continental Army successes indicated that their patriotic cause was not necessarily doomed to disaster.

Church bells pealed right through the day when American in-

* New Jersey's Richard Stockton was captured and so brutally treated that he signed a British amnesty proclamation, for which he was shunned by his former rebel friends and associates for the brief remainder of his life. The homes of fifteen of the signers, including Stockton, were destroyed by the British.

dependence was proclaimed. Bonfires lit up the night. There were cheering and parading and rousing public speeches. In Baltimore, as in other cities and towns, an effigy of George III was carted through the streets and then put to the torch. In New York, a statue of the king at the Battery was knocked off its pedestal and melted down for bullets to fire at His Majesty's troops. It was a moment for rejoicing. America was free. Its prospects were grand and glorious.

Within six months, however, jubilation had faded. The Continental Army had dwindled to a fraction of the multitude that had been drawn up outside Boston to confront the British. It had been trounced by the redcoats on Long Island, forced out of New York and driven into ignominious retreat.

There was little to indicate that these were temporary setbacks or strategic ploys to lull the enemy itno complacency. The army displayed alarming signs of simply being no match for the British. Congress had to face the fact that independence, though gloriously declared, would not be easily achieved. "Our people knew not the hardships and calamities of war," a member of Congress commented, "when they so boldly dared Britain to arms."[16] After the defiant flourishes which had accompanied cutting loose from the motherland, adjustment to the realities of the situation was proving exceedingly painful.

Expectations that France would rush to the aid of the American rebels to get even with Britain for past humiliations were transformed into prolonged diplomacy, not helped by battlefield indications to the French that, if they did rally to Britain's wayward colonies, they might find themselves heading for further humiliation. Expectations that Americans would flock to the colors by the tens of thousands to fight for liberty and justice proved illusory, leaving Congress to fumble its way through a maze of recruiting problems because, if there was no army in this War of Independence, there was nothing. At the same time, the value of newly printed Continental currency was collapsing, complicating the task of financing the soaring costs of the war.

To make matters worse, Congress had to deal with problems of its own continuity. Most of its original members were gone or about to leave. Some, like Franklin, Jay and John Adams, were taking up diplomatic assignments abroad. Some, like Washington, Dickinson, and Philip Schuyler of New York, had donned the uniform of the Continental Army. Some, like Jefferson, John Rutledge and Samuel Adams, were leaving for home to transform what had been royal colonies into independent states, with laws and constitutions and governments answerable only to their own property-owning citizens, it being understood that the Continental Congress was only a temporary expedient.

With a few exceptions, the men who succeeded them in Congress were less gifted and less memorable. A foreign observer* commented, "All but a few of the superior [delegates] have disappeared."[17] Young James Madison noted when he arrived to take his place in Congress that there was "a defect of adequate statesmen"[18] among his colleagues there. Delegates from North Carolina reported home that "the exertions of Congress are no longer competent." Enraged by the contrast between the old Congress and the new, Alexander Hamilton demanded, "The great men who composed our first council, are they dead, have they deserted the cause, or what has become of them?"[19]

Though there was a war on and America was losing it, many of the lawyers, merchants and planters who now came to Philadelphia displayed great reluctance to tear themselves away from their practices, businesses and plantations, their comings and goings rarely influenced by affairs of state. Nor, when they were in attendance, did the new intake take happily to sitting long hours trying to resolve the problems they inherited and others which were created daily. Titus Hosmer of Connecticut, an early riser, complained that some of his colleagues were "so much immersed in the pursuit of pleasure or business that it is very rare we can make a Congress before near eleven o'clock." One of the original congressmen, feeling distinctly out of place, exclaimed, "Good God! How different from the glorious spirit with which we embarked in the Cause of Liberty."

Delegates did not remain long in Congress before finding some means of being relieved of their irksome public duties. One congressman wrote that they changed so quickly, it was little use even learning their names. Often, barely had a delegate grown conversant with details of the issues which required his attention, and with congressional procedures, than he handed over to a successor who also had to start unraveling those mysteries.

---

* Pierre Duponceau, aide to General von Steuben.

None of this discouraged them from speaking their minds. One of their number lamented the presence of so many "gentlemen who love to talk as much as they" and thought such garrulousness responsible for the delay in getting business transacted. When Robert Livingston of New York was returned to Congress in 1779 after a three-year absence, he said he went back with "the reluctance of the shipwrecked wretch who embarks again after having once safely landed." John Dickinson's simile on his leaving Congress was even more evocative: "No youthful lover ever stript off his cloathes to step into bed to his blooming bride with more delight than I have cast off my popularity."[20]

When the British occupied Philadelphia in 1777, sending Congress scrambling for safety to York, many of the delegates who met there continued to concern themselves with trivialities though their flight was a dramatic setback, deserving a more dignified showing. Henry Laurens of South Carolina, president of Congress during its York exile, observed, "Some sensible things have been said, and as much nonsense as ever I heard in so short a space."[21]

The winter before, a false alarm about a threatening British advance had also sent Congress scurrying out of Philadelphia. Baltimore, to which it fled, was then little more than a village, which John Adams called "the dirtiest place in the world." North Carolina's William Hooper went into greater detail:

> This dirty, boggy hole beggars all description. . . . When the devil proferred our Saviour the Kingdom of the World, he surely placed his thumb on this delectable spot and reserved it to himself. . . . As to the inhabitants, Congress can boast no acquaintance with them but what arises from their daily exorbitant claims upon our pockets.[22]

Baltimore was so disagreeable that many delegates didn't bother to show up there at all. Warnings were issued by conservatives about the formation of a radical clique there. Though there had been such a clique from the beginning, it was more apparent in Baltimore because radicals seemed less deterred from attending by discomfort and inconvenience.

Absenteeism had already been an established habit in Congress, as Hooper had complained in a letter home from Philadelphia: "I am fatigued almost to death. Nine colonies . . . are required to compose a Congress. Neither Georgia, Maryland, Delaware or New York have been for some time past represented so that your humble servant is compelled to a constant unremitting attendance."[23] In York, during the wretched winter of 1777–78, attendance was neither constant nor even occasional for many delegates. While the troops languished at Valley Forge not far away, it wasn't always possible to proceed with the business of the Revolution. Attendance at sessions frequently dwindled to less than a quorum. Once, when summoned to a night sitting, Thomas Burke, the hardworking, irreverent Irish-born delegate from North Carolina, minced no words in informing the messenger sent to fetch him that it was too late and he would not attend. His attitude and language ("The devil take me if I will come!") provoked a demand that Burke be censured. But it couldn't be done, because a quorum was required to administer such chastisement and without Burke there was no quorum.

Later, as spring set in, some of the habitually absent delegates did put in appearances. It prompted one of the more dedicated delegates to note wryly, "We are come to the season when certain birds of passage return who seldom appear in our flock during the winter."

Accommodations in York were cramped, and amenities were limited. Most delegates lived two to a room in lodgings and took their meals at local taverns. For some, the situation was intolerable. "Believe me," wrote Cornelius Harnett of North Carolina, "it is the most inhospitable scandalous place I was ever in. If I can return once more to my family, all the Devils in Hell shall not separate us."[24]

During all this time, Congress, for all its weaknesses and whinings, was doing what it could to herd the states together into some sort of federation. A handful of congressmen dreamed of a Greater America, befitting the vast continent whose fringe it had so far tamed. But there was no sudden mass conversion to the concept of a single American nation to which the states would relinquish their newly gained, much cherished sovereignty. All the delegates were suspicious of any move that might sooner or later limit freedom. Many had no doubt that the proposed Confederacy of States could turn out to be an even greater tyrannical power than Britain. Edward Rutledge, who had pressed so hard for prerevolutionary unity, was resolved to "vest Congress with no more power than is absolutely essential" so that the liberties of Americans, and particularly South Carolinians, might not be endangered.

Nevertheless, France, whose military and financial assistance was growing increasingly essential, had to be shown that the American people were capable of molding themselves into a nation to which aid could be productively extended. Could France be expected to direct its help toward a confusing jumble of separate American states? How much would Virginia get? What would be sent to Pennsylvania? Would a people incapable of uniting be capable of winning, no matter how convinced they were of the justice of their cause?

The debate over the terms for confederation was protracted and often abusive. It dealt with the powers to be exercised by the central government, how the states should share the expenses involved, how voting rights should be apportioned, how claims to western territories should be handled, and other issues upon which there were widely differing and sometimes diametrically opposed views. No confederation could seriously be contemplated without reference to the divisive territorial squabbles between states. Connecticut still laid claim to parts of Pennsylvania's Susquehanna Valley. The territory around what is now Pittsburgh—snatched from the French only a dozen years before—was still claimed by both Pennsylvania and Virginia. New Hampshiremen who claimed land in Vermont were charged with criminal trespass in New York when they ventured into that disputed region.

John Banister of Virginia moaned that the "affairs of the greatest magnitude . . . lie dormant and give place to local trifles."[25] Another delegate sighed, "We make slow progress . . . as every inch is disputed, and very jarring claims and interests are to be adjusted. . . . I almost despair of seeing it accomplished."

When, despite continuing gripes and grievances between the states, agreement on Articles of Confederation was finally reached in November 1777, only Virginia was prepared to ratify them. The other states gave their approval, some grudgingly, not too long afterward—except Maryland, whose territorial dispute with Virginia still rankled, as its delegation made clear to Congress:

> Although the pressure of immediate calamities, the dread of their continuance from the appearance of disunion . . . may have induced some states to accede to the present confederation . . . it requires no great share of foresight to predict that when those causes cease to operate, the states which have thus acceded to the confederation will consider it as no longer binding and will largely embrace the first occasion of asserting their just rights, and securing their independence. Is it possible that those states who are ambitiously grasping at territories to which . . . they have not the least shadow of exclusive right will use with great moderation the increase of wealth and power derived from those territories when acquired than they have displayed in their endeavors to acquire them? We think not. We are convinced the same spirit which hath prompted them to insist on a claim so extravagant, so repugnant to every principle of justice, so incompatible with the general welfare of the states, will urge them on to add oppression to injustice.[26]

Such fraternal suspicion was to be a feature of Congress right through the war. When, in the interests of democracy, it was proposed that the hearings in York be thrown open to the general public, the suggestion was wisely voted down. The wranglings of the first all-American government would hardly have had the desired effect on a people paying the price of war. A New Jersey delegate, the Reverend John Witherspoon, president of the College of New Jersey (the future Princeton University), who attended congressional sessions in his academic cap and robes, pointed out that "should the idea get abroad there is likely to be no union among us, it will dampen the minds of the people, diminish the glory of our struggle, and lessen its importance."[27]

With an eye toward France, another congressman asked, "What contract will a foreign state make with us when we cannot agree among ourselves?" He needn't have worried. France had reasons of its own to want to ally itself with the rebels. It wasn't overly concerned about congressional quibbles. What mattered was the Revolution's military performance. When the French came to believe that, with a little help, an American victory was a real possibility, the alliance was ceremonially forged—and differences in Congress were momentarily submerged. Independence seemed assured. Patriots no longer stood alone.

The pleasure of congressional conservatives at this momentous development was tinged with regret. The alliance with France meant that reconciliation with Britain was totally out of the question. Only the clash of arms could now produce a solution. Ironically, the British now offered their former colonies all that even the radicals had wanted three years earlier, on the eve of the war. Allegiance to the king, while remaining within the British Empire (little more than a formality), was all that would be required of them. To sweeten this proposition, it was noised about that prominent Americans could expect personal considerations from His Majesty if reconciliation was achieved—money certainly, perhaps also elevation to the nobility. There was talk of Washington being made a duke.

These suggestions drew only contempt from those who were possible candidates for such rewards, though radicals were suspicious that their conservative colleagues were still so enamored of things British that they might be tempted to sell out the cause of independence. "Surely Congress will never recede from our French friends," Patrick Henry wrote nervously to a friend, as if such a possibility existed.

It was, in fact, unthinkable. Too much blood had been spilled. Too great a commitment to unqualified independence had been made. And the British evacuation of Philadelphia, allowing Congress to return from York, seemed to show that America's military fortunes were on the upswing. Englishman John Lind may not have been exaggerating when he said, "Had an angel descended from heaven with terms of accommodation which offered less than independence, [the Americans] would have driven him back with hostile scorn."

The return to Philadelphia brought much relief to congressmen who had found York uncomfortable, confining or less than worthy of their presence. But it did little to improve the efficiency of the revolutionary government which still had to cope with the seemingly impossible task of financing the war and provisioning the army. Various committees and consultative groups were formed by Congress to expedite matters. But they also regularly bogged down in confusion and argument. Not without reason, accusations were flung about that individuals involved represented private rather than public interests. A particularly ugly tiff between Silas Deane and Arthur Lee, about Deane's alleged abuse of office when both were founder members of America's overseas diplomatic corps, promoting French aid for the Revolution, bubbled over into Congress, where their respective advocates argued bitterly over charges of corruption, profiteering, incompetence and insubordination. Cyrus Griffin of Virginia complained, "We are plagued to death with quarrels and recriminations." Some congressmen took their accusations and arguments to the newspapers, which were already doing very well out of airing disputes between delegates and states. John Jay said there was as much intrigue in Congress as in the Vatican.

Endlessly short of provisions and money to pay the troops, the army command was infuriated by these degrading displays. When Washington visited Congress at the end of 1778, he wrote a friend that he found

> abundant reason to be convinced that our affairs are in a more distressed, ruinous and deplorable condition than they have been in since the commencement of the war. . . . Party disputes and personal quarrels are the great business of the day while the momentous concerns of an empire, a great and accumulated debt; ruined finances, depreciated money, and want of credit . . . are but secondary considerations and postponed from day to day, from week to week.

This theme was repeated again and again during the closing years of the war. Surveying the work of Congress, South Carolina's John Mathews declared a year later, "The American cause never stood so near the pinnacle of destruction as it this day does." A year after that, in the winter of 1780, General Nathanael Greene noted, "I have been among the great in Philadelphia and have a worse opinion of our cause than ever."[28]

Major John Armstrong, later to be a senator from New York and later still secretary of war, was scathing about congressional delegates: "Their wisdom has long been questioned, their virtue suspected and their dignity a jest." How could a dedicated revolutionary think otherwise if, when all was finally said and done, it was just barely possible to scrape together enough congressmen to ratify the treaty which finally brought peace to America and confirmed the independence for which so many Americans had died?

The hope of a glorious future for Congress which John Adams had uttered when the Founding Fathers first gathered in Philadelphia eight years earlier seemed to have foundered along the way:

> It is to be a school of political prophets, I suppose, a nursery of American statesmen. . . . From this fountain may there issue streams which shall gladden all the cities and towns of North America forever. I am for making it annual, and for sending an entire new set every year . . . that we may have politicians in plenty.

Despite the feeble performance of Congress at a time of national anguish and perplexity, no American totalitarian dictatorship emerged of the kind which sprouted in France and Russia during the turmoil of their revolutions. It is one of the most remarkable aspects of the American Revolution and of America itself. Through all the frustrations and fumblings, liberty remained a watchword, even when the consequence was glaring inefficiency.

The beginnings of America's Congress make a peculiar tale. This every-changing body of men managed, despite everything, to provide a fulcrum upon which the revolutionary movement could balance. It managed to defer potentially unmovable obstacles to American unity till after the war when the framers of the American Constitution could cope with them under less pressure. It succeeded in projecting at least an image of an American nation-in-the-making with which France would be prepared to risk allying itself and which Britain would ultimately be willing to recognize.

It is breathtaking to imagine what the Revolution might have been like had Congress consisted, from beginning to end, of a body of brilliant, competent, reliable men. Or, perhaps, it didn't really matter. This was an armed uprising. It had to be won or lost in the field.

5

AMERICA'S FIRST ARMY

It will not be believed that such a force as Great Britain has employed . . . could be baffled . . . by numbers infinitely less, composed of men oftentime half-starved, always in rags, without pay, and experiencing every species of distress which human nature is capable of undergoing.

—GEORGE WASHINGTON[1]

Not for a moment, as the Revolution erupted, did the British doubt their ability to make short work of the colonial yokels who dared to take on the king's formidable fighting forces. One of His Majesty's generals boasted that with a thousand grenadiers he could "go from one end of America to the other and geld all the males, partly by force and partly by a little coaxing."[2]

The British had good reason to be confident. The odds were weighted heavily in their favor. They had a strong, well-trained army. The Royal Navy was at least twice the size of any other maritime force then in existence, and, with all the insubordinate colonies vulnerably arrayed along America's Atlantic coast, it posed an equally serious threat to the rebels. In addition, the British could call upon tens of thousands of experienced European mercenaries to help do the fighting.*

* Before hired German infantry took the field in the colonies on behalf of His Britannic Majesty, an effort had been made to rent phalanxes of Russian troops to help crush the rebellion. Empress Catherine the Great, not wanting to get involved,

Opposing the British in this conflict were a covey of colonies which, at that stage, didn't even presume to call themselves a nation. They joined the fray with different degrees of enthusiasm, some with extreme reluctance. Between them, they could field only some scraggly militia units composed of barely trained part-time soldiers. And their inhabitants included countless Americans who did not approve of the war because of loyalty to the enemy, aversion to any sort of conflict or sheer indifference. An unbiased assessment of the contending forces as the war began would have made the challenge to the British seem incredibly reckless.

But the tide of history cresting toward rebellion assumed its own momentum. The cause of liberty—as defined with moving eloquence by rebel spokesmen—took on obsessive, heroic proportions which overrode strategic calculations or cool contemplation of the prospects. When Ethan Allen seized Fort Ticonderoga in northern New York from the dumbfounded British in the first days of the struggle "in the name of the Great Jehovah and the Continental Congress," few in the ranks of the rebels doubted that he was indeed acting on behalf of both. (Other reports said that what Allen had actually cried out to the British commander of the fort was, "Come out of there, you damned rat!")

The Ticonderoga episode was an audacious coup, the stuff that patriotic dreams are made of. It stoked the furnaces of American morale. But the conflict was just beginning. It would be pock-marked by heartbreaking setbacks and excruciating hardship.

A drain-away of fighting men through desertion plagued the rebel cause right through the war, undermining morale and limiting military options. Not only was it a problem that could not be resolved; it was hard even to define accurately. Was a soldier who took off into the woods because the army did not feed, clothe or pay him or treat his wounds adequately really a deserter? Certainly not in his own eyes. Was a man deserting when he abandoned the Continental Army to sign up with the militia of his home state, which, while also dedicated to the cause of liberty, was less demanding of his services and paid better? What about militia units attached to the Continental Army which left en masse

---

scotched the idea, but not before pro-American Member of Parliament Edmund Burke grieved, "I am on thorns. I cannot, at my ease, see Russian barbarism let loose to waste the most beautiful object that ever appeared upon this globe."[3]

for home, officers and all, whether they were needed or not? It wasn't as if they were bowing completely out of the conflict or going over to the enemy.

However the problem was defined, it was so chronic that senior officers often did not know how many men they had at their disposal to fight the battles of the Revolution. There might be ten thousand troops one day and just a fraction of that number the next.* In a major assault on a British position in the South, the general in command believed he had seven thousand men when, in fact, there were only three thousand. Confident of victory, he found his attack turned into a wild, uncontrollable retreat. Time and time again, strategy had to be reconsidered because the forces upon which calculations had been based were no longer available. Even toward the end of the war, when the troops were moving south to trap the British army at Yorktown, they were hurried with a minimum of ceremony through Philadelphia so as not to expose them to temptations to lose themselves in the city.

Some men felt justified in heading for home—twenty, thirty at a time—because they judged their officers to be fools, incompetents or petty tyrants who seemed to have forgotten that the war was being fought for liberty. Men from New England, with their fierce egalitarian traditions, often were not prepared to follow officers they had not themselves chosen or whom they did not know. Even when they were led by friends and neighbors, they weren't necessarily willing to perform all the disagreeable or seemingly pointless tasks that go with soldiering simply because those friends and neighbors told them to.

That many men deserted because they had wives and children and crops to look after was understandable. In small communities and remote areas, the absence of the men all year round—and particularly at harvest time—could mean starvation and disaster. The men simply could not be spared. One officer wrote home that not a day passed without a soldier, with tears in his eyes, showing him a letter from his wife telling how bad things were at home: "I am without bread and cannot get any. The committee will not supply me. My children will starve, or if they do not, they must

---

* In *The Morale of the American Revolutionary Army* (page 72), Allen Bowman says, "At least a third of the regular troops enlisted in the revolutionary army became deserters."

freeze. We have no wood, neither can we get any. Pray come home."[4]

Some men left the army because they had not expected the war to last so long. They stayed only as long as they had intended to stay, no matter how desperately they were needed and no matter what pleas their officers made. Some deserted because the realities of war were different than they had anticipated. They just didn't want to get hurt or killed. New settlements in Kentucky and elsewhere along the frontier became havens for soldiers who decided to turn their backs on the conflict. Washington complained that deserters who were caught were sometimes set free by "the people."

It was suspected that some officers encouraged men to desert so that they would have excuses to take off themselves, ostensibly to track down shirkers. "We shall have to detach one-half of the army to bring back the other," Washington groaned.[5] One of his generals suggested sending northern troops to fight in the South and southern troops north, making home much farther away and thus helping "cure the itch" for heading there before time.

The problem was so serious that no rigid response to it could be formulated by the army command. Deserters were sometimes executed. But at times, Washington felt he had no option but to sanction a lenient "furlough" policy, with only minor penalties inflicted on men who went absent without leave—reprimands, small fines, a few lashes of the whip—so that men who took time off from the war would not be discouraged from returning to duty.

Often the number of men who had deserted or were on furlough equaled or exceeded the number still in the ranks. When the situation grew truly desperate, officers were forbidden to grant furloughs without Washington's approval, an indication of how small the army had grown and the petty detail with which the commander in chief had to concern himself.

Frustrating though the desertion problem was, it was remarkable that even more men did not go absent without leave, or that Congress had any army left at all in this historic struggle. Supply shortages were gruesome. Washington had to appeal personally to Congress and to the Commissary General in Philadelphia for food for his men. General Greene protested bitterly that at times his troops fainted from hunger. General Anthony Wayne diverted his men from planned battles to forage for food.

Nor was food the only item in chronic short supply. There were times when more than half of Washington's forces—an army on the move—were inadequately shod or completely barefoot. American troop movements could sometimes be tracked through the snow by blood trails from the men's feet. One brigade, which was not unique in its tribulations, reported that of its 367 men fit for duty, only 143 had serviceable shoes, 37 had coats, and 198 had blankets—in winter!* The Virginia assembly was told, "Cold and nakedness have swept off four fold more of [the] troops than all the malice of a cruel enemy."[6] Malnutrition, hypothermia and other maladies were widespread. Medical care was primitive where it existed at all. Men who were seriously ill often had nothing but the frozen earth to sleep on. When the army was in winter's quarters at Morristown, New Jersey, some men were buried like sheep under the snow. Units were sometimes without a single field officer fit for active duty.

Congress and state assemblies passed resolution after resolution, promising to come up with clothes for the army, food, guns, reinforcements. But they rarely did so in a way worthy of the principles for which they said they were rebelling. One senior officer blamed the endless chatter and delay on lawyers, even then reflexively suspected of deviousness by Americans, who were present in substantial numbers in both Congress and local legislatures. "Pettifogging lawyers . . . begin to peep in great plenty," he said, calling "this pest of creatures no less pernicious to the peace and welfare of the state than the locusts were to the growth of herbiage in Egypt."[7]

The failure of civilians to supply adequate provisions for their fighting men aroused feelings which couldn't have been more bitter had the aim been to make the army incapable of fighting. Both officers and men were enraged to discover that local merchants—ostensibly patriots like themselves—sent goods the army badly needed to be sold not only in far-off corners of the colonies where prices were known to be better, but even to the

* Desperate for uniforms with which to clothe his men as well as to help instill discipline in troops fighting the tightly disciplined redcoats, Washington was flabbergasted when an eagerly awaited shipment consisted of red uniforms. Glorified sketches in history books of the rich variety of colorful uniforms with which the revolutionary army was supplied are a mockery of men who would have settled for far less just to help them keep warm.

enemy. Many people who did supply the army cheated it shamelessly.* Congressman Samuel Huntington of Connecticut grieved that while "the country abounds with the necessary resources, . . . private gain seems the only object of too many individuals." His namesake, Colonel Ebenezer Huntington, was less restrained in expressing his contempt for civilians and their indifference to the fate of the army:

> I despise my countrymen. I wish I could say I was not born in America. . . . The rascally stupidity which prevails, the insults and neglects which the army have met with, beggars all description. It must go no further. They can endure it no longer. I am in rags, have lain in the rain on the ground for forty hours past, and only a junk of fresh beef and that without salt to dine on this day, rec'd no pay since last December, and all this for my cowardly countrymen who flinch at the very time when exertions are wanted, and hold their purse strings as tho they would damn the world, rather than part with a dollar to their army.

To try to keep troops on active service, Congress did in fact allocate dollars. The men were offered bounties to enlist and reenlist. But the question of bounties presented disagreeable problems as well. Many men who joined the army, accepting the reward for signing on, slipped away to join state militias where enlistment bounties were higher. At one stage, when Congress authorized Continental Army bounties of as much as $200 for men who enlisted (up from ten dollars at the beginning of the war), New Jersey was offering $220, Georgia was offering $300, and Virginia was offering $750. Fed up, Washington warned he could not guarantee special Continental Army attention in the war to states creaming off his troops with inflated monetary rewards.

* "Americans repeatedly sold defective food, clothing, gunpowder and other supplies to their own army. Wagoners drained brine from the barrels of pickled meat to lighten their loads, then charged at the full weight for shipping spoiled meat; meatpackers drained the brine and replaced it with water, which kept up the weight but ruined the meat; barrels of flour arrived at camp with the flour in the middle scooped out; cobblers used old scraps to make shoes that looked good but quickly fell apart; the army received bundles of blankets that, when opened, revealed that each blanket was only a fraction of the proper size; gunsmiths cheated the government when hired to repair arms; large quantities of gunpowder were 'bad and not be depended on.' "—Charles Royster, *A Revolutionary People at War*, 274.

Aside from offering better money, state militia enlistments were usually for no more than six months, while Washington had no doubt it would be impossible to train men and fight a war if he could count on his troops staying in service only half a year.

State militias were supposed to be available to Washington when he planned his strategy. But they could not be relied upon. Washington complained, "They come in, you cannot tell how, go, you cannot tell when, and act, you cannot tell where; consume your provisions, exhaust your stores and leave you at last in a critical moment."[8] Several times, attacks on the British were prematurely launched because the brief enlistment period of militiamen attached to the army, and needed for those assaults, was about to expire. Lafayette marveled at the way militia units might leave for home regardless of battlefield circumstances. "You might as well stop the flood tide," he said, "as stop militia whose times are out."[9]

When expected French assistance did not materialize for the battle of Newport in 1778, so many militiamen left for home that the army there was reduced by half its strength at a stroke. In upstate New York, at a critical moment in the Revolution, just before the battle for Bemis Heights, the New Hampshire militia arrived in the line in the morning and left at midday. (It returned to distinguish itself in battle a few days later.)

General Greene complained, "With the militia, everybody is a general. . . . They must go to war their own way or not at all." As at Newport, there was nothing to guarantee they would stay if things turned nasty. At the battle of Camden, the North Carolina and Virginia militias, though outnumbering the British, fled without firing a shot. Criticized for not protecting his flank in a battle with the redcoats by bracing up against a marsh, General Daniel Morgan explained that if he had used the marsh for cover, the militiamen under his command would have made for it once the battle had commenced and "nothing could have detained them."[10] Morgan said that the best way to deploy militia was to put them in the center of the line with picked troops behind them to shoot down those who tried to run away.

Militia units often served with great daring and dedication, but even when they did, regional antagonisms between them could complicate the job of the commander, who would have preferred to concentrate on other matters. Friction was habitual between

New England and southern militia contingents and between coastal units and units made up of their backwoods country cousins. There were times when promises had to be made that militia would not have to serve in states other than their own, which limited their usefulness when such boundaries were meaningless in combat.

The quality and morale of the men called to the colors was also of continual concern. In states which had to resort to conscription to make up congressional quotas, the results were never all that was hoped for. In Virginia's Augusta and Rockbridge counties, for example, mobs seized and destroyed draft documents. Elsewhere in Virginia, a mob frightened off draft officers and then defiantly retired to a nearby tavern to drink the king's health.

In 1781, ten percent of the recruits arriving from New England, where the fighting had started in a blaze of glory six years earlier, were so unfit for duty that they were sent home.[11] There was a sizable number of rejects from other states as well because men who were drafted could and did pay others to take their places, and often it was older men, misfits and even young boys who were sent to fill in; they were available at less cost than able-bodied substitutes. Some states relieved themselves of their prison populations by shipping off convicts as "volunteers" to meet congressional quotas. Not surprisingly, many of those men took off through the woods at the earliest opportunity and were never seen again. Their idea of liberty differed from that of Congress.

All this put a tremendous strain on the fighting spirit of the men who remained on active duty, with an inevitable impact on their performance. Officers were demoralized as much as ordinary soldiers. It mortified Washington, who counted on his officers to whip his army into shape. He suggested in a moment of annoyance that nothing "but the breaking of two or three officers in every regiment will effect a radical cure of their negligence, inattention and . . . downright disobedience."[12]

Morale was no problem for the men who formed up outside Boston in 1775, laying siege to the city at the start of the Revolution. They did not yet consider themselves rebels against the king, but they were itching to tangle with the redcoats occupying the city. Their cause was just and their confidence was absolute. A

British officer said they were "worked up to such a degree of enthusiasm and madness they are easily persuaded the Lord is to assist them in whatever they undertake."

However, they did not constitute an organized fighting force. There was little discipline in their ranks. These were citizen-soldiers. They came and went as they pleased and drilled only when they were of a mind to. Their supply situation was chaotic. No responsible officer could seriously have contemplated using those men, highly motivated though they were, for a major assault on British positions. Some idea of what they looked like to outsiders was given by a British surgeon, probably prejudiced but not altogether blind, who visited their encampments outside Boston in 1775: "This army . . . is truly nothing but a drunken, canting, lying, praying, hypocritical rabble, without order, subjection, discipline or cleanliness; and must fall to pieces of itself in the course of three months."[13]

The redcoats had problems, too. They were also short of supplies and were ravaged by scurvy and smallpox. But theirs was a tightly disciplined fighting force. Had they broken out of Boston and scattered their disorganized besiegers (this was a full year before the Declaration of Independence), the Revolution might well have been extinguished before it was launched. It would have been a long time before another American colonial force of any consequence would again have gathered to confront the British Army.

In most of the colonies, the revolutionary impulse was still incubating. A successful British assault might have stiffened the backbone of those—including many in Congress—who opposed the insurrection at that stage or who feared its consequences. It might have encouraged them to resist radical pressures and stand fast before the stampede to revolution became unstoppable.

The British might have done all this had their commander, General Sir William Howe,* not trembled at the recollection of the monstrous price in casualties his forces had paid for his Bun-

---

* The British forces in America had four successive commanders during the War of Independence. General Thomas Gage, commander since 1763, was succeeded by Howe in 1775—shortly after the battle of Bunker Hill, at which Howe had been operational commander! Howe was succeeded in 1778 by General Sir Henry Clinton, who was succeeded by General Sir Guy Carleton in 1782. Carleton was commander in chief of British forces in America when the peace treaty ending the war was signed.

ker Hill victory on Boston's Charlestown peninsula in June of that year, 1775—a fantastic British bungle. (Instead of sending suicidal waves of redcoats against entrenched rebel positions, he could easily have sealed off the rebels on the narrow neck of land on which they were defiantly dug in and starved them out.)

Resulting British timidity had given Washington an advantage when he rushed to Massachusetts in July 1775 to take personal charge of the troops as soon as he was named commander in chief of the Continental Army. It permitted him to face a confused stalemate rather than imminent catastrophe as he took on the task of creating a national army for a nation that did not yet exist. With his war already in progress, he began fashioning that army from ingredients which were not always compatible or pliable—untrained local alarm companies, colonial militia units with ideas of their own about what they would and would not do, and streams of volunteers whose enthusiasm tended to wane as they faced the dreary reality of slow-paced siege soldiering.

From the very beginning, the army confronted Washington with problems that would have shattered a lesser man and irreparably destroyed the reputation of a lesser commander. He hoped to field twenty thousand fighting men within six months of assuming command. But by the deadline he and Congress had set, less than half that number had been recruited. Many who did sign up could not be relied upon, and many who could be relied upon remained stubbornly resistant to military training.

Nor was it only the enlisted men who presented problems. Owing their commissions to family connections or social status rather than to military experience, some officers had no idea whatsoever what their duties required of them. Many high-ranking officers in local militias declined to accept lower rank in the Continental Army, or did so grudgingly.

Desperate for action to retrieve a situation that seemed to be slipping away from him as the weeks and months passed, Washington four times considered mounting assaults on the British with the questionable forces at his disposal. Four times he was talked out of it by his generals, who dreaded the consequences of fiasco. Within a few months of this phony war, the men who had rushed to the line hankering after battle had grown impatient and restless. As the first winter drew near, many of them took off for home to see to their neglected families, crops and livestock. Seeing them go, others without such pressing commitments drifted off as well. Some departed simply because they felt they had been there long enough and it was time for other patriots to do their duty. By November, Connecticut militiamen had decided they had served their time and set off homeward, "hissed, groaned at and pelted" by the men they filed through on their way out of camp. Soon some of those men were homeward bound as well.

Jealousies, resentments and ambitious connivings among senior officers were rampant. John Adams would later snarl, "I am wearied to death with the wrangling between military officers, high and low. They quarrel like cats and dogs. They worry one another like mastiffs, scrambling for rank and pay like apes for nuts."[14] Colonies demanded that special consideration be given their favorite sons when command appointments were distributed. As a result, twelve generals were named to serve under Washington when, considering the situation, seven would have sufficed.

Special consideration did not necessarily mean that those given senior appointments were content with what they got. When Joseph Spencer of the Connecticut militia, named a brigadier general in the Continental Army, learned that Israel Putnam, also of Connecticut, had been made a major general, he abandoned his troops outside Boston and went home to sulk. Just a few months after assuming command, Washington, jolted into despair and bewilderment by the behavior of his senior officers, wrote, "Such a dearth of public spirit, and want of virtue, such stock-jobbing, and fertility in all the low arts to obtain advantages of one kind or another . . . I never saw before and pray I may never witness again . . ."[15]

Such vexation was understandable in a commander whose supply situation remained absurdly precarious. At one stage, two thousand of his men—one fifth of the army as it then existed—had no firearms at all. So short of weapons was the army that an order was issued that "no soldier, however dismissed, is to carry away any arms with him that are good and fit for service." That included the weapons which men owned privately and which they had brought with them to the siege of Boston.

Still there weren't enough weapons, and not many of those who had guns found much use for them. At a time when few bullets fired in combat hit their targets, at a time when sustained, largely wasted field-of-fire volleys were standard in battlefield confrontations, Washington found—and the discovery stunned him into silence for half an hour—that he had only enough powder to issue to his soldiers at most nine cartridges apiece! General Putnam sounded off in fury: "Powder, powder! Ye gods, give us powder!"[16] At that point, Benjamin Franklin's suggestion that American troops might be equipped with bows and arrows did not seem frivolous.

After repeated pleas from Washington, Congress was finally induced to issue a summons to the "several colonies of New Hampshire, Rhode Island, Connecticut and the interior towns of Massachusetts Bay, that they immediately furnish the American army before Boston as much powder . . . as they can possibly spare." Nevertheless, support from these areas closest to the front was hardly overwhelming, nor is it likely that the response would have been different had it been commonly known that there were days during the siege of Boston when whole sections of the American siege line were left completely undefended.

To aggravate the situation still further, Washington was so short of trusted aides that he had to expend much time and energy on chores that should have been left to his staff or even junior officers: making certain the camp areas were regularly policed; giving instruction on the care and maintenance of latrines; forbidding sentries to talk to the enemy. His most trusted adviser and friend, Colonel Joseph Reed, returned from Massachusetts to Philadelphia because his presence was required there to deal with certain matters for his law firm. Another key aide, Edmund Randolph, returned to Virginia to look after the estate of an uncle who had just died. No wonder Washington was prompted to confess, "I have often thought how much happier I should have been if, instead of accepting a command under such circumstances, I had taken my musket on my shoulder and entered the ranks or, if I could have justified the measure to posterity and my own conscience, had retired to the back country and lived in a wigwam."[17]

He resisted that temptation, stayed, and got the men to buckle down and throw up fortifications in depth, making the siege of Boston credible. More important, Colonel Henry Knox (the chubby Boston bookseller who would later be America's first secretary of war) and his men performed the astonishing task of manhandling forty-three cannon, some of which weighed more than a ton, from the captured British armory at Ticonderoga across hundreds of miles of rough country to the outskirts of Boston in deepest winter—along with enough lead and flint to make them operational.

Determined finally to break the Boston stalemate, Washington seized upon an inexplicable British failure to secure the Dorchester Heights commanding the city. He had his newly delivered artillery rammed into position on those heights, leaving the British no choice but to evacuate Boston, a move which did not distress the British commander at all. General Howe had not been happy locked up there, the butt of ridicule back in London for being unable to disperse undisciplined rabble.

Though simple observation and sad experience demonstrated time and time again that the bulk of the Continental Army couldn't be counted on, its core consisted of dedicated, determined men. These tenacious patriots, America's winter soldiers, stayed on when others found reason not to. Without them, the Revolution would have quickly collapsed, a futile adventure. They weathered the worst and reacted to adversity in the same spirit as General Nathanael Greene, who snapped, "We fight, get beat, rise and fight again." But in many ways, the ultimate success of the Revolution was due, not to those heroes but, like the rebel success in Boston, more to British bungling and hesitancy than to anything else.

The British repeatedly squandered opportunities that were theirs by the nature of things or were handed them on a plate by the inexperienced Americans. It even took the British command two years of war to adjust to the fact that the rebels presented a challenge that would not fizzle out of its own accord.

An example of British folly was the failure to shift the redcoats evacuated from Boston directly to New York. Instead, they were briefly diverted to Halifax, Nova Scotia, away from trouble farther south. It is true that reinforcements were on their way, and, after being cooped up in Boston under trying circumstances, they needed rehabilitation. But New York loyalists had already proved themselves to be numerous and active. (New York's mayor,

David Mathews, was implicated in a plot to assassinate George Washington.*) The British would have been able to settle in comfortably in New York, as they did when they finally reached it five months later, in August 1776. More to the point, a British presence earlier might have split the colonies by keeping New York from agreeing to the Declaration of Independence, which it only reluctantly endorsed a full week after independence had been approved by Congress. Also, had they sailed directly from Boston in March, while New York was only thinly defended by rebel forces, they might not have had to fight for the city.

It was, however, not a difficult campaign for them. Washington was able to field eighteen thousand men for defense of the city, more than he would again have at his disposal at any time in the war. But these men, outnumbered by British forces almost twice as numerous, were scattered impossibly throughout the area because the British might land anywhere—on Long Island, on the tip of Manhattan, up the Hudson, or at a dozen other choice locations. Washington did not dispute the warning of General Charles Lee that, with the British controlling the sea approach, New York could not be successfully defended. But to surrender the second-largest city in America within a few weeks of independence, without even a token struggle, would have bit deeply into American morale. It would have shattered his relations with Congress and more than canceled out his triumph in forcing the redcoats to turn tail at Boston.

What made the decision even more difficult for the commander in chief was the realization that the quality of his troops was still frighteningly doubtful. Many of the men who had benefited from training during the Boston siege had been dispatched as reinforcements for the American campaign farther north, designed to draw Canada into the Revolution. Their places had been taken by raw recruits and inexperienced militia so awed by their task that when the long-expected British fleet showed up off Sandy Hook and two British vessels ran the gauntlet of American shore batteries up the Hudson, many men abandoned their posts and trotted along the shore to watch them, like children at a parade. The

* This was before the British captured the city. Mathews was part of an abortive British-funded conspiracy to provoke a munity among American troops and eliminate the commander in chief.

troops were suitably chastized in general orders the following day: "Such unsoldierly conduct must grieve every good officer and give the enemy a mean opinion of the army."

Washington concentrated half his troops at what was then the village of Brooklyn (population four thousand) on Long Island. Brooklyn Heights commanded the entrance to New York Bay as effectively as Dorchester Heights commanded Boston. This time, however, the British did not pull out. Instead, having landed unchallenged, they almost destroyed the American army there and then.

While Hessian mercenaries, moving in as expected from Flatbush, attacked the front of the American line, British troops, guided by a loyalist Brooklyn farmer, slipped around to turn the American flank. Trained in close combat, the enemy diliberately drew American fire and, before reloading was possible, charged in with bayonets. The novice American soldiers were outnumbered, outwitted and terrified. Officers who had never been in battle before were quickly confounded. They were unable to do what was expected of them, much less respond effectively to unanticipated developments.

Many men stood their ground and fought courageously. Watching Marylanders go into battle, Washington declared, "Good God! What brave fellows I must this day lose." Others did not stand the test, panicking and bolting when confronted with the ferocity of the attackers. One in every nine Americans engaged in that battle was lost that day—killed, wounded or taken prisoner. So complete was the American rout that it will always remain a mystery why the British commander failed to follow it up by cutting off and capturing the remaining American forces and Washington as well, and administering what could have been the terminal blows to rebel hopes.

The American position seemed hopeless. They had lost many of their officers. They were trapped on an island which numbered comparatively few rebels among its civilian inhabitants. Nevertheless, the British did not act immediately to press their advantage, and Washington was able the next night to superintend a masterly retreat across the mouth of the East River from Brooklyn to Manhattan. In that one night, nine thousand men made the crossing, leaving their heavy cannon behind only because they sank in the mud of the shore.

* * *

It was the first major battle of the war and an unmitigated American reverse. Nor did it end there. Once safely in Manhattan, demoralized militiamen began dispersing willy-nilly. Six thousand of the eight-thousand-man Connecticut contingent drifted away homeward, as did many others. They were to some extent replaced by new troops which had been en route before the Long Island debacle, but these were untrained, undrilled and unprepared for what was to come. Morale was so low among the defeated Americans that Washington was reluctant to have stragglers or plunderers punished for fear of provoking mutinies.

What was more, Manhattan Island, his new bailiwick, could no more be defended than Long Island. When the British, inexplicably taking their time again, finally landed there two weeks later, at Kip's Bay near where the entrance to a tunnel linking Manhattan and Queens squats today, Washington was compelled to keep retreating. Many of his remaining troops were already scurrying northward.

In one incident, the sudden appearance of a few British soldiers sent a larger American unit scrambling for safety without firing a shot, leaving Washington and his aides, who had been trying to rally the men, without so much as a musket among them. So appalled was the commander in chief by this pusillanimous display that his normally reliable self-control snapped. He drew his sword and vainly tried to force his panicking troops back into line. He and his aides themselves managed to avoid being taken prisoner only because they were mounted and able to gallop humiliatingly away. "I have often read and heard of . . . cowardice," an American officer fumed at the behavior of the men, "but hitherto have had but faint idea of it. . . . I could wish the transactions of this day blotted out of the annals of America."[18] It was harsh judgment on soldiers who probably had never been in combat before that moment when the British troopers in their bright uniforms and uttering fierce cries rushed at them, their bayonets glistening in the sun.

In London, the news from Long Island and New York was deliriously received. People there had been baffled by the absence of expected reports telling how the upstart rebels had been trounced by British might and right. Now King George could express the hope that "deluded and unhappy" Americans would return to "a just and constitutional subordination."

Shamed and stung into desperate action by their abject flight, the Americans made several bold attempts to block the British advance. But New York City was a hopeless cause for them, and their retreat across New Jersey to escape the enemy was a classic tale of a shattered army on the run, forced to forage for food or steal supplies from hostile locals, demoralized and unable to stanch an alarming hemorrhage of desertions. Beholding what was left of the Continental Army on this pitiable trek, one observer suggested that a fresh enemy force of just five hundred men "might have demolished the whole."

"I shall continue to retreat before [the British]," Washington explained, "so as to lull them into security." Rationalization though it was, it appeared to work. The British commander, General Sir William Howe, seemed determined not to send his forces rushing forward to overtake the bedraggled Americans, despite the urgings of his exasperated junior officers. Howe was subsequently hard pressed to explain why he had been so negligent, limply suggesting that he had never received orders to annihilate the Continental Army.

He was, in fact, in a peculiar position. In addition to being the British military commander for the early part of the war, he had been instructed to see if some method could be found for peacefully ending the rebellion. Furthermore, like many enlightened Englishmen, he was not totally unsympathetic to the rebel cause and hoped that agreement at some stage might make a slaughter of his American adversaries unnecessary. In British-occupied New York, he was wont to snub Americans who remained loyal to Britain, some of whom were men of rank and distinction. When the British were about to withdraw from Philadelphia, Howe advised a prominent loyalist there to make his peace with the rebels, thus almost conceding defeat though the war was still far from over. It is likely that he agreed with his brother, Admiral Howe, the British naval commander, that "almost all the people of parts and spirit were in the rebellion."

Whatever the British commander's reasons, Washington was fortunate that a more determined officer did not command the enemy forces. As a military man desperately aware of his own predicament, he could not understand "what hindered them from dispersing our little army and giving a fatal blow to our affairs."[19]

By that time, the rebels had been forced to absorb news of the miscarriage of their Canada adventure. Rebel leaders had assumed that Canadians (mostly of French origin) were as anxious as themselves to be rid of British tyrannical rule. American forces were dispatched to lend support and hasten the process.

General Richard Montgomery led a thousand men up the Hudson and Lake Champlain to seize the town of Montreal as a prelude to moving against the greater prize of Quebec. At the same time, one of the most astounding escapades of the war was undertaken by the men who were to form the second prong of the Canada invasion. Colonel Benedict Arnold led these men through the Maine wilderness to meet up with Montgomery beneath the walls of Quebec.

Theirs was a harrowing trek. Their means of transport, meant to speed up their passage, were flat-bottomed boats which at times had to be dragged, pushed and carried over miles of rugged terrain. Where navigation was hazardous on the rock-studded Kennebec River, Arnold and his men waded up to their necks in freezing water, pushing and pulling their boats forward, sometimes having to clear the way by breaking surface ice. During the night, their wet clothing froze to their bodies. To keep that from happening, some of the men stayed on their feet all night trying to dry themselves. Some of their supplies were washed away or contaminated by leakage, and one quarter of the entire force turned back en masse, taking with them more than their share of the food supplies. Aside from eating their mascot dog, the remaining men were sometimes reduced to chewing on shaving soap, nibbling on candles and gnawing on cartridge boxes to ward off starvation. Many dropped by the wayside and died. But Arnold and 675 of the 1,100 men with whom he had started out stayed the route.

Their excruciating experience turned out to be in vain. Despite their perseverance and stamina, the Americans simply did not have enough troops on the spot to storm Quebec successfully. Many of those who had not begged off en route were determined to head for home as soon as their enlistments expired, within days of their link-up with Montgomery's men. This compelled Montgomery to schedule an assault on Quebec sooner than was wise. His plan to launch his attack on the first stormy night ahead, when the British were unlikely to be on the alert, was leaked to the British commander by an American deserter, robbing the rebels of the essential element of surprise. Montgomery, leading his men, was shot dead almost immediately. Benedict Arnold was wounded and the expeditionary force was driven back.

Few Canadians had risen to assist the rebel forces. Catholic French Canadians preferred the British to the Catholic-baiting New England Protestants. There was to be a further effort later to enroll them in the fight for liberty. Some Canadians of British origin did join the Revolution, but most remained unimpressed by either rebel rhetoric or rebel military achievement.

As a people, Americans seem always to have been manic-depressive, responding to the latest setback with unrelieved dejection and to the latest good news with joy bordering on bliss. Word of the failure to hold New York loosed an orgy of despair, convincing many who had previously been hopeful of victory that the American cause was lost. However, when Washington's men stood fast at Harlem Heights, forcing overconfident redcoats to withdraw under fire, morale soared and patriotism was rampant. As Washington's troops tramped wearily in retreat through New Jersey, men peeling off in droves and going their own way, even Congress was prepared for the worst. But when the Americans staged a surprise raid on the Hessian encampment at Trenton on Christmas night 1776 to score a badly needed victory, morale once again surged upward. An English observer noted, "The minds of the people are much altered. A few days ago they had given up the cause for lost . . . now they are all liberty-mad again."

As befitted an English gentleman and a seasoned European soldier, General Howe was much less excitable than the mercurial Americans. As far as he was concerned, there was a time for fighting and a time for hibernation. When the winter of '76–'77 closed in over the American landscape, the British commander retired to New York, where he could enjoy the favors of his mistress, Elizabeth Loring, the attractive wife of a compliant American commissary officer in the British Army. This casual attitude was not well received by American loyalists. Convinced that the rebels were on the verge of total collapse, they urged Howe to get on with the job of snuffing out the Revolution:

Awake, arouse, Sir Billy,
There's forage on the plain.
Ah, leave your little filly,
And open the campaign.

Aside from the personal pleasures he would have had to forgo, and aside from shunning winter combat as a matter of experience and tradition, Howe believed that after a season in the frozen fields of the countryside, the rebels would be prepared to concede that their uprising was ill-conceived and doomed and that British rule wasn't half as bad as their leaders insisted. He called his men back from most of Jersey to winter quarters near New York. Ever vigilant, Washington rushed bedraggled but plucky units forward to claim that inhospitable region, which, having experienced extensive plundering by Hessian troops, looked somewhat more sympathetically on the rebel cause than its inhabitants had previously. Once more, adrenaline was pumped through the American bloodsteam in good measure. Once more, a wave of optimism swept the states, as they now had become, their colonial identity jettisoned forever.

But the surge in morale was short-lived. Despite the promises of Congress and individual states, the army was still pathetically strapped for supplies. There was nowhere near enough food, clothing, blankets or medicine. Desertion remained habitual. Discipline remained haphazard.

Nevertheless, Washington performed the remarkable feat of keeping his army in being—though it was sometimes down to barely three thousand men!—and ready to confront Howe when his redcoats, ferried by sea from New York, landed at Chesapeake Bay to march on Philadelphia a year after independence had been declared there. The battle of Brandywine was another incident in which British forces overwhelmed inexperienced American troops (whose officers hadn't even reconnoitered the terrain over which they were to fight) and then neglected to follow up their victory. Howe again hesitated, permitting the Americans to withdraw, and then marched on to seize nearby Philadelphia, a smaller prize than the destruction of the Continental Army would have been.

Congress had fled by the time the British advance guard arrived, no adjournment vote having been taken. Sufficiently aware of the fate that awaited them if captured, congressmen did not stand on ceremony. They filtered out of town like fugitives. Washington made an effort to redeem the reputation of the army at nearby Germantown with a shrewdly calculated assault, which was, however, turned to the advantage of the enemy when his officers got their signals muddled. Shots were exchanged between American units, and the troops panicked headlong into retreat in a blinding fog.

Disillusioned by his personal circumstances, an American officer captured at Germantown declared, "I really believe the game is up. . . . Everybody is tired and those red-hot Virginians who were so violent are all crying out for Peace."[20] But American expectations had sunk so low by then that the mere fact the rebels *might* have won at Germantown if things had worked out as planned served to keep American spirits from collapsing altogether.

As 1777 drew to a close, Washington badly needed either a quick, convincing victory or a respite. The former not being likely, he went about seeking winter quarters for his men. General Johann Kalb, who was later to be killed in combat in South Carolina, confided to a friend that he believed Valley Forge had been chosen on the advice of fools, speculators or traitors. It was bleak, desolate and exposed to the cruel whims of winter. It was in fact chosen because Washington thought it could be defended if the British tried a surprise attack and, at the same time, was close enough to Philadelphia for him to keep an eye on the enemy there.

There are few places more appropriately designated as American national monuments than Valley Forge. There are few places where Americans—each of whom could have deserted long before—suffered more for their homeland under conditions which even devout optimists might have been excused for considering hopeless. One in every four soldiers who wintered that year at Valley Forge died there. General John Sullivan bemoaned the circumstances in which the troops found themselves that Pennsylvania winter: "The whole of them without watch coats, one half without blankets and more than a third without shoes, stockings or breeches, and many of them without jackets . . . and not a few without shirts."[21] Some officers were "so naked they were ashamed to be seen."

The men made camp at Valley Forge in mid-December 1777, but not until mid-January were they all under cover, in huts they built from the timber of nearby forests. Even then there was only the frozen earth for a floor and crouchinig near smoking fires for warmth. An impression of their misery was hauntingly evoked in the diary of army surgeon Albigence Waldo:

> I am sick—discontented—and out of humor. Poor food—hard lodging—cold weather—fatigue—nasty clothes—nasty cookery—vomit half my time—smoked out of my senses—the Devil's in it—I can't endure it—why are we sent here to starve and freeze—what sweet felicities have I left at home—a charming wife—pretty children—good food—good cookery—all agreeable—all harmonious. Here, all confusion—smoke and cold—hunger and filthiness—a pox on my bad luck. Here comes a bowl of beef soup—full of burnt leaves and dirt, sickish enough to make a Hector spew—away with it boys—I'll live like the chameleon upon air.

Refusing to accept that an army should turn against the people it served, Washington declined to act on advice, including some from congressmen, that he simply seize desperately needed provisions from farmers and others in the area. But he was disgusted by the avarice of local civilians who charged outrageous prices for food for their hungry army. Even worse were the feelings aroused by those of them who preferred to peddle their wares to the British in Philadelphia, who did not haggle over payment. Some who were caught paid a price themselves. A miller named Thomas Butler was given 250 lashes for trying to sneak flour into Philadelphia under cover of darkness. Farmer William Maddock was fined £100 sterling for trying to bring cattle for the British to slaughter at a time when rebel soldiers, of an evening, would sing out black-humor choruses of "No meat! No meat!" across the frozen landscape.

Through sickness, death, and desertion, the Continental Army, rebuilt the previous summer, again dwindled to almost negligible proportions—if only numbers were considered. General James Varnum, who was at Valley Forge, underestimated the pluck of the men who were there, too, when he observed that the situation was such "that in all human probability the army must soon dissolve."[22]

Though a creature of Congress, the army endlessly complained of the inability of congressmen to grasp the military requirements of the Revolution. In the early part of the war, Congress's cack-handed appointment of foreigners to the revolutionary officer corps provoked a clamor of complaint. The shortage of experienced officers was unquestionably worrying. Recognizing the dangers involved, Congress authorized Silas Deane, when he was dispatched as emissary to France in 1776, to sign up experienced French officers, particularly military engineers, to help fight the British.

Many of the foreigners who joined the Continental Army performed valuable services. Von Steuben, the Prussian drillmaster at Valley Forge, had shamelessly exaggerated his previous experience, but he did more than anyone else to turn American soldiers into disciplined fighting men. Thaddeus Kościusko from Poland was influential in formulating the strategy which led to the British defeat at Saratoga, and later fought with distinction in the South. Lafayette was valued adviser and confidant to Washington, a classic loner, and helped smooth sometimes strained relations between the American and French allies.

But Silas Deane's assignment to recruit officers led to a string of troublesome abuses. An inexperienced diplomat seeking to cultivate influential Frenchmen, Deane came under pressure from those he sought to befriend in Paris to sign on men who had neither experience nor ability. Most were self-seeking adventurers. Some condescended to serve the American cause provided they were given senior commands. Some came with letters of introduction from French dignitaries whom congressmen, desperate for a French alliance to save the Revolution, were reluctant to offend. Some were junior officers who arrived expecting to be awarded higher rank in the American army which they would then be able to carry back to France, thus quickly gaining seniority that otherwise would take them years to acquire. Some, not troubling to solicit introductory letters at home, simply showed up in Philadelphia, having heard that America was a land so short of talent, imagination and gentility that even the lowliest French lieutenant might soon charm his way into acquiring a colonel's epaulets.

Congress at first felt obliged to enroll these presumptuous hopefuls. It granted them commissions and left it to the army to deal with their grandiose expectations. When their reception by the army wasn't all they had expected, some left for home, taking with them the inflated ranks they had acquired. But others remained and were a great distraction and nuisance to Washington and other senior American military men. Particularly offended were American generals over whose heads some foreigners were promoted by Congress. Several of them threatened to resign their commissions. "Our officers think it exceedingly hard," Washington told Congress, "after they have toiled in this service and probably sustained many losses, to have strangers put over them, whose merit, perhaps, is not equal to their own but whose effrontry will take no denial."

One French officer of doubtful talents but understood to be a favorite of the king of France arrived with an entourage of twenty-eight staff officers and sergeants of his own, expecting to take command of all American artillery and engineering forces. His accidental death by drowning soon after his arrival came as a relief to both Congress and Washington.

The situation grew so unmanageable that Thomas Jefferson, risking giving offense, urged "French gentlemen" not to come to America, and another congressman moaned, "They are flocking over in such numbers that I do not know what we shall do with them." Word gradually spread overseas that America wasn't quite the land of opportunity it had been cracked up to be, and the influx was gradually stemmed.

What was not stemmed were the complaints and grumblings in the army about men being made to go hungry and in tatters while not being paid. Particularly enraged were officers who were bankrupting themselves by serving the Revolution. A horse, which was often essential but was not always provided, could cost an officer the equivalent of ten years of his army pay. If he stayed long enough in one place, settling his laundry bill could eat up all his pay.*

By 1778, up to twenty officers a week were asking leave to resign their commissions. Some wanted out simply because they couldn't afford to stay in the army; others because they saw many civilians making a lot of money from the war and thought it was about time they did the same. When France joined the war and its expeditionary force landed, French officers sometimes invited their American opposite numbers to dinner. The invitations were rarely accepted, because American officers couldn't afford to reciprocate with any semblance of dignity.

Not by coincidence did France's decision to risk allying itself with the rebels come hard on the heels of the rebel victory at Saratoga in northern New York at the end of 1777. Saratoga was the first major American victory in the war, and it was devastating. It was the bloody finale to a daring plan by the British to send their forces slogging down from Canada to New York to slice New England off from the rest of America. They would then pursue a war of attrition to tire out the less tempestuous southerners and people in the middle states and make them more amenable to a settlement with the motherland.

In blocking this ambitious venture way up near the Canadian border, the rebels not only mauled the British army but obliterated any hopes the British command had for the divide-and-conquer strategy most likely to crush the Revolution. The Saratoga saga finally persuaded the French that despite their earlier performance and continuing difficulties, the Americans could win, and that by joining them in the war they were not likely to find themselves trapped in a costly fiasco. When previously pressed for an alliance, they had hesitated and dawdled. Now they rushed to embrace the patriot cause openly before the rebels could be tempted to back out of the conflict by renewed military setbacks or by British concessions which they knew were in the pipeline.

---

* George Washington wrote, "No officer can live upon his pay. . . . Hundreds having spent their little all in addition to their scanty public allowance, have resigned because they could no longer support themselves as officers. . . . Numbers are . . . rendered unfit for duty for want of clothing, while the rest are wasting their property, and some of them are verging fast to the gulf of poverty and distress."[23]

Relief and revived confidence was the response in America to the French connection. "I believe no event was ever received with more heartfelt joy," Washington exclaimed, officially informing his army that it had "pleased the Almighty Ruler of the Universe propitiously to defend the Cause of the United American States . . . by raising us up a powerful Friend among the Princes of the Earth." It was not exactly the terminology king-hater Tom Paine would have employed.

But though Saratoga aroused great optimism and ultimately proved to be the turning point in the war, the worst was still to come. It would be another five years before the peace treaty would finally be signed. Before then, leading rebels—Washington among them—would again sink to the depths of despair, doubting the ability of the Continental Army to withstand the battering of the British forces, doubting the willingness of Americans to put up with the unrelieved hardship of war, doubting even the value of the foreign alliance they had welcomed with such great expectations.

At first there was good reason for confidence. A fleet of warships was said to be en route from France to put paid finally to the devastating advantage the redcoats derived from Britain's seaborne mastery of the Atlantic coast. What was more, thousands of French troops reportedly were on board to march to the aid of American land forces when the fleet sailed in.

It was exciting. It was exhilarating. It was also premature. Optimism generated by the formation of the alliance frittered away when it became apparent that the Americans had badly miscalculated the likely French contribution to the war effort. They expected the French entry into the conflict to produce reasonably quick results. But it was another eighteen months before any meaningful French involvement in military operations would take place. And it would be a full three years of hardship and adversity before the alliance would prove decisive.

Americans weren't the only ones to be disappointed. Once committed to the war, the French were depressed to see that the rebels were not in nearly as strong a position as they had been led to believe after the Saratoga victory. Nor was the revolutionary spirit as widespread as they had expected. Count Rochambeau, the French commander, reported home, "Do not count on these people nor on their resources. They have neither money nor credit. Their forces only exist momentarily. . . . When they are to be attacked in their own homes, they assemble only during the time of personal danger to defend themselves."[24]

There was also a question of who was in charge. Accustomed to command, autocratic senior French officers were not overly pleased with the determination of American commanders, whom they considered really only farmers and tradesmen, to presume to decide on battle plans for the alliance. More than one French officer would end up believing that the ultimate military success of the Revolution was a French achievement to which American forces had lent assistance.

Initial strategy was for the French armada arriving on the scene to act on American intelligence reports and bottle up and destroy a British flotilla sheltering in Delaware Bay. Then it would cruise northward to assist the Americans in the long-overdue recapture of New York City. It was straightforward. Elusive victory seemed around the corner. But when the French, taking a very long eighty-seven days to cross the Atlantic, arrived in July 1778, it was too late for the first part of the plan even to be attempted. The British ships had moved on by then. When he pursued them to New York, the French admiral decided the enemy fleet was too formidable for the firepower at his disposal, so battle was avoided there as well.

It is possible that the French were simply being shrewd, that they believed that driving the British out of their bastion in New York was not to their advantage, that it would induce the British to come to terms with the rebels, thus ending the war prematurely as far as French interests were concerned.

The next joint operation, in August 1778, was to be in Rhode Island, where French vessels were to put their marines ashore to join American infantry in the capture of Newport from the British. But the unexpected arrival of the British fleet offshore and a storm which did damage to ships of both navies discouraged the French from proceeding with the plan, despite anguished American insistence that Newport was ripe for plucking. Decimated by desertions when French intentions to pull out of the engagement became clear, the American forces withdrew.

France's reputation as an ally and a friend in need was badly dented by these proceedings. When the French fleet put in at Boston Harbor for repairs, its sailors on shore leave ran into an anti-French riot. Several were beaten up, and one of their officers was bludgeoned to death. Hot-tempered General Sullivan, who had commanded the American forces in the Newport fiasco, described the French withdrawal there as a "stain on the honor of France." Sullivan angrily declared that French behavior had "revived all the ancient prejudices against the faith and sincerity of that people" and encouraged Americans "most heartily to curse the new alliance."[25] Worried rebel leaders hastily stepped in to calm the situation and prevent an early rupture with their badly needed ally whose loans were keeping the revolutionary economy from complete collapse.

The French next showed up at Savannah in October 1779, having spent the intervening time in the more agreeable waters of the West Indies. A combined American-French land-sea assault on the British-held city seemed so certain of success that a call for a British surrender was made prior to the battle. The British commander, playing for time to strengthen his defenses, asked for twenty-four hours in which to consider raising the white flag. In the end, however, possibly because the French commander insisted on launching his attack prematurely (he declined to wait until preparations could be made for storming the British fortifications), Savannah showed again how prone the rebels were to snatching defeat from the jaws of victory. Subsequent successes at Charleston, Camden and elsewhere gave the British control of much of the South. In 1780, it seemed possible that what was then the Deep South was being levered out of the Revolution.

So dismayed had the French been by the Savannah setback, which they attributed to American bungling, that they sailed for home—both their major efforts to assist their youthful ally having been botched. A suggestion was dispatched from Paris that the rebels really had to do more to win their own war.

In the summer of 1780, a French expeditionary force finally landed at Newport, which had been evacuated by the British. It did virtually nothing for most of the following year except charm local inhabitants. But its presence there kept the British from shifting forces garrisoned in New York to the South, where the redcoats had racked up a string of successes, overrunning Georgia and South Carolina, and where General Nathanael Greene was given the unenviable assignment of salvaging the rebel position.

By late 1780, America had endured five grueling years of

death and destruction. At best, the rebels had a stalemate to show for it, though many of them would have considered that a generous overestimate. The army might have expected increasing dollops of aid and consideration from Congress and the states as the civilian authorities came to grips with their responsibilities. But it remained ragged and destitute, surviving hand to mouth. This was a full three years after the celebrated victory at Saratoga, but Greene, surveying the troops of his new command, wrote to a congressman, "The wants of this army are so numerous and various that the shortest way of telling you is to inform you that we have nothing." Washington too had no good news to report:

> Scarce any State in the Union has, at this hour, an eighth part of its quota in the field and little prospect that I can see of ever getting more than half. . . . Instead of everything in readiness to take the field, we have nothing, and instead of having the prospect of a glorious offensive campaign before us, we have a bewildered and gloomy defensive one.

Thomas Jefferson said the morale of some Virginia militiamen was so low that there was "no hope of being able longer to keep them in service."[26] But it was in the South early in 1781 that the tide showed signs of turning in favor of the rebels.

General Daniel Morgan seemed to be inviting fresh disaster by picking the meadow at Cowpens, South Carolina, where there was no escape route for his men, as the place to stand and fight. But he inflicted a stinging defeat on the overconfident British, encouraging southern militiamen, demoralized by defeat and neglect, to rally once more to the cause. Guerrillas under the command of "Swamp Fox" Francis Marion and "Carolina Gamecock" Thomas Sumter and dragoons led by "Lighthorse Harry" Lee began nibbling away at British positions, retaking outposts and threatening more secure coastal strongholds. The British forces were still largely intact. But the growing number of their setbacks, while none of them was momentous, grew increasingly unsettling. Whatever the other factors in the war, it was now beginning to become apparent to the British that the land was too big and too unruly for them to subdue, except in bits and pieces, and most of those not for long.

Their victory in the battle at Eutaw Springs, South Carolina, in September 1781 was a costly success for the British. They lost a lot of men there. But the fact that a brilliantly executed rebel surprise assault was fought off by them seemed to indicate that rebel optimism might once again be premature. If Washington had proceeded with his intention to mount a major assault on the British in New York, it probably would have been premature. The redcoats were braced for him there, and his probing attacks were easily brushed off. At the advice of the French, he thereupon turned his attention to the sizable army of British troops that, hoping to force Virginia out of the war, were congregated around Yorktown.

At last getting their signals straight, the American and French commands synchronized battle plans. French troops, shunted southward from their positions in Rhode Island, where some had to be pried away from their newly acquired sweethearts, marched on Virginia. With French troops landed by sea, they constituted a force roughly equal in size to the American troops who also converged on the region in strength. Together, they boxed the British army in at Yorktown in October 1781 while the French fleet, in an audacious maneuver, sped up from the West Indies to bottle up the James and York rivers and block a British withdrawal or reinforcement. There was no way out.

The British had had enough. It looked to them as if the war could, at best, only drag on and on. It had grown increasingly unpopular at home. Even ministers of the crown were sick of it. And now their army had suffered a colossal setback. It was time to wash their hands of these turbulent colonies.

The war was, in effect, over. For Americans, however, the agony lingered on. The army could not be sent home, partly because there was no absolute guarantee that there would be no resumption of hostilities* and partly because there weren't enough funds to pay the men off. Morale problems persisted, and mutiny was, as it had been through most of the war, a recurring threat.

Even just before the showdown at Yorktown, long-term Penn-

* There were, in fact, further skirmishes, though no further major battles. Washington wanted to follow up the Yorktown triumph by mounting American-French assaults on British positions at Wilmington and Charleston, but the French withdrew their forces to tangle with the British in the West Indies, where they later took a beating.

sylvania troopers who had gone through the worst rebelled in disgust over accumulated grievances. They formed a board of sergeants to negotiate with senior officers on their behalf after they became convinced they were being tricked into staying on in the army for longer than their original enlistments. Prior to Yorktown, there had been a persistent danger that men would desert to the British, rather than just go home, because the British offered them the back pay which Congress kept promising but rarely delivered.

As early as 1777, a New England brigade low in supplies and behind in pay refused orders to join the bulk of the army in Pennsylvania. In that incident, a captain shot and killed a ringleader to break the mutiny and was killed himself before other officers quelled the revolt. At West Point two years later, hungry troops were talked out of mutiny only after others had been summoned to force them back into line. In 1780, a New York lieutenant was forced to commit the outrage of enrolling Indians to corral absconding mutineers, killing several of the rebellious troops in the process. Even in 1783, at the war's official conclusion, unpaid soldiers marched on Philadelphia to claim what was theirs, sending Congress scuttling to safety in Princeton, out of reach of its own enraged troops.

Saratoga and Yorktown were the only major American victories in a war which consisted mostly of lesser campaigns, battles and skirmishes, in some of which American fighting men excelled. At Bennington, Vermont, in the summer of '77, much-maligned, poorly trained New England militiamen routed experienced Hessian mercenaries. At Stony Point, New York, in the summer of '79, rebels demonstrated soldierly daring sufficient to impress the most haughty of British officers. The exploits of George Rogers Clark in clearing the British from much of the Mississippi and Ohio valleys ('78–'81) are among the most exciting deeds in the annals of the American frontier. But throughout the war, most encounters between the British and the rebels ended in rebel setbacks.

Not until France made good its promise and provided effective naval and infantry support at Yorktown (where, incidentally, French troops rushed into battle shouting *"Vive le Roi!"*) did the Revolution undeniably gain the military initiative. At no point until Yorktown could the rebels be certain that an encouraging win might not soon be neutralized by a demoralizing setback. Not until Yorktown could they be absolutely confident of final victory. It was a long, hard and, for the most part, discouraging war.

6

THE COMMANDER UNDER FIRE

My enemies take an ungenerous advantage of me; they know the delicacy of my situation, and that motives of policy deprive me of the defense I might otherwise make against their invidious attacks.

—GEORGE WASHINGTON[1]

During his first years as commander in chief of the Continental Army, George Washington had the misfortune of being regarded by an important group of his fellow revolutionaries as that most sad and sorry of American outcasts, a loser. He had lost in Long Island and New York. He had lost at Brandywine and Germantown. He had even permitted the British to capture the capital of the Revolution and had thus obliged disgruntled congressmen to scramble in undignified haste out of Philadelphia to save their necks.

His successes—at Trenton and Princeton—had raised American hopes, but his critics claimed they were really skirmishes rather than battles, having little long-term strategic significance. It was an exaggeration to declare, as did merchant Elkanah Watson at the end of 1776, that "we . . . considered ourselves a vanquished people." But the situation was grim, and, as a result, Washington—though soon to be dubbed Father of His Country—became the target of a concerted effort to deprive him of his command and authority and to consign him to obscurity.

So ineffectual had been the performance of his Continental Army, so little could be said in its favor, that criticism of Washington, even open abuse, was inevitable. It came from some of the most influential men in rebel ranks. Among them were some who had been his most ardent advocates, men like John Adams who had strongly backed Washington's nomination as army commander, Pennsylvania politician Thomas Mifflin who had initially been proud to serve as his aide-de-camp, and fellow Virginian Congressman Richard Henry Lee. Their change of heart, and the sniping of others as well, presented to Washington a tormenting challenge which compounded his military difficulties and intensified his bouts of anguish and despair.

He was badgered. He was plotted against. His orders were ignored. Congress casually bypassed him in dealing with his subordinates. Men who might have been expected to be discreet openly spoke insultingly of his abilities. And all of this came to a head while Washington and his men languished at Valley Forge and the future looked dismal enough for the Revolution without additional divisive pressures.

By virtue of his position and the pressing nature of his duties, he was poorly placed to defend himself. To try to explain, to give excuses for the army's difficulties by pinpointing what he saw as the causes, would have provided the British with both strategic intelligence and additional inducement to exploit the plight of his troops. Despite the comforts of their winter's hibernation in Philadelphia, they might even have been encouraged to embark on a campaign against the exhausted rebel forces at Valley Forge. In a letter to a confidant, Washington lamented that his critics knew he could not "combat their insinuations, however injurious, without disclosing secrets which it is of the utmost value to conceal."

Some of those who were most vitriolic in condemning Washington must have realized full well how inadequate were the forces at his disposal and how badly they were provisioned. They included men who had served under him and had experienced much of what he was experiencing. Nevertheless, they believed he was not making the best use of the resources he did have and was, therefore, proving increasingly incapable of commanding the army of the Revolution.

Faced with Washington's incessant pleas for supplies, congressmen began thinking of him as a nag and a nuisance who, with his "whining complaints" about shortfalls in provisions and the failure to provide funds to pay the troops, was making excuses for his own inadequacies. Having trouble raising funds to finance the Revolution at a time when its success was hardly secure, some were puzzled when the commander in chief of the army bothered them with demands for pensions for his officers and for the women who might become their widows. It seemed hardly a subject to concern personally the man who should have dedicated himself entirely to thrashing the enemy, a task for which he had so far demonstrated no great flair. Didn't he know what a commander was supposed to do? Was that why the performance of the army was so lamentable? Was it true, as some distinguished rebels suggested, that Washington's grasp of military matters left much to be desired?

Insinuations that he was unfit for his command sometimes pressed beyond the bounds of decency. New Jersey Congressman Jonathan Sergeant accused him of being responsible for "such blunders as might have disgraced a soldier of three months' standing."[2] The Pennsylvania assembly grotesquely suggested that retiring his exhausted troops to Valley Forge may have been convenient for the men but it was a dereliction of duty when there was a war to win. Benjamin Rush, former congressman, distinguished army surgeon and the father of American psychiatry, said Washington's "slackness and remissness" were "so conspicuous that a general langor must ensue"[3] unless there were major new developments. Connecticut Congressman Eliphalet Dyer insisted the army required "total reform," implying that a change in command was overdue. Congressman Abraham Clark said, "We may talk of the enemy's cruelty as we will but we have no greater cruelty to complain of than the management of the army." It was falsely claimed that Washington's forces which had failed to stop the redcoats from seizing Philadelphia outnumbered the British three to one when, in fact, they had themselves been outnumbered.

To point to the shortage of troops, the shortage of supplies, the failure of state militias to provide promised backup—even if such explanations could have been kept from the British—might still not have redeemed Washington's reputation among his detractors. To them, it still would have seemed that all he was doing was delaying the moment of total defeat, that his drawn-out holding operation might not hold much longer, that a different commander could do better because it wasn't likely he could do worse. Judging only by the achievements of the army at that stage, it was not an altogether unreasonable conclusion to draw. Sizing up the situation, even some of Washington's devoted officers and advocates had doubts and qualms.

Washington's troubles began not long after his assumption of command. Whether he sought his job is impossible to tell. As a Virginia delegate to the Continental Congress he had not much to say but had taken to showing up at congressional sessions in his uniform as a colonel in the Virginia militia. It may have been only to demonstrate his readiness to do his part if fighting became necessary to convince Parliament to respect the rights of British Americans, but it made a strong impression. However, when it was rumored that he might be nominated army commander, he urged friends in Congress to block it. And when he was nevertheless chosen to be commander in chief, he declared, "I do not think myself equal to the command I am honored with." It was probably the most humble statement ever made by an American general and undoubtedly one which some people soon came to believe to be no less than accurate.

Washington's nomination had, suprisingly, been backed in Congress by Massachusetts radicals. A Massachusetts man, Artemas Ward, was already in titular command of the rebel forces around Boston and expected to be confirmed in the post. But it was recognized by most New England congressmen that if someone from Massachusetts were chosen to lead the army, which was then operational only in Massachusetts, and if the situation deteriorated or the stalemate dragged on, the support of other colonies might wither away. There were already indications that many people were tiring of Boston's fuss and bother. By backing Washington, New England delegates sought to weld the other colonies to the cause. However, having helped get Washington appointed, some in Massachusetts soon found reason to resent him—and not only Bostonian John Hancock, who never excused the reserved, courteous Virginian for having attained the position which he believed he himself deserved.*

At first Washington's dignified, soldierly bearing and his total dedication to the rights and liberties of British Americans made an impression strong enough to dispel any doubts harbored by rebels who would have preferred a different commanding general for the army. His announcement that he would accept no pay, only reimbursement for his expenses, was also well received. For a symbol of unity for the colonies at that moment of truth, Congress would have been hard pressed to pick a more suitable man.

However, though they welcomed outside support for their confrontation with the British at Boston, New Englanders were not too happy with the way Washington named southerners and others as his senior aides when they believed those positions should have gone to local men, many of whom had taken up arms in support of liberty when Pennsylvanians and Marylanders were still debating the proper course of action.

Nor did the new commander endear himself with his disdain for the New England officers he found in charge when he arrived in Massachusetts. "The most indifferent kind of people I ever saw," he said and cashiered several of them, some "for drawing more pay and provisions than they had men in their companies." There were objections also to the way Washington relieved local merchants of monopolies over supplies for the Continental Army around Boston in order to establish a more coherent and economical supply flow.

As for the New Englanders who formed the ranks of the Continental Army when he arrived, the new commander, nettled by "an unaccountable kind of stupidity in the low class of these people," was appalled by what passed for discipline. It was not uncommon for sentry posts to be left unguarded when sentries grew hungry and went off in search of something to eat or grew lonely and went looking for company. Soldiers regularly decided for themselves where they would be positioned in the defensive line. With disease already taking its toll, Washington was also dismayed at the state of field sanitation. Men relieved themselves where they wished, which was disagreeable as well as unhealthy.

---

* Describing Hancock's reaction when Washington was nominated, John Adams said, "Mortification and resentment were expressed as forcibly as his face could exhibit them."

Washington's determination to change all that, drastically and immediately, riled many of the men. Being both irregulars and New England individualists, they did not take kindly to being ordered about. Nor did they appreciate being forced, at the risk of being flogged, to pay close heed to the distinction between officers and ordinary soldiers. And when, in view of the citizens'-army character of the forces, discipline could not be rigidly enforced, townsfolk in the area objected to the way the commander was unable to keep his troops from engaging in petty crimes against Americans when they should have been directing all their mischief toward the British.

Some were indignant at the way Washington, not the most adroit of politicians, found little time to cultivate local rebel dignitaries—good men, dedicated patriots, worthy of his attention. They could not appreciate that, aside from his natural reserve, his shortage of suitable staff officers gave him little time for the usual courtesies.

Even at that early stage, Washington's military judgment was questioned by many locals. Towns along the coast were aggrieved because he declined to fragment his forces by sending units to protect them from possible British seaborne incursions. He could not explain, of course, that he feared that his army was still so questionable a fighting force that it might disintegrate if the British actually tried to break out of Boston. Suspecting that the enemy had planted spies everywhere, he kept that worry from all but his closest aides, so that poor military judgment and dereliction of duty rather than strategic calculation was seen as his reason for rejecting the pleas of worried townsfolk along the coast. He was tormented by the situation:

> So far from having an army of twenty thousand men, well armed, I have been here with less than half that number, including sick, furloughed, and on command, and those neither armed nor clothed as they should be. In short, my situation has been such that I have been obliged to use art to conceal it from my own officers.

Though Washington had come to rescue Boston from British oppression, it is not surprising that some New Englanders were instinctively irritated by him. As a former British Army officer and a southern patrician, he had standards of behavior, both military and personal, which clashed with local modes and attitudes, not only the way southern and Yankee attitudes still clash. He was personally offended by everything that contributed to the lack of discipline of the men (furious when he saw a Massachusetts captain who happened to be a barber shaving a Massachusetts private) and by the unsavory, ungentlemanly jockeying for favor among officers. He was depressed by having to spend hours resolving disputes over rank. He was mortified by having to beg units to do their duty. It clashed with his sense of propriety. It was uncivilized.

In a fit of exasperation, he wrote to a cousin that New Englanders were "an exceedingly dirty and nasty people."[4] To other intimates, he complained of the unreliability of New England militia units. Word of his feelings filtered back to New England and also reached New Englanders in Congress. It aroused much indignation. John Adams angrily demanded, "Does every man to the southward of Hudson's River behave like a hero, and every man to the northward of it like a poltroon?" To many, it was proof that a slave-owning, haughty southern gentleman who was used to cantering around his plantation like a noble lord each morning, whose wardrobe had been tailored in London, and who wore silk stockings and silver buckles on his shoes, was simply incapable of appreciating the straightforward, unpretentious, democratic spirit of New England, whose sons had taken on the redcoats before Washington had entered the fray and who would always be there when needed.

Local grievances, regional antagonisms, personal prejudices and the sniping and griping would have had little significance if the army under this determined, single-minded commander could produce convincing victories. Congress could jabber away endlessly and issue stirring proclamations from time to time, but things could actually be made to happen only in the field. As head of the army, Washington was the central symbol of the battle for the restoration and protection of American liberties. The hopes of the rebels—even of those who instinctively distrusted a Virginia nabob—rode with him. When his men forced the British out of Boston, the aloof commander was a hero to all, an accomplished soldier, a tribune of the people. Congress voted him a gold medal. He was a man unquestionably worthy of both his command and the respect of all Americans. But not for long.

When Long Island and New York fell, when it became apparent that the British withdrawal from Boston—that magnificent triumph for freedom and justice—had been no more than a strategic retreat, when the army was sent reeling back in disarray, doubts about Washington's military skills began accumulating like grime, and not only in New England. Joseph Reed, the adviser Washington most respected, and General Charles Lee, the commander's most senior subordinate, exchanged messages in which they questioned Washington's competence. Reed wrote to Lee, "I do think it is entirely owing to you that this army, and the liberation of America, so far as they are dependent on it, are not totally cut off"[5]—as if the commander in chief were no more than a liability. They agreed that "a fatal indecision of mind in war is a much greater disqualification than stupidity"—an unmistakable suggestion that Washington lacked decisiveness at a time when it was indispensable. Their views came to his attention and distressed him deeply.

Alarmed by the army's setback and determined not to lose control of the Revolution, Congress exercised its power to oversee army affairs. It exercised the right to make senior army appointments which, at times, undermined Washington's authority in the field. Ambitious officers took time off from their duties to cultivate congressmen, lobbying them with accounts of their own skills and views, which did not always do justice to the skills and views of their commander in chief.

Such behavior encouraged would-be military experts in Congress to scrutinize Washington's battle plans. He was, at the beginning, required to refer so many of his decisions to Congress for consideration and approval that he warned no war could be fought that way, that unless there was a letup, "ten days more will put an end to the existence of our army."[6] Fearing the worst, Congress relaxed its grip on the commander in chief. But by then it had become routine in some revolutionary circles not to expect too much of him.

General Horatio Gates deserves more attention than he usually receives for the extraordinary role he played in the Revolution. Barely remembered today, Gates was, briefly, one of America's earliest national heroes. In scoring the only truly important, exclusively American military victory of the war, the troops under his command at Saratoga finally demonstrated, after so many frustrations elsewhere, that a rebel triumph over the British in the Revolution was a distinct probability. In the process, as Washington's bedraggled troops headed dejectedly for rest and rehabilitation at Valley Forge farther south, Gates became a figure around whom the commander in chief's increasingly vocal band of critics could congregate. Here was the man to win the war that was being lost. Massachusetts Congressman James Lovell wrote Gates, "The army will be totally lost unless you come down and collect the virtuous band who wish to fight under your banner."[7] Comparing Gates and Washington, Benjamin Rush saw "the one on the pinnacle of military glory [and] the other outgeneralled."

Nor were other army officers immune to the implications of the contrast between Washington's string of setbacks and Gates's encouraging success. Not a few were quick to noise it about that they also had better ideas on how to run the army. Timothy Pickering, who had risen to be adjutant general, made disparaging remarks about the way things were being done. Others did the same, with greater or lesser discretion. General Israel Putnam, as dedicated a revolutionary as could be found in America, had already once ignored Washington's orders to dispatch needed reinforcements, because he believed he could make better use of the requisitioned troops. The faithful Nathanael Greene observed, "the General does want decision; for my part, I decide in a moment." More charitably, Johann Kalb said Washington's excessive modesty often led him to neglect his own judgment and act on the advice of lesser men.

Congress, which had chosen Washington by acclaim two years earlier, now consisted largely of new delegates with no personal recollection of the high hopes which had overriden regional and political differences when that unanimous choice had been made in Philadelphia. Few felt personally obliged to come to Washington's defense as the plot against him thickened. Even his urgent plea that Congress reform the quartermaster department, the better to provide for the ill-served troops, was not seriously received.

Dr. James Craik, the army's chief surgeon, wrote Washington, "Base and villainous men, through chagrin, envy, or ambition, are endeavoring to lessen you in the minds of the people."[8] Fearing confusion and division if the mutterings against the commander continued, Henry Laurens, then president of Congress and Washington's devoted ally, warned, "We are tottering and without the immediate exertion of wisdom and fortitude, we must fall down." But with Gates the hero of the moment, the sniping at Washington became a behind-the-scenes campaign to replace him with this new victor of the North and thus save the Revolution from disaster.

The assault on Washington's reputation and position was, for the most part, kept out of the public arena. The army was held together partly by the personal loyalty of many of the troops to their commander. Active opposition to Washington was largely confined to a group of well-placed political personalities and military men. Biographer James Thomas Flexner says the commanding general was a natural target for discontented Americans, that "he was blamed by farmers whose cows had been stolen or died of natural causes, by businessmen who had lost money, by underfed soldiers and officers not promoted, by childless women and men with stomach ulcers." But his critics realized that, despite everything, the commander in chief remained overwhelmingly popular with most Americans committed to the Revolution. To try openly to remove the Revolution's paladin from the field of battle could be to destroy the Revolution itself, as well as everything they believed in and were fighting for. He had to be eased out with as little fuss as possible.

Expressions of concern about Washington's continued popularity among Americans were not uncommon. John Adams had already voiced his vexation at the "superstitious veneration that is sometimes paid to General Washington."[9] Connecticut Governor Jonathan Trumbull, who did more than most to drum up supplies for the army, hinted that he felt much the same way: "A much exalted character should make way for a general." Some genuinely feared the possibility that, having escaped the tyranny of King George III, Americans might find themselves saddled with a new King George. Benjamin Rush was convinced Washington's popularity was a danger to American liberties.

An anonymous printed diatribe was circulated in Philadelphia suggesting that Washington was a total incompetent. When for reasons of security (as well as a natural reticence) he made a point of discouraging military gossip at his Valley Forge headquarters, just as he had outside Boston, he was accused of trying to run the war secretly to avoid criticism. Contrary to standard procedure, Gates, still his subordinate, took to ignoring Washington, dispatching his communiqués from the North directly to Congress rather than through the appropriate chain of command. When Washington reproached him, Gates presumed to assure his commander that Congress would, of course, pass on to him all he needed to know.

It must have been particularly wounding to hear from Henry Laurens that among those secretly lining up against him were some in whom Washington "reposed an implicit confidence." He was, however, probably not surprised to find included in the ranks of his detractors a charming, well-spoken Irish colonel by the name of Thomas Conway who had long served in the French Army, who had mesmerized Congress with accounts of his considerable military expertise, and who made little secret that he considered Washington's command abilities "miserable indeed."

Brazenly, Conway did not conceal that he had come to America and had offered his services to the rebel cause in order to advance his own career. It was his intention to return to Paris as a major general, thus earning the rank of brigadier general in the French Army. But anybody who seemed genuinely capable of helping turn the tide was welcomed by Congress, and Conway was listened to, even after he had peevishly protested that another foreign officer, subordinate to him in the French Army, had been given a rank senior to his in the Continental Army.

Despite this petulance and other indications that Conway's devotion to the cause of liberty was not unqualified, the judgment of this foreign military expert, who thought so little of Washington, bolstered the position of patriots who sought the commander in chief's ouster. They were particularly pleased when word of Conway's promotion over the heads of some of the commander's most valued senior officers led Washington to exclaim, "It will be impossible for me to be of any further service if such insuperable difficulties are thrown in my way." Here, finally, was Washington hinting that he could be driven to resign.

It might have happened. Another army commander—Gates probably—might have taken over. Washington might have returned to his Mount Vernon home and sat out the rest of the war there. He might not have been America's first President, and the capital of the United States might have borne a different name.

The instrument to be used to accelerate Washington's departure from the army was to be the Board of War. That body had earlier been set up by Congress when it was anxious to guarantee civilian control over the military. It was more often than not totally ineffectual. Military matters were dealt with by board members who had little understanding of strategy or tactics. Many questions which deserved urgent attention got bogged down in indecision, delay or outright neglect. Now, as Washington's adversaries moved in for the kill, the Board of War was transformed and military men were appointed to sit on it. Horatio Gates, Washington's archrival, was named by Congress to be its president and, in effect, the commander in chief's superior. It was a barely disguised insult. He couldn't be demoted or discharged, but his critics hoped this provocation would encourage him to leave under his own steam and make way for a commander capable of winning the war.

No sooner had Gates taken charge than Conway, known to be detested by Washington, who considered him a nincompoop and a popinjay, was named by Congress to be inspector general of the Continental Army and sent off to Valley Forge—where he was not wanted and where he was so frigidly received that he did not stay long. Not long afterward, Lafayette, who had become a great admirer of Washington and who was greatly valued by Congress because of his influence in France, was detached from the commander in chief's entourage. Without Washington being consulted, he was dispatched to command another invasion of Canada. The purpose was to deprive Washington of influential French support as the campaign against him approached its climax. It would also let Gates bask in reflected glory from the Canadian triumph Lafayette was expected to produce but didn't because the invasion, badly planned and poorly provisioned, was canceled before it began. For some in rebel ranks, Washington had momentarily become a prime target. They were convinced he was a liability to the Revolution. He had to be jettisoned as quickly as possible.

Washington's aide Alexander Hamilton, who was actively involved in defending his commander's reputation, believed that the conspiracy would have succeeded had the conspirators acted with greater subtlety, discretion and wisdom. As it was, their plot fell to pieces at just about the time they believed it would succeed.

They had made tactical errors. They had made their intentions transparent before they had managed to force Washington into a corner. They had underestimated the fact that he had friends as well as enemies in high places. Their effort to blacken Washington's reputation as a soldier was too offensive and becoming too blatant for Congress as a whole to tolerate without jeopardizing its own stature. The attitude of some of Washington's subordinates bordered on mutiny, which couldn't be tolerated.

Nor did Conway prove to be an asset to the dump-Washington clique. Driven exclusively by ambition, Conway showed himself to be a conniving sycophant—first unreservedly disparaging the commander in chief, then seeking to ingratiate himself with him by suggesting that the modest Virginian ranked alongside Frederick the Great as a military genius.

Such duplicity cost Conway his credibility. After Congress, to his shock and surprise, accepted his resignation, he was wounded in a duel with one of Washington's aides and returned to Europe. ("A longer stay in this country will endanger my hopes of promotion in France.") He had managed to extract the rank he sought of major general in the Continental Army, but his hopes of benefiting from his American adventure were only partly fulfilled. He surfaced again some years later as governor general of French forces in India.

Gates had by that time also beat a humiliating retreat. Unflattering comments Conway had made about Washington in a letter to him (a reference to a weak general running the country) were brought to Washington's attention. With cold dignity, which he maintained throughout these unsavory proceedings, the commander in chief made it known that he was aware of what had passed between the two men. Rattled, Gates foolishly insinuated that Washington had stooped to having his private papers "stealingly copied," only to be stopped short by the disclosure that it was one of his own aides, while drunk, who was responsible for the leak. Aware that he had overstepped the bounds of propriety and had been made to look foolish, while Washington had been made to seem a tower of strength plagued by termites, Gates made humble apologies and bowed out of the intrigue.

The plot, so inadequately manned, so flimsily executed, but so painful to Washington while it lasted, had petered out. Though without anything more to show for the achievement of his army than there had been earlier, Washington emerged in a stronger position than ever before. Cowed by developments, baffled, weary and with far more on its plate than it could handle, Congress backed away from what was left of the controversy. It surrendered all control of the army to the man whose ouster some of its members had been prepared so recently to contemplate.

Never again would Washington be seriously challenged by Congress. To the regret of some delegates who still feared his emergence as a military dictator, he was now recognized as irreplaceable. He was able to move forward from Valley Forge, not with greater hope of logistical support (that would never be put right), but without fear of further intrigue within army ranks or within the revolutionary leadership.

A troubling question remains as to whether those who sought to oust Washington were wrong to do so. New England egalitarians who were rubbed the wrong way by the mannerisms of southern patricians and mountebanks like Conway had special reasons for feeling as they did about him. But, discounting them, was the dump-Washington movement based on anything other than a genuine belief that the commander in chief was losing the war? His setbacks were real and ominous. The shortage of trained officers and recruits, the fickleness of state militias, the mass desertions and the supply inadequacies were genuine excuses. But wasn't it possible that another commander might have been more imaginative, more inventive, more capable of overriding those drawbacks?

Did Washington fail to understand America's true military potential as it then existed? Trained as a British officer, he tended to discount guerrilla tactics, which were, nevertheless, employed by rebels against the British with striking effect where Washington was not in direct command—in the South, in the West and in the buildup to the victory at Saratoga. Scorning the militia and other irregulars, he was an advocate of conventional soldiering as it was then practiced by the great armies of Europe. Those armies were manned mostly by the dregs of society, and, unlike the situation with regard to America's people's army, their casualty rates were rarely serious considerations for their officers and governments, for whom victory was usually the only thing that mattered. Washington sought to forge from scratch an army of civilians, most of whom had to be bribed or lectured into sticking around for more than a few months at a time, and he meant that army to confront the finest infantry in the world—experienced, disciplined, superbly drilled—and to do so according to the enemy's own rules of warfare. It made the string of costly, heroic American setbacks almost inevitable.

No one could deny Washington's courage. Time and time again, at great personal risk, he appeared on horseback in the midst of battle to rally the men and urge them forward. Soldiers who fought in his battles worshiped him for that. But one of the primary tasks of the senior commander is not to be killed or captured, which might have happened to Washington several times with serious consequences for the Revolution.

He took other risks which were even more dangerous. In positioning his troops at Brooklyn Heights early in the war, he left the men no escape corridor and could have lost most of his army right there had the British command been more alert. The battle of Trenton, in which retreating American forces turned around and overwhelmed a Hessian brigade, produced a badly needed morale booster, but it depended strongly on Hessian patrols not detecting American movements and, if it had failed, would have been an even greater blow to the patriot cause than the loss of New York.

Washington was the earliest American devotee of big guns. He had his cannon hauled from place to place. But it was at great cost in time, energy and maneuverability, and they were rarely used to great effect.

It may be that the failure of Washington to create the disciplined professional army he so badly wanted saved the Revolution from collapse. Such an army, had it existed, might have been met and annihilated once and for all by the far more experienced, far better armed British forces. As it was, the British were never able to obliterate the disjointed, disorderly American challenge, so often presented by irregulars who made their own rules of combat. That challenge kept cropping up no matter how many times regular units of the army were thrashed in the field. Not till French troops belatedly joined him at Yorktown could Washington piece together a strong enough force to master the redcoats in a set-piece confrontation. It may be that he was the victor in the war despite his limited strategic imagination.

There was, however, far more to being commander in chief of

the revolutionary army than planning battles. None of Washington's critics realized the extent to which his unflagging dedication in the face of monstrous adversity provided the symbol of what little unity there was between the states when initial enthusiasm flagged and the going got rough. None of them fully understood that the commander in chief's popularity among rank-and-file rebels—unmatched by any other single personality—was a key cohesive factor at a time when Americans first began to think of themselves as Americans. None recognized how his perseverance, despite the sniping of revolutionaries he respected, kept the army from disintegrating altogether—and, no matter how far short it fell of planned full strength and how limited its success, there had to be the core of an army as a focus of concentrated rebel determination.

Nor should anyone have underrated French confidence in this dignified, gracious soldier, as close as any American came to matching the idealized European image of an aristocrat. A less impressive figure might have made the French hesitate even more than they did before actually committing themselves to the rebel cause. And had Washington been forced out, and had the army then fragmented as his advocates believed it would, the French would have been unlikely to throw their weight behind an assortment of quaint, unpredictable militias.

Whatever else was said about Washington, no one presumed to doubt his wholehearted devotion to the Revolution, though some loyalist journals, printed under British protection in New York, expressed the hope that he would come to his senses and renew his allegiance to the king of England:

> *Let Washington now from his mountain descend,*
> *Who knows but in George he may still find a friend.*
> *A Briton, though he loves his bottle and wench,*
> *Is an honester fellow than parlez vous French.*[10]

That some patriots had been sufficiently frustrated by the way the war was going to seek to replace Washington is not surprising. Americans had by then already become addicted to the philosophy that what works is good, what doesn't work is bad and should be changed without delay. But in retrospect, suitable substitutes were not available. Nathanael Greene proved to be a superb, dedicated soldier and imaginative general, but he still was to prove himself when Washington's reputation was under fire. In any case, he had neither the personal stature nor the political connections to be in the running for the top army job. John Hancock, who had both and who wanted the job very badly, was a politician and a businessman rather than a soldier, and he was from Massachusetts at a time when, in view of the danger of alienating other states, New Englanders were not really eligible.

As for Horatio Gates, the leading contender, only frustration at the dismal course of events in the war could have prompted military men among Washington's critics to consider him a likely candidate. It was easy enough for less knowledgeable detractors to draw a contrast between Gates's victory at Saratoga and Washington's sequence of defeats. But it should have been apparent to more perspicacious patriots that it was only different circumstances which made the latter seem a bungler and the former suddenly appear to be the champion the Revolution needed.

Gates was nothing of the sort. The British forces moving south from Canada to split the states and crush the Revolution incubated their own defeat. Their entrapment at Saratoga was already in the making by the time Gates took command in the North after New England militia units refused to serve under General Schuyler because he was haughty and arrogant. Even before Schuyler was forced out, British supply lines had grown impossibly overextended and were growing more labyrinthine every day.

By comparison, British forces with which Washington had to contend farther south could, and did, regularly call on Royal Navy backup, which meant their supply lines were never out of control. It also gave them a tactical mobility which was denied Washington: they could, at will, put men ashore anywhere along the coast and lift them out again, an advantage the commander in chief, harried though he was, could never overlook.

There was also the Indian factor. While Washington watched in anguish as his men came and went, attacks on settlers by Indians serving the British cause in the North prior to the Saratoga showdown provoked local support for Gates of the kind Washington could only envy.

As for Gates's martial talents, they were not much in evidence in the Northern campaign. Greater credit for the rebel victory there should have gone, as it did when the dust finally settled, to

General Daniel Morgan and Benedict Arnold (also a general by then) for their daring and imaginative assault tactics.

But on the basis of the Saratoga victory, Gates was assigned command of the army in the South following the collapse of the bid to oust Washington. It was hoped that he would put a stop to the British drive through the South which looked as if it could cascade clear across the Carolinas. However, his southern command and the high regard for his abilities both abruptly crumbled at the battle of Camden, at which Gates's forces were routed in one of the worst setbacks in the war and in which he himself undertook a remarkable personal retreat, galloping back sixty miles on horseback before nightfall. It is not easy to imagine what might have happened to the army with such a man at its head.

Nor is it easy to contemplate Charles Lee as commander in chief, though some congressmen had thought of him rather than Washington when the matter was first considered. Lee was a veteran officer who could boast of considerable battlefield and command experience in the British Army when he had been younger. He had settled in Virginia several years before the Revolution and had been an early advocate of armed combat to protect British American liberties. He proved a valuable aide to Washington in the early part of the war, though he was not always quick to obey orders if he thought them misconceived. This was a particularly awkward matter for Washington, who, a gentleman through and through, was in the habit of framing orders as suggestions to his senior aides. Lee could therefore protest that no real disobedience was involved.

Lee was an arrogant, irascible man, blunt to the point of rudeness, who had grave doubts about the competence of his commander from the beginning. He probably had grave doubts about the competence of anyone but himself. Fellow officers resented him because he was overbearing and discourteous toward them (he preferred the company of his dogs). He also had a lean and hungry look which compounded the disagreeable impression he made. His temperament would certainly have made his relations with Congress—troubled enough for a tactful man like Washington—impossible. And how might he have handled the hypersensitive, proud, squabbling senior officers who so often seemed on the verge of resignation?

Lee, whose experience should have saved him, was taken prisoner by the British in December 1776—a strange affair in which he was captured by a redcoat patrol while overnighting at a tavern miles from his encampment. Many years after the Revolution, it was discovered that suggestions he made to the British while he was their prisoner on how to crush the rebellion—a thrust through the middle colonies—indicated that his allegiance to the rebel cause was not as firm as was thought. But when he was freed in a prisoner swap, Lee returned to active duty with the army. He was given command of patriot forces harassing the British as they evacuated Philadelphia, whose occupation by them had served no strategic purpose.

The crunch in that operation came at Monmouth, New Jersey, where, instead of executing a fairly simple assault, Lee's men retreated at his orders. It turned into a chaotic flight, halted by Washington, who happened upon the scene. The commander in chief took personal command, reformed the line and saved the army from another mauling. Stopped in flight, Lee explained to his furious commander that though he had been assigned a key role in the Monmouth assault plan, he had never thought much of the operation. The normally composed Washington is reported that day to have indulged in foul language of a kind his staff had never heard him use before. Lee's subsequent rows with fellow officers led to two inconclusive duels and to his eventual dismissal from the army by Congress. A bitter man to begin with, he remained one till the end of his days: "I desire most earnestly that I may not be buried in any church or church yard . . . for since I resided in this country, I have had so much bad company while living, that I do not choose to continue it when dead."

There is reason to believe that Lee may have been a more imaginative, more flexible strategic thinker than Washington. He did not scorn the value of irregulars. He may have been right in thinking of the Monmouth campaign as a pointless risk when French assistance was believed to be on its way. But his behavior at Monmouth after accepting the role he was assigned there was intolerable. It took more than military savvy to fill the shoes of the commander in chief.

It took heroic endurance in the face of appalling and unrelenting disadvantages. It took an unwavering sense of duty that could not be undermined or distracted by petty resentments or the abuse of critics. And despite Washington's patrician nature, it took underlying respect for the men he led.

Had Lee been chosen commander to begin with instead of Washington, or had Gates or anyone else replaced him during the war, it would have meant more than merely a different army command. If history is punctuated with the appearance of indispensable men and their achievements, Washington was certainly one of them and his ability to survive the efforts to push him aside was one of his achievements.

7

LIFE, LIBERTY AND THE PURSUIT OF SOMETHING ELSE

There never has been so fair an opportunity of making a large fortune since I have been conversant in the world.

—Robert Morris[1]

Early in 1781, when the rebels still had good reason to fear that the outcome of the Revolution was very much in doubt, Thomas Jefferson, by then governor of Virginia, conveyed a complaint to General Nathanael Greene from his state assembly. Jefferson told Greene that he had been informed that rebel troops under the general's command had illegally made off with horses belonging to patriotic Virginians, and had behaved very badly in the process. Clearly uncomfortable at having to do so, Jefferson requested details on what had happened to the horses, some of which were of great value, and indicated that their return would be much appreciated.

Greene, who was trying to drive the British out of part of the South which they had overrun, replied with restrained fury. He said he was sorry if mistakes had been made, if insults had been administered, if the appropriate seizure documents had not been handed over to the unfortunate horse owners, if, in some cases, studs had been seized instead of geldings. But he felt it necessary to explain to the man who had drafted the Declaration of Independence that the army—stumbling from setback to setback—still faced collapse, that it desperately needed horses, and that the liberties of the American people were more important than a few animals. Greene must also have bristled at the realization that some of the people on whose behalf Jefferson had complained probably were doing well out of the war.

They were not alone. Money was to be made from the struggle for independence by those who knew how. A one-sided controversy raged throughout the conflict between those who insisted that "he who increases his wealth in such times as the present must be an enemy to his country" and those who quietly beavered away at extracting fortunes from adversity.

And adversity is a mild description for the chaos which descended on the economy of America. None of the patriot leaders had imagined that financing the war and managing a war economy would prove so fraught with discord, perplexity and despondency. It turned out to be a nightmare of roaring inflation, discredited currency, squalid scrounging for crushingly expensive provisions, pauperization of small farmers, and recriminations between revolutionaries about who was responsible for everything that was going wrong.

As with the Revolution itself, to finance the war Congress started out confidently enough. It issued paper money, backed not by gold or silver, or even by the authority of a central government, but by faith in a glorious cause. America would not be found wanting. The necessary funds would be provided. The British, and Americans themselves, would be shown the pluck and unity of purpose of the "associated colonies." By the time two years had passed, the printing presses of newly independent America were churning out paper money with reckless abandon, though the faith of America in the glorious cause was proving less than overwhelming.

Depreciation was inevitable, and not simply to make technical adjustments to the economy. The value of the Continental dollar plummeted. Where they could, people turned instead to hard currency—Spanish dollar coins, doubloons, shillings, anything that wasn't paper. By 1777, the "Continental" was worth a third less than its original value. By 1779, it was down to the equivalent of ten cents. By 1781, one hard dollar could buy a thousand paper dollars. Tavern keepers took to refusing to serve soldiers because they could pay for their drinks only with American money.

More than the economy was endangered. Richard Henry Lee feared that the inundation of money would make a mockery of the Revolution and undermine the liberties for which the rebels were fighting. Gouverneur Morris grieved that "the torrent of paper money hath swept away with it much of our morals and impaired the national industry to a degree truly alarming."[2] Joseph Reed confessed, "I could never have thought . . . I should have heard Frugality, Spirit and Patriotism laugh'd at, but so it is." Indeed, many people turned their attention away from thoughts of freedom and independence and concentrated on more pressing matters.

Prices were soaring wildly. Flour cost two thousand percent more in 1781 than it had at the beginning of the war. Butter was twelve dollars a pound. Salt rose from thirty cents to thirty dollars a bushel. Tea was ninety dollars a pound. Wood was thirty dollars a cord for cityfolk who couldn't chop their own. To buy a suit and a hat in Philadelphia might cost those who could afford them two thousand dollars. Thomas Paine paid three hundred dollars for a pair of stockings. Prices changed at short notice. A dollar might buy less at dinnertime than it could at breakfast. Abigail Adams complained to her husband, John Adams, "That a scarcity prevails of every article, not only of luxury but even the necessaries of life, is a certain fact. Everything bears an exorbitant price."

Anticipating greater returns if they bided their time, merchants kept their goods off the market, thus guaranteeing that prices would rise. Goods were hard to come by even without such conniving. Where they could, shrewd businessmen cornered the market in items in short supply and were thus able to charge what they liked, whether for shoes or fabrics or coffee.

Though not as dramatically, wages soared as well as prices, causing problems for employers and the businesses they ran, some of which were essential to the war effort. With the economy expanding to meet the requirements of a war, and with the men away in the army or militia, labor was at a premium. Workers whose rising wages couldn't keep pace with the escalating cost of living could readily shift to higher-paying jobs. Carpenters at the fort at West Point, erected to guard the upper Hudson River against the British up in Canada, went on strike when they learned that wages for carpenters elsewhere in America had risen more than theirs. Soldiers assigned to military construction projects were embittered by the realization that they earned a fraction of the wages of civilians alongside whom they worked. All sorts of trades and businesses were affected. A printer confessed that "the increasing wages demanded by my people, without end or limitation, . . . and the great difficulty in procuring paper" were "extremely perpexing."

Congressmen were not immune to the consequences of the runaway inflation. Room and board in Philadelphia rose from four dollars a week in 1776 (not including alcoholic refreshment) to one hundred dollars a week three years later. Nathaniel Peabody of New Hampshire complained, "The expense of living [in Philadelphia] is intolerable, beyond conception, and almost insupportable."[3] Some congressmen whose presence in the capital might have been considered obligatory in view of the economic and military situation went home because they felt they couldn't afford to stay.

Many people opposed on principle to strong, potentially tyrannical government underwent a change of heart. They called for the passage of laws to govern the economy, restore a sense of proportion and bring things under control. But Congress was unable to brake the inflationary spiral. To reduce the ever-growing volume of printed money, it announced a massive public loan. But the four percent interest offered proved unequal to the risks Americans believed they were being asked to take. Lotteries were concocted to raise funds to prosecute the war. The response was no less disappointing.

To shift some of the pressure to the states, Congress urged newly formed state assemblies—whose halls and chambers reverberated with as much libertarian oratory as Congress once had—to raise taxes for the Continental treasury. Not to frighten them, no tax quotas were set. Though some money was raised by the states, little of it was forwarded to Congress. The states explained that they had expenses, too. One congressman said that appealing to the states to pay up was like preaching to the dead.

When state quotas were finally fixed, congressional coffers still had little to show for it, though the states gradually tightened up their own tax collection procedures. Americans who had gone to war rather than tolerate unjust taxes found themselves obliged to pay much steeper taxes than ever before. For some in Massachusetts, for example, they amounted to ten times their prewar assessments. An upstate New York man said, "It will not be in the power of the collector to collect the whole [of the taxes due] as some persons . . . are not worth half the sum they are taxed."[4]

Isolated from their markets but taxed on land values nevertheless, some small farmers faced ruin because of their tax assessments. They lost livestock and even their homes to the tax collector. Artisans unable to pay up to help finance the state's contribution to the war effort had the tools of their trade seized for forced tax sales. To make certain that taxes were collected, tax men in Rhode Island were jailed if they failed to bring in their allotted quotas. The tax collector became as much an enemy as the British and was often more of a threat. Despite efforts to assess taxes equitably, there were incidents of violence against collectors in Massachusetts, Pennsylvania and other states. People took to recalling that the Boston Tea Party, a proud moment for revolutionaries, had been a justifiable act of lawlessness provoked by unfair taxes.

Tax collection, even where it was methodically carried out, did nothing to stabilize the economic situation. In desperation, Congress urged states to bring in price controls to permit the overheated economy to cool off. Measures to that effect were introduced in many places despite the objections of conservatives among the rebels. John Jay maintained, "It is inconsistent with the principle of liberty to prevent a man from the free disposal of his property on such terms and for such considerations as he may think fit." A backlash was forecast. It was said that while fighting British tyranny Congress would lay itself open to accusations of promoting an even greater and more rigid tyranny. People evading price controls would do so in the name of liberty, debasing the rhetoric of the Revolution as well as its currency.

Free-market advocates predicted that the controls would, in any case, be ineffective. They were right. Wherever they were imposed black markets sprang up and provided otherwise unavailable goods at prices above legal limits. Merchants kept nonperishable goods off the market altogether, waiting for the authorities to realize what they were up against and back away. A lot of "smart money" was going into real estate, which, then as now, was not as exposed to the ravages of monetary uncertainty. It was a particularly attractive investment at a time when confiscated or hastily abandoned loyalist properties were coming under the hammer and could be scooped up for much less than their worth.

Capital was also invested in buying up goods in regions where price controls were imposed, for disposal in places where only the rules of the marketplace applied. It was thus possible, for example, for the price to be twenty-five dollars for a bushel of wheat in states where controls were in effect and where wheat was therefore hard to come by, and eighty dollars where there were no controls and where wheat was therefore more likely to be available to those who could afford it.

An effort to stamp out this damaging disparity by banning interstate shipments of scarce goods was doomed to failure. Anyone who remembered how easily Americans had smuggled things past pre-Revolution British customs controls could have predicted as much.

In places, revolutionary committees and gangs of embittered housewives roughed up merchants and forced them to open their warehouses and release hoarded goods onto the market at acceptable prices. There were riots against high prices and profiteering in Boston and Philadelphia. Such acts, spontaneous and sporadic, had little overall effect, except to magnify animosities between patriots who were poor and patriots who were not. Controls or not, regardless of consumer fury, despite the lamentations and warnings of rebel leaders, prices continued to climb.

Soon even the pretense of holding them in check had to be abandoned.

The effect on the army of the unstoppable inflationary surge was devastating. Washington groaned that "a wagon-load of money will scarcely purchase a wagon-load of provisions."[5] Married men's pay, when it came, was barely enough to feed their families. New Jersey troops told their state assembly that four months' pay for a private would not buy his family a bushel of wheat. Some soldiers could easily be relieved of all their earnings during a payday binge while settling up with credit-extending purveyors of rotgut which they called rum, who faithfully followed the troops. Men were sometimes paid in interest-bearing certificates which were to be redeemed after the war. For ready money, soldiers often sold those certificates to speculators at a fraction of their value.

Having learned from experience not to rely on the quartermaster, officers struggled to acquire provisions for their men from extortionate merchants who shunned the Continental dollar. To cope with the supply situation, Congress asked the states to pay some of their designated taxes (which weren't coming through in the form of money anyway) in beef, pork, corn and wheat for the army. Colonel Alexander Hamilton, grown deeply cynical, was not far off the mark when he forecast the result:

> The states will never be sufficiently impressed with our necessities. Each will make its own ease a primary object, the supply of the army a secondary one. The variety of channels through which the business is transacted will multiply the number of persons employed, and the opportunities of embezzling. . . . Very little of the money raised in the several states will go into the Continental treasury, on pretense that it is all exhausted in providing the quotas of supplies.

Most agonizing for the army were the shortages of food. The inability to organize a workable system of food requisition and supply was cruel punishment, especially in seasons when random foraging couldn't adequately meet the needs of the men. Hungry soldiers on the move regularly had to make do with whatever they could find—green corn snatched from fields they passed or unripe fruit plucked from orchards they filed through. It turned men's stomachs and put them out of action. In winter, when even such doubtful nourishment was impossible to come by, some would seek sustenance by thickening their watery soup with hair powder. In Norwalk, Connecticut, troops touched off a riot by stealing grain from a warehouse when local people barely had enough to go round. Army surgeon James Thacher, with troops manning a strategic outpost at Highland, New York, just north of West Point, was appalled by the situation:

> For three days past, I have not been able to procure food enough to appease my appetite; we are threatened with starvation. That a part of the army charged with the defense of a post so highly important to America should be left in such an unprovided and destitute condition, is truly a matter of astonishment, and unless a remedy can be found, our soldiers will abandon the cause of their country, and we must submit to the yoke of Britain.[6]

Successive reports told a tale of desperate scavenging and consumption of inedibles over and over again—for the men in the abortive invasion of Canada, during the retreat across Jersey, at winter's quarters in Valley Forge and at Morristown the following year, and during the campaigns in the South. More often than not, America's first army was a hungry army.

It was, however, not prepared to tolerate starvation. As a congressman ominously pointed out, "Men with arms in their hands will not starve when provisions can be obtained by force." Everywhere the army went, it left behind stories of soldiers officially commandeering or simply stealing what they wanted. Farmers in many places took to growing, then hiding, only what they themselves needed, because they knew that their surplus produce was likely to be confiscated. The imminence of battle took on an extra meaning for people nearby. A rebel officer observed, "Those who are nearest to where the scene of action is to be must expect to give up everything they have which is wanted for the enterprise."

Nor were civilians the only victims. Military supply trains dispatched to deliver provisions to army units farther down the line were stopped en route while soldiers liberated what they needed. It wasn't only depreciation of Continental money which prompted the civilian teamsters who ran those supply trains to demand payment in advance for delivery. They knew from experience how meager their deliveries might turn out to be by the time they reached their destinations.

Weapons and ammunition were also lifted from the supply trains by the troops regardless of the needs of their intended recipients. Weapons had previously been supplied when needed by shipments from England. There were, at the beginning of the war, no mills in America for grinding out gunpowder, nor banks of strategically situated furnaces for casting bullets and cannon balls. Washington lamented, "Nothing distresses me more than the universal call that is upon me from all quarters for firearms which I am totally unable to supply."

Firearms were requisitioned from civilians, though that source of supply hardly provided enough to satisfy the needs of the army and the expanded militias. There had to be much improvising. Blacksmiths were much in demand to make and repair weapons. Waterspouts, sash-window weights and other items of lead were requisitioned to be made into shot. Bibles were transformed into cartridge cases. Not until sizable cargoes of French weapons slipped through the British blockade two years into the war was the situation eased.

But the shortfall in other materials and provisions remained desperate throughout the conflict. General Greene was not the only one to sanction the seizure by troops of whatever they needed. Washington was deeply distressed by such scavenging. He feared it would turn the civilian population against both the army and the Revolution. He confessed that an "ill-placed humanity" and a "reluctance to give distress may have restrained me." But soon his qualms gave way to unsentimental reality, and he allowed that "our affairs are in so deplorable a condition as to fill the mind with the most anxious fears" and make his men rob "the country people of their subsistence from sheer necessity."

It would have pleased him to be able to pay for everything, but the worthlessness of Continental currency and army IOUs of various descriptions made that impossible. Washington was informed in 1781, "Credit may be said to be at an end; the innumerable certificates granted by the quartermaster and commissary departments and by the authority of the state have extinguished all confidence."[7]

Confidence had really shriveled away long before, despite drastic measures to keep it alive. People who had refused to accept American paper money in payment had risked imprisonment and denunciation as traitors. In Virginia, people who had refused to take the depreciating Continental dollars in payment of debts automatically forfeited all interest in those debts. But it was an illusion to believe the value of the dollar could be sustained when even counterfeiters found that their handiwork was worth less than the paper it was printed on. This was true even when counterfeit bills were better than perfect. In one case the legitimate dollar bill could be distinguished from the imitation because "Philadelphia" was misspelled on the back of the genuine article but not on the fake.

Though not commonly conceded to rate a place alongside Jefferson, Franklin and Adams in the pantheon of the Revolution, Robert Morris probably was, after George Washington, the most indispensable American in the War of Independence. Without him, the conflict might well have dragged on inconclusively for several more years. In 1781, with Congress on the verge of bankruptcy, with the Continental dollar recognized as an instrument of torture rather than a financial tonic, with troops in a mutinous mood because they hadn't been paid and weren't being fed, Morris was called upon to become superintendent of finance, in effect America's first secretary of the treasury. By that time Congress had become so overwhelmed by its responsibilities that Benjamin Rush described it as "abused, laughed at and cursed in every company."[8] In such a situation, Morris, a man of imagination and drive, became the guiding force in congressional affairs and formulator of congressional policies which, at the time, had to be concentrated on salvaging the Revolution.

Having consistently criticized the reckless printing of unbacked money and the casual attitude toward expenditure, Morris, upon assuming his post, immediately changed the direction of the American economy—or tried to. He pressed ahead with hard money policies. He insisted on fiscal responsibility. He introduced rigid economies. His goal was to instill faith in what Congress declared to be American money. Whether it would have made much difference to the prosecution of the war is impossible to say.

What is not in doubt, however, is that Morris, shortly after accepting his herculean assignment, performed a remarkable deed. He shrewdly marshaled the funds at his disposal to pay the troops, issue the supplies and provide the transport the army needed for its role in the joint French-American campaign against the British at Yorktown. He was thus instrumental in producing the decisive triumph for the rebel cause when the outlook was still far from promising. For that, Morris deserves greater reverence from Americans than he has ever received.

It is, however, highly unlikely that he will ever be so honored. There were aspects to Morris's character and various dealings which do not fit the conventional image of a national hero. Had he not contributed as much as he did to winning the war, he might have earned just a footnote in history for losing a lot of money speculating prematurely on a patch of untamed land which would later be transformed into Washington, D.C.

As it was, his mercantile drive and unabashed self-interest remained among his primary recognizable motivating impulses, even when he was serving the Revolution in a senior capacity. A successful businessman before the war, he declined to accept the job of revolutionary superintendent of finance until he was permitted to continue at the same time with his personal business enterprises, which were increasingly lucrative because of war shortages.

Earlier, as a member of the secret congressional committee assigned the task of importing supplies for the troops, he had access to inside information which enabled him to make very profitable investments. Employing and partnering people who worked as purchasing agents for the government, he was in a position to enhance his own takings considerably. Other businessmen sought him out because it was known that to include Morris in a deal was almost a guarantee of substantial profits. He bragged to a friend, "There is plenty of room to make as much money as you please."

There were protests that too much money earmarked by Congress for supplies went as commissions to Morris's firm. The contract he negotiated (with himself as chief congressional negotiator) to supply gunpowder to the army guaranteed him a commission even if the gunpowder was seized by the British and never reached rebel forces. While managing congressional funds, he was accused of unloading a cargo he owned onto the public books after hearing that it had been captured at sea by the British, thus saving himself from the financial loss entailed. An investigation found no irregularity in that transaction—it was, in fact, a complicated matter—but there was no denying that Morris, a rich man before the war began, did enormously well out of the conflict.

A firm believer in free enterprise and in the obligations of a merchant to make a profit wherever he could, Morris was untroubled by suggestions that his personal interests conflicted with the greater good. Though he originally doubted the value of breaking the American connection with Britain, and though he delayed a month before signing the Declaration of Independence, he was a committed patriot who foresaw the "power, consequence and grandeur" of America. But his mercantile drive was finally the ruin of him. He plunged too deeply into land speculation after the war, spent three years in a debtors' prison, and died broke and forgotten.

But this inglorious fate could not detract from the key role he played in saving the rebel cause from additional misery. Nor was he alone among exalted rebels in looking after his private interests during the war. Congressman Samuel Chase of Maryland, one of the earliest advocates of forceful action against British tyranny, made a killing in grain which he cornered to sell to the French fleet. By virtue of his position, he knew that the French would soon be arriving with their food supplies depleted, prepared to pay what was asked. His shrewd maneuver more than doubled the cost of flour at a stroke, and not only the French had to pay the inflated market price.

Dr. William Shippen, director general of army hospitals, speculated in materials needed by the hospitals and managed to live exceedingly well despite his relatively meager salary. No less a patriot than Nathanael Greene, who rebuked Jefferson over requisitioned horses, was not averse to speculating in scarce commodities, though this otherwise fearless general saw the wisdom in keeping it a secret.

The quartermaster general did not have to worry about concealing the improvement in his personal finances as a consequence of his military assignment. Until Congress reconsidered toward the end of the war, he and his assistants were officially authorized to divide a commission of one percent of all funds—a tidy sum—they disbursed on behalf of the army. Not content with such gains, Thomas Mifflin, when he was quartermaster general, awarded lucrative government contracts to his brother. Like

Commissary General Jeremiah Wadsworth, Mifflin left his job considerably richer than he started in it, though both shared, through inexperience and incompetence, responsibility for the army's supply problems.

Not only those in privileged positions profited personally from the Revolution. Any man who could lay his hands on a hogshead of rum and a wagon to follow the troops could turn them into the makings of a flourishing enterprise. Rather than join the army, many men signed up as sailors on congressionally sanctioned privateers and did well selling the goods from British vessels they seized. A businessman could painlessly put himself in the clear by paying off his long-accumulated debts in dollars that were practically worthless.*

Some profiteering was based on the systematic abuse of public office. In *The Power of the Purse*, E. James Ferguson notes:

> Almost all federal procurement officers were merchants, and it was an uncontradicted belief, occasionally proved, that they speculated with public money, embezzled funds and supplies, used public wagons and ships to transport their own goods, and deliberately bid up prices in order to increase their commissions on purchases. A further drain on federal resources arose from excessive personnel employed in noncombatant service with the army. A host of soldiers and hired civilians were kept at tasks requiring only a fraction of their time.

Though it had little effect, mercenary attitudes were widely deplored. Henry Laurens suggested that it was very hard "for a rich or covetous man to enter heartily into the Kingdom of Patriotism." That he would be barred from the Kingdom of Heaven apparently did not need repeating. Washington moaned that

* Many Virginia planters had been deeply in debt to British merchants before the war.[9] Member of Congress Benjamin Harrison owed £2,000 (a substantial sum at the time). Thomas Jefferson was said to have owed about £10,000 to firms in London and Glasgow. It became common practice to take advantage of measures passed by the revolutionary Virginia assembly authorizing repayment of sterling debts to British merchants in newly printed, much depreciated Virginia currency. Those who had neglected to settle up in this fashion during the war reacted badly when called upon to do so less advantageously after peace had been restored. One was quoted by George Mason as having asked, "If we are now going to pay debts due to British merchants, what have we been fighting for all this while?"

"stock jobbing, speculating, engrossing, &c, &c, seem to be the great business of the day, and of the multitude, whilst a virtuous few struggle, lament and suffer in silence."

As Washington's friend and neighbor Carter Braxton noted, for many Americans patriotism had its limits when it came to profit and loss. Braxton observed that, despite the war, English products "are so much preferred that America now winks at every importation of their goods." A merchant in Boston secretly advised his agent in London to mix English and Dutch goods when he shipped them, so that no one would know he was doing business with the British. Comparing Americans with the Biblical Israelites in the desert, New Hampshire Congressman Josiah Bartlett declared, "We are a crooked and perverse generation, longing for the fineries and follies of those Egyptian task masters from whom we have so lately freed ourselves."[10]

Trading with the enemy was rife. The good people of patriotic Providence ferried provisions out to British warships in Gardiners Bay because the English paid well, and not in American money. It was argued by those who were rebuked for such practices that the British would get what they needed anyway, so why not give patriots and the Revolution the benefit of their money? A French officer serving in the Continental Army saw it differently. He saw it as an American disease: "Money is their God, money is the controlling idea in all their actions. They think only of how it may be gained. Everyone is for himself. No one is for the general good."[11]

8

THE SILENCED MAJORITY

The only source of uneasiness amongst us arises from the number of [loyalists] we have in every state. . . . Some are so from real attachment to Great Britain; . . . many, very many, from fear of British forces; some because they are dissatisfied with the general measures of Congress; more because they disapprove of the men in power and the measures of their respective states. . . . If America falls, it will be owing to such divisions more than the force of our enemies.

—Committee of Secret Correspondence, Continental Congress, October 1, 1776

In meeting halls and taverns, from pulpits and public platforms, in town squares and city parks clear across the colonies, the intoxicating words of freedom rang out with reverence and fervor, inspiring Americans to pledge their lives and fortunes in the struggle against tyranny. Here was a cause worthy of their ingrained defiance and fighting spirit. And it wasn't only their cause. As articulate advocates of rebellion told them, it was the cause of all mankind. As their parsons and pastors told them, their cause was the cause of virtue and rectitude. The British had gone preposterously astray if they thought Americans could be intimidated. Accounts of their wretched deeds and presumptions intensified revolutionary zeal. Americans had embarked on a just crusade.

But that was only part of the story. Though legend has it otherwise, the American Revolution was not an uprising of a united people. Support for the revolutionary cause was widespread, but most Americans wanted no part of it. The Revolution was launched, led and promoted by a minority of visionaries who, with a host of their supporters, spurred, guided and sometimes stampeded the reluctant majority toward a destiny it viewed with incomprehension, indifference, suspicion, anxiety, or disdain.

So obstinately did many Americans repudiate independence and all it stood for that they fled as refugees to other lands to escape from it. One hundred thousand of them—one in every twenty free Americans then living—felt they could no longer remain in America because of the Revolution. In terms of today's population, that would be equivalent to some twelve million Americans going into exile—a staggering thought.

And the ones who fled—mostly to Canada and England—did not, by their departure, completely rid the country of people who saw no sense in the Revolution. Regardless of loyalties, comparatively few Americans could pick up and go, trusting that someone would shelter and feed them and their families in a strange country far away. Most of them were tied to their land or their livelihoods. The dissidents who fled to distant shores were far outnumbered by those who couldn't afford to bolt or just refused to leave despite being intimidated, penalized by local revolutionary posses, and sometimes physically assaulted.

In Plymouth County, Massachusetts, elderly Israel Williams, who was loyal to Britain and who had not long before declined a British appointment in the colonial administration because of "infirmity of body," was locked in a room of his house with the chimney sealed and kept there until he had almost suffocated from the smoke.

In North Carolina, loyalist Daniel Maxwell, suspicious about rumblings against him, hid in the woods near where he lived and watched his rebel neighbors plunder his home.

In Delaware, loyalist Robert Strafford Byrne was submerged in water until he was prepared to condemn the British "ministerial sons of bitches" and promised to leave the region.

In Charleston, George Walker refused to drink damnation to the king of England. It was enough reason for him to be tarred and feathered, paraded through the town and pelted by onlookers with whatever came to hand.

Bostonian Edward Stow had his house daubed with excrement and his skull fractured by a hardwood stick for refusing to support the rebel cause.

After studying in England, young Samuel Shepherd returned to Virginia, to find that a few casually uttered loyalist sentiments in a tavern earned him whispered advice from friends not to think aloud about such matters.

To avoid the attention of rebel vigilantes, Philadelphia schoolmaster Robert Proud withdrew from society and lived "in a very private and retired way, even like a person dead amidst the confusions, and conversing more with my books than with persons."[1]

Loyalists who were prepared to submit and convincingly embrace the cause of independence and liberty were absolved and spared further harassment. The temptation to give in was often irresistible. One loyalist wit quipped that Americans were "by force and oppression compelled to be free."[2] For many, that was no exaggeration. Loyalist farmers who stood their ground found their livestock mutilated. They couldn't get their corn ground or their horses shod except in areas not yet under rebel control, which diminished sharply as the rebellion took hold. They often were forbidden to venture farther than one mile from their farms.

Loyalist carpenters and other artisans were boycotted, and people who dared to break the boycott fell themselves under risk of rebel reprisal. In some places, loyalists were taxed to make good all robberies committed in their neighborhoods. They were barred from going to court to recover debts owed to them and were generally denied the protection of the law. Not even those assaulted in the streets on suspicion of harboring forbidden opinions could expect the law to intercede on their behalf.

In some places, allegiance to the king was enough to earn an American a jail sentence. The homes of wealthy loyalists were plundered, and sometimes also the homes of those who were not wealthy. The wife of farmer Norman MacLeod, who had been jailed for fighting for the loyalist cause, fled in fear after her home had been repeatedly pillaged by local patriots.

These were not isolated incidents. They happened throughout America, throughout the war, even though independence was not the wish of most Americans. The British said it wasn't, but that was to be expected. They weren't inclined to lend credence to the rebel claim of massive popular support for the Revolution. The

British were, however, not alone in their reckoning about who backed whom. No less a revolutionary than John Adams declared that at the beginning the American verdict was one third in favor of independence, one third against and one third uncommitted.

Even without such an appraisal from someone who might have been expected to claim otherwise, there is plenty of evidence testifying to the extent to which Americans did not support the Revolution. There is, in fact, enough evidence to raise questions about whether, judged by its own standards, the rebel cause was truly justified. The goal of the Revolution was government deriving its authority "from the consent of the governed." No one could pretend such consent was forthcoming in 1776. Whatever other vindication they had (and history subsequently provided some), when weighed against their own principles, the Founding Fathers were on shaky moral ground in organizing the American Revolution and seeing it through to victory. Only by discounting the mood of the majority could they have been considered the voice of the people.

To try to determine exactly how many Americans were patriotic rebels against Britain and how many were not is a vain exercise. There was no head count then and there can't be any now. But there are clues to a breakdown.

As Washington and his men trudged wretchedly in retreat through New Jersey a few months after the Declaration of Independence, he found so little support there that he called it enemy country. New York and Pennsylvania were so nearly divided that if they had not been sandwiched between unshakably rebellious New England to the north and Virginia to the south, they would have opted out of the Revolution. Indeed, the British were well received by local residents when they occupied New York City and Philadelphia, the two largest American cities at the time.

In Philadelphia, when boycotts and blockades imposed by the rebels were lifted during the brief British occupation, business boomed and theaters thrived as never before. While the army went hungry at nearby Valley Forge, British forces more agreeably winter-quartered in the City of Brotherly Love had no trouble acquiring provisions from obliging farmers in the area. In what was to be New York State, even before the war began, Congress felt obliged to excommunicate Queens County, decreeing that all trade and intercourse with its inhabitants be stopped because they were "incapable of resolving to live and die as free men." Attitudes prevailing in Queens were to be found as well in nearby New York City into which Queens had not yet been absorbed.

In the South, too, the Revolution was very far from being universally acclaimed. South Carolina and Georgia joined the Revolution only very reluctantly and were almost detached from it during the war. At the height of the conflict, Virginia militiamen declined to venture into the Carolinas to join other rebel forces in confronting the British there. As for Delaware, Thomas Jefferson was informed by a prominent rebel that two thirds of the people there were "notoriously known in their hearts to be with the enemy," and a British official boasted that Delawareans supplied "everything we wanted."

There were even stubborn pockets of loyalists in New England, where the rebels had been in virtually complete control from the very beginning. Townships on Martha's Vineyard and along the Connecticut coast were not alone in casting their lot with the British rather than the Revolution until rebel pressure forced them into line. When the British landed at Newport, Rhode Island, they were given an escort of honor by local loyalists.

Many families were bitterly split by conflicting allegiances and convictions. Benjamin Franklin was the father figure of the Revolution, but his own son, William Franklin, was a leading loyalist. General Henry Knox, the Revolution's artillery wizard, was the son-in-law of loyalist Thomas Flucker, who fled to England. Revolutionary General John Stark was the brother of British Army Colonel William Stark, who died in combat fighting the rebels. The father of Declaration of Independence signer Thomas Heyward was a loyalist. Massachusetts Attorney General Jonathan Sewall, a prominent loyalist, was John Hancock's brother-in-law. The three nephews of loyalist Lieutenant Governor William Bull of South Carolina were all patriots. Samuel Hale, cousin of revolutionary spy and hero Nathan Hale, was a loyalist.

Numerous less illustrious families were similarly cleft. In many cases, close kin took up arms on opposing sides. Each was convinced of the justice of the cause he espoused and the wickedness of the one he set himself against.

As the Revolution took shape, Benjamin Franklin, who would

be partially reconciled with his son by mail after the war, tried to explain why so many Americans withheld their support from it: "The novelty of the thing deters some, the doubt of success others, the vain hope of reconciliation [with the British] many." A foreign participant in the war was less analystic. General Louis Le Bèque Duportail, the French commandant of engineers in the revolutionary army, reported home, "There is a hundred times more enthusiasm for this Revolution in any Paris café than in all the colonies together."[3]

Duportail's flippant observation reflected the disgust which festered in the army when patriotic zeal fizzled out in the country after the initial explosion of do-or-die enthusiasm. Revolutionary committees remained vigilant and active. Loyalists were still hounded and neutralists were kept in their place. Patriotism was still the watchword and the British still scorned. But it was impossible for a soldier in the field or an officer at headquarters to overlook the cynicism, the foot-dragging and the profiteering that began to undermine revolutionary morale as soon as the first rebel setbacks were recorded in 1776.

So many patriots proved to be so fickle, so wavering, or so totally negligent when it came to active support for the Revolution that it can be doubted whether their hearts were really in it. It was fortunate for the revolutionaries that their cause did not depend exclusively on the determination and tenacity of all who professed to be rebels against tyranny.

The grotesque shortfall of material civilian support for Washington's hungry, ragged troops demonstrated most pointedly how limited was the backing for the Revolution among ordinary Americans. A Continental Army colonel did not exaggerate when he charged at the height of the war that "the people at home are destroying the army by their conduct much faster than [the British] can possibly do by their fighting."

Many people could not see what stake they had in the struggle. At the time, nine out of every ten Americans worked the land. Most of them were subsistence farmers, not impoverished but only just managing to get by. Their chief concerns were their crops and livestock and, along the frontier, the menace of hostile Indians. An overly long winter, a rampaging spring flood or the mysterious disappearance of a horse overnight meant more to them than the rights or wrongs of British rule, which affected them practically not at all. Some had rarely seen either a redcoat or a tax collector. A victory for the Revolution would make them no more free than they were already. They would not be able to toil less hard to coax a living from the land.

The rhetoric of freedom was stirring, but they were as far removed from the libertarian ferment of the bustling coastal towns and cities as city folk—who made up no more than ten percent of the population—were from the precariousness of existence on the fringe of the continental wilderness. A tax on tea or a British clamp-down on insubordinate Boston meant little to pioneers who had made for the tall timber or had settled on the lush meadows of western Pennsylvania, northern New York or what would one day be the state of Kentucky. Those among them who became rebels did so because they were persuaded the country they loved was under threat rather than to redress any particular grievances. If they had ever encountered tyranny, it was likely to have come from bailiffs from the nearest town, with whom they would still have to deal after the war, rather than from anyone engaged on the overseas affairs of the king.

People who unequivocally rejected the Revolution rather than trying to stay clear of the convulsion sweeping the colonies were of a different breed. These were the true loyalists; Tories, the rebels called them. (In England, Tories were, as they still are, the most ardently royalist political faction. The word "Tory" was originally Irish and meant outlaw.)

Some American Tories were officials of the colonial administration—governors and their staffs, judges, customs officers, clerks, etc.—who had a professional commitment to the status quo. But a host of Americans in less exalted positions and callings also turned their backs on the rebellion. One group of loyalists who were banished from Massachusetts for refusal to toe the rebel line included laborers, farmers, a printer, a cabinetmaker, a chandler and other small shopkeepers. A list of Tories in Delaware against whom legal action was taken included a physician, a bricklayer, an innkeeper and a milliner.

As might have been expected, many loyalists were rich men and women who sniffed chaos and anarchy in popular demonstrations of any kind. They dreaded the prospect of mob rule. More is known about their kind—the De Lanceys of New York, the Pepperells of Massachusetts—than about less affluent Tories, which sometimes left the impression that loyalists usually were upper crust. While wealth was a factor in many cases, it did not necessarily influence allegiance, except that a rich loyalist was less likely to be roughed up by his neighbors and therefore more likely to escape punishment if he lay low.

Some of the richest men in the colonies—including John Hancock and revolutionary army General Philip Schuyler—were rebels from the beginning. George Washington and Thomas Jefferson were far from poor. Indeed, large landowners in Virginia generally backed the Revolution despite their wealth and privileged status, while those in New York generally did not. One of the latter, identifying himself as "Westchester Farmer," defined their position: "If I must be enslaved, let it be by a king at least, and not by a parcel of upstart, lawless committee men. If I must be devoured, let me be devoured by the jaws of a lion, and not be gnawed to death by rats and vermin!"[4]

Had it not been for ordinary, patriotic American farmers who fought for independence, there would have been no revolutionary army to speak of. But many newly arrived farm people had received free passage to the colonies from Britain and patches of back-country land from the British authorities. They were disinclined to show their gratitude by turning on their benefactors. So many Scottish folk who settled in Georgia were loyalists that the state later passed a law which, for a time, banned further immigration from Scotland.

Some loyalists came to their allegiances in a roundabout way. A hardworking American tenant farmer resented his American landlord comfortably ensconced in the big house in the valley far more than he did the king over the water. He was inclined to choose sides accordingly, or to refrain altogether from choosing sides. In the hill country of the South, scrub farmers lost little love on plantation owners, rich, remote men, nabobs who owned most of the fertile land of the region, whose black slaves did their work for them, and several of whom were committed revolutionaries sounding off about the meaning of liberty.

American businessmen had the strongest material reasons to object to British rule. They resented laws which protected British monopolies in goods which the colonies could have dealt in just as readily and just as profitably. "We are entitled to life, liberty and the means of sustenance by the grace of Heaven and without the King's leave," protested the Boston Committee of Correspondence. There were complaints too that the colonies were regularly used as dumping grounds for otherwise marketable British goods.

Merchants also suffered more than most of their countrymen from British taxes. However, just prior to the Revolution, the colonies enjoyed a feverish spell of growth and prosperity out of which the merchants particularly did very well indeed. Many had substantial trading links with Britain and the British West Indies which they wished to retain, or had profitable domestic business operations they did not want disrupted by an armed contest with the motherland. After the war began, even patriots among them found ways of slipping past embargoes and boycotts to import British goods for which there remained an insatiable market in America despite the conflict.

Among the loyalists were some Americans who maintained that kings (or Parliament at least) should rule and ordinary mortals should obey. But among them also were individuals whose unwavering dedication to liberty and justice matched that of the most stalwart of the Founding Fathers. These were men and women who, like many English people today, genuinely held British law and culture to be worthier than any conceivable alternative.

Even some patriots worried about what would follow if the Revolution succeeded. Abigail Adams wondered in a letter to her husband, "If we separate from Britain, what code of laws will be established? How shall we be governed so as to retain our liberties?" John Adams, who never wavered in his dedication to the patriot cause, was himself disconcerted when, in the early days of the rebellion, he encountered a known rogue who was also a patriot because of his belief that he would never again have to worry about being brought before a court of law.

Loyalists had no doubt that the outlook for Americans would be dismal if the system of justice under which they had lived was swept away. Some succumbed to hysteria at the prospect of being denied British protection. Joseph Galloway warned that if America broke away from the motherland, nothing would stop invading foreigners or native ruffians from "entering your houses . . . , seizing your property, and carrying havock and devastation wherever they head—ravishing your wives and daughters, and afterwards plunging the dagger into their tender bosoms, while you are obliged to stand . . . the helpless spectators."[5] For people who thought that way, the rebels were not only mistaken; they were dangerous vandals as well.

The crumbling of British control was shattering to Americans for whom such control was synonymous with civilization itself. It was as if the codes of law and principles of virtue by which they guided their lives had suddenly been rendered null and void—by committees! Seeing a man being run out of town in Wilmington, North Carolina, for daring to smile at the unmilitary spectacle of a ragtag gathering of local rebel militiamen, a loyalist woman pathetically wailed, "Oh, Britannia, what are you doing while your obedient sons are thus insulted by their unlawful brethren?"

For some Americans, rebellion conjured up an apocalyptic vision of death and devastation. They issued warnings that the British would mount a fearsome campaign against the rebel threat to the king's authority, just as they had against the French challenge in America a few years earlier. Like many people today, they believed that no sufficiently convincing reason had been offered by advocates of the hard line to justify the bloodshed and destruction that could be the consequence of risking or provoking an armed conflict. There were forecasts of "the blood of thousands bedewing the ground and the whole wealth of the continent, the whole labour of a century, vanish'd in air." Americans were warned they would see "our houses . . . burnt to ashes, our fair possessions laid to waste."[6] Britain, it was said, "has been long tender of the rod but be assured the time approaches when she will exercise it with severity." For some it was a truly frightening prospect. For many, it later became a terrifying reality.

Some Americans did not openly reject the rebel cause till well into the war, when the worst forecasts of the prophets of catastrophe appeared to have come true and when further challenge to British might seemed futile. William Smith, chief justice of New York, did not declare his allegiance to the crown until 1777. That same year, Reverend Jacob Duché, chaplain of the Continental Congress, a man who had deeply moved rebel leaders when he urged them to "stand fast . . . in the liberty wherewith Christ hath made us free," wrote to an astonished George Washington, urging him to abandon the Revolution and castigating the "bankrupts, attorneys and men of desperate fortune" who had by then become congressmen. "How fruitless the expense of blood!" Duché grieved.[7] Despairing of victory for the Revolution, Silas Deane, who had been America's first official envoy in Europe, in 1781 urged an accommodation with Britain and an end to the fighting.

Alienation from the American mainstream came as bitter irony to those loyalists who had started out vigorously challenging transgressions against the liberties of their compatriots. Isaac Low of New York, John Zubly of Georgia and Robert Alexander of Maryland, all early members of Congress, had criticized British taxes and trade restrictions; but as the cause they and others like them supported grew increasingly radicalized, they found themselves ideologically stranded. Things were going too far, too fast.

They had started out believing in the sanctity of American liberties and ended up wholeheartedly deploring the rebellion founded, they believed, on grievances which, though genuine, had become highly inflated and were in any case capable of being amicably settled. They had envisioned a British America with its rights and privileges guaranteed, but still sheltering within the protective embrace of the empire. For them, rebelling over a tax on tea, as the Boston radicals had done, was equivalent to amputating your foot to cope with a boil on your big toe. They were, however, doomed to be treated unkindly in the history books, at best ignored, at worst made to look treacherous.

For people who profoundly cherished both their British and American identities, the rebellion aroused much anguish. Their predicament was recorded with painful clarity by Hector St. John Crèvecoeur:

> Shall I discard all my ancient principles? Shall I renounce that name, that nation which I held once so respectable? . . . On the other hand, shall I arm myself against the playmates of my youth, my bosom friends, my acquaintences? The idea makes me shudder.

Crèvecoeur, who is better known for having written with great charm and affection about the splendors of American rural life, ultimately forsook America and left for England, exasperated by rebels who were perpetually "bawling about liberty without knowing what it was."

Those who shared his feelings were confirmed in their disgust at rebel behavior by the prewar politics-of-the-mob practices of the Sons of Liberty and sundry revolutionary committees. These committees were generally self-appointed or chosen by local rebels. William Eddis, a surveyor of customs at Annapolis, had no doubts about the situation:

> I am heartily disgusted with the times. The universal cry is Liberty, to support which an infinite number of petty tyrannies are established under the appelation of committees; in every one of which a few despots lord it over the calm and moderate, inflame the passions of the mob, and pronounce those to be enemies of the general good who may presume in any way to dissent from the creed they have thought proper to impose.[8]

In Massachusetts, Jonathan Sewall, offended not only by the politics of rebels he encountered, declared, "They swear and drink, and lie and whore and cheat, and pull down houses, and tar and feather, and play the devil in every shape . . . and yet they cry out for Liberty!"

So many Americans did not support the Revolution that it would be reasonable to suppose that they played a significant role during those fateful years. Remarkably, they did not. Geographically, they were widely enough distributed to have undermined rebel unity. Statistically, there were enough of them to have influenced the course of American history. But they exercised no such influence. They were the silenced majority—overruled, intimidated, emasculated.

The warnings of those who dreaded the devastation of war were smothered by the pronouncements of patriots. People who preferred to stay clear of the struggle learned that such an option is not always available when political passions are aroused. Defiant loyalists found that their refusal to conceal or deny their convictions was both risky and finally futile. William Nelson has observed in *The American Tory*, "The loyalists in the American Revolution suffered a most abject kind of political failure, losing not only their argument, their war, and their place in American society, but even their proper place in history."

It is true that history is rarely kind to losers, but they themselves were largely responsible for their feeble showing. Unlike the rebels, comparatively few of them were ideologically or emotionally geared to band together in a self-sustaining campaign as aggressive and demagogic as the one which gave the rebels the initiative and the momentum to dominate the American scene and silence opposition.

As things threatened to fall apart, as cries for liberty grew more forceful, even the more highly placed among the loyalists tended to withdraw from the rough-and-tumble of colonial politics. They had little stomach for power struggles and no wish to expose themselves to the rough justice of the committees and the mobs.

Also responsible for their failure to defend their views more energetically was their certainty that the rebels—outlaws and rowdies that they were—would quickly be dealt with by the British or would fall out among themselves and self-destruct, a distinct possibility in view of tactical differences between rebel factions.

But even in places where they were to be found in substantial numbers, loyalists often found their position untenable virtually from the start. Perhaps it couldn't be otherwise when they were subjected to the kind of harassment from their compatriots that would shame and horrify most Americans today. An embittered victim complained: "The loyalist who was true to his convictions, creed and king was detested, reviled . . . , mobbed, ostracized, or imprisoned, and all this at the will of a committee, self-constituted and responsible to no one."

Such harassment had the effect of isolating loyalists not only from their rebel neighbors and associates but also from those who, though holding no strong feelings in the dispute, preferred not to risk being tainted by association with outcasts. Incapable of organizing their own defense, loyalists relied on the British authorities to cope with the situation—that was what the King's Peace was supposed to be all about. They could only look on in pained bewilderment as it became clear that what they considered treason and villainy had become respectable and patriotic and that the British would ultimately cave in.

Loyalists could fume at rebel lawlessness. They could protest at the pestilence of rebel sedition. They could insist that the Continental Congress had less legal authority than a parish vestry. They could commiserate with each other as their personal miseries accumulated. But they could do little but watch the Revolution bud, then flourish, and finally triumph, as their British protectors, dazed by the improbable endurance of the ragged rebel forces, proved incapable not only of winning but even of usefully deploying the Americans who volunteered to fight under their banners.

It would be unjust to dismiss the loyalists as toadies to the British or as cowards or reprobates, although there were certainly some of all three in their ranks. But the rebels, newly proclaimed as patriots, had once also considered themselves loyal subjects of the king. It was they who had changed course. It was they who had turned what had been a loyal protest against official improprieties into an armed rising.

By the time it became clear that the Revolution would not be crushed, when it was obvious that the sacrifices of dedicated rebels more than compensated for the cynicism of the many who merely mouthed the words of rebellion, most Americans had been converted to the cause of independence. Victory is very persuasive. Also, the British had squandered their advantages. They had repeatedly created rebels where there had been none before.

Loyalists in New Jersey had second thoughts after they had been roughed up and robbed by redcoats and Britain's German mercenaries. Southern loyalists were appalled and terrified by the British promise of freedom for black slaves who enrolled in British forces to fight the Revolution. British-inspired Indian raids on rebel civilians disgusted and horrified many who had scorned the rebellion. But a remarkable number of Americans clung tenaciously to their allegiance to the motherland, keeping to the path they had originally chosen even though it led them to oblivion.

Once the war had begun and passions had been aroused, few rebels felt any sympathy for Americans who declined to denounce their loyalty to the king and who suffered at the hands of their patriotic neighbors, committees and mobs as a consequence. Before the Revolution was proclaimed, however, some rebel leaders were deeply concerned about the mistreatment of people whose only crime was to cling to dissenting convictions.

Such abuses of personal freedom were hardly consistent with the catechism of liberty. John Adams feared that the rough-and-ready methods employed by "rude and insolent rabbles" in the name of liberty would besmirch their just cause. Rabble there may have been among those who invoked the menace of the mob to silence loyalists, but other elements were active as well. Sounding a theme that would be heard in later times too, one observer contended that "the chief abettors of violence" were "young men of good parts but spoiled by a strange, imperfect, desultory kind of education which crept into fashion all over America."

A climate of unrest and upheaval generated an explosive momentum all its own. Physical attacks on individuals could be savage. Most harrowing was the tarring and feathering. It was a grotesque, medieval torture of English origin, applied to many whose crime was refusal to renounce loyalty to the king. The victim would be stripped of his clothes. Hot tar straight from the barrel of the boiling, thick, adhesive substance would then be ladled over his body, sometimes over his head as well. It could cause serious burns and, if it entered his eyes, blindness. The tar, which quickly hardened, sometimes took weeks to remove. It often left enduring scars where the skin had been burned or had been torn off in the removal process. The experience could, of course, also scar a man's mind.

Feathers were not always applied. That was done only to make the victim more of a spectacle. Sometimes, after the tarring and feathering, he would be put on a pole, a leg on each side of it, which was then carried on the shoulders of two burly men, with a man on each side to keep the victim upright and in place. He was then paraded through town, followed by a jeering crowd. Sometimes, more mercifully, the tarred-and-feathered loyalist was simply chucked into a ditch to find his way home as best he could.

There were many cases like that of Thomas Randolph, a barrel maker of Quibbletown, New Jersey,

> who had publickly proved himself an enemy to his country, by reviling and using his utmost endeavours to oppose the proceedings of the Continental and Provincial Conventions and Committees, in defense of their rights and liberties. . . . [He] was ordered to be stripped naked, well coated with tar and feathers, and carried in a wagon publickly round the town; which punishment was accordingly inflicted. And as he soon became duly sensible of his offense, for which he ear-

> nestly begged pardon, and promised to atone, as far as he was able . . . , he was released.

Ann Hulton, sister of the British customs commissioner in Boston, described how a mob seized an old storekeeper who was

> stript naked, one of the severest cold nights this winter, his body covered all over with tar, then with feathers, his arm dislocated in tearing off his cloathes. He was dragged in a cart with thousands attending, some beating him with clubs and knocking him out of the cart, then in again. . . . The doctors say that it is impossible this poor creature can live. They say his flesh comes off his back in stakes.

Myles Cooper, loyalist president of New York's King's College, later to become Columbia University, was in his apartment at the college when he was warned that a crowd of those who took exception to his political views was on its way, intent on "shaving his head, cutting off his ears, slitting his nose, stripping him naked and setting him adrift." Cooper slipped out a back window and was led to safety by one of his students. The next morning he boarded an English vessel and made for England.

Organized, calculated intimidation was widely practiced and widely successful. Thomas Jones, a New York Supreme Court judge, maintained that loyalists outnumbered rebels four to one among the voters of New York City. But when the question of whether New York should send delegates to the Continental Congress arose, "a large and select party of the most violent republican partizans . . . formed themselves into a company, armed with bludgeons and quarter staves, . . . and threatened destruction to any person who should oppose the election of delegates."

In Jamaica, Long Island, ninety-one freeholders out of 160 in the township signed a declaration asserting they had never given their consent for the choosing of the local committee to name congressional delegates. Their protest changed nothing. In Georgia, only five of the twelve parishes sent representatives to a provincial assembly which met to appoint the delegates. Though comparatively few North Carolinians had voted for their delegates to Congress, rebel committees there declared persons who rejected the authority of Congress to be "objects of resentment of the public," to be treated as enemies of liberty.

In towns and villages across the colonies, self-appointed committees of inquisitors sounded out leading local figures and others whose allegiance was in doubt. Those who hesitated in their replies or were less than enthusiastic about such rebel causes as the "Association" ban on trade with Britain fell under suspicion. They were often required to make humiliating apologies or explanations if they wished to avoid punishment. Only occasionally could a loyalist find humor in the situation:

> *To sign or not to sign! That is the question.*
> *Whether t'were better for an honest man to sign*
> *And to be safe—or to resolve,*
> *Betide what will, against "associations"*
> *And by retreating, shun them. To fly—I reck*
> *Not where—and, by that flight, t'escape*
> *Feathers and tar, and thousand of other ills*
> *That loyalty is heir to: 'tis a consummation*
> *Devoutly to be wished. To fly—to want—*
> *To want?—perchance to starve! Ah, there's the rub!*[9]

A tongue-in cheek petition, purporting to be from a group of Philadelphia women, begged to have them excused from a boycott on English tea for social reasons:

> The petition . . . humbly sheweth that your petitioners, as well spinsters as married, having been long accustomed to the drinking of tea, fear it will be utterly impossible for them to exhibit so much patriotism as wholly to disuse it. . . . Your petitioners would . . . represent that coffee or chocolate or any other substitute hitherto proposed . . . must destroy the brilliancy of fancy and fluency of expression, usually found at tea tables, when they are handling the conduct or character of their absent acquaintences.[10]

But in most of America, toying that way with the rebel cause was no laughing matter. A Kent County, Delaware, lawyer who presumed to write a pseudonymous letter to a local newspaper expressing loyalist sympathies was so terrified by his inquisitors that he felt it the better part of valor to apologize meekly to the local Committee of Correspondence: "With sorrow and contrition for my weakness and folly, I confess myself the author of the letter. . . . I do profess and promise that I will never again oppose those laudable measures, necessarily adopted by my countrymen for the preservation of American freedom, but will co-operate to the utmost of my abilities. . . ."[11] The committee thereupon "Resolved unanimously that [we] do think the . . . recantation fully satisfactory."

A Virginia schoolmaster who voiced loyalist sentiments had to humble himself even more convincingly:

> I do most heartily and willingly, on my knees, implore the forgiveness of this country for so ungrateful a return made for the advantages I have received from it . . . and hope, from this contrition for my offense, I shall be at least admitted to subsist amongst the people I greatly esteem.

Silas Newcomb, a Cumberland County, New Jersey, man, fared even less well. He was branded an enemy of liberty, to be ostracized, for refusing to concede that it was evil to drink banned English tea and for providing no indication that he would cease that abominable practice in the future.

Not only loyalists fell under threat of punishment. A climate of accusation permitted slights, grudges and long-standing differences to be acted upon. It was, as a contemporary observer noted, "a fine time to gratify low private revenge," with the accused required to protest his dedication to liberty and explain away real or imagined infractions which might have been interpreted as allegiance to the crown. Loyalists, trying to keep their heads down, had to be particularly careful. One recorded that he "had the misfortune to affront one of the Committee men, by not giving his daughter a kiss when I was introduced to her." This was said to have angered the father so much that he set vigilantes to spy on the man to report on whatever transgressions he might commit against the liberties of Americans. "Sorry," the offender concluded ungallantly, "I did not give the ugly jade a kiss."

He would have been more than sorry had he suffered the fate of those loyalists who were imprisoned during the war in the abandoned Simsbury copper mines in Connecticut, a hellhole the story of which mercifully is largely forgotten today. Prisoners sent there were said to "bid adieu to the world." The mines, more than sixty feet underground, were reachable only by ladder. Pots of charcoal were laid out by the prisoners to try to dispel the perpetual stink of foul air which filled the caverns. Vermin abounded and water perpetually leaked from the cavern roof and walls. Some loyalists confined in the mines had been captured fighting for the British; some were incarcerated there merely because they refused to renounce the king.

Loyalist clergymen found themselves in a difficult position. It was their sacred duty to lead their flocks along the path of righteousness, which denied them the option of keeping silent for safety's sake. One who considered himself concerned with the saving of souls, not with politics, tried and failed to distance himself from the conflict. "Even silence," he lamented, "is now considered . . . as evidence" of opposition to the rebel cause.[12] He ultimately felt obliged to flee for protection to British-occupied Boston.

Reverend Jonathan Boucher of Maryland, once a friend of George Washington, took to preaching at his church with a loaded pistol on the lectern. Boucher wrote, "I refused to set my hand to various associations and resolves, all, in my estimation, very unnecessary and unjust; in consequence of which I soon became a marked man. . . . I daily met with insults . . . I received letters threatening me with the most dreadful consequences if I did not desist from preaching."

According to Boucher, he was informed one day that a group of rebels had gathered at his church and that some of them intended to fire their pistols at him as soon as he reached the pulpit. Persuaded by friends not to mount the pulpit, he was nevertheless soon surrounded by men bent on doing him harm.

> It occurred to me that there was but one way to save my life—this was by seizing Sprigg [leader of the band of rebels], as I immediately did, by the collar, and with my cocked pistol in the other hand, assuring him that if any violence were offered to me, I would instantly blow his brains out. I then told him he might conduct me to my house . . . This he did, and we marched together upwards of a hundred yards, guarded by his whole company—whom he had the meanness to order to play the rogue's march all the way we went.

Boucher soon decided he had no choice but to flee the region and later emigrated to England. Other loyalist clergymen were similarly harassed. In Connecticut, Reverend Samuel Peters noted that "for my telling the church people not to take up arms, etc., it being high treason, etc., the Sons of Liberty have almost killed one of my church, tarred and feathered two, abused others; and on the sixth day destroyed my windows and rent my clothes." Reverend Jonathan Odell of New Jersey, who fled to British-occupied New York, said, "I thought it my duty to shut up my church and discontinue my attendance on the Public Worship from the fatal day of the Declaration of Independency."

Those were Episcopalians, mindful of their Anglican heritage. They tended to identify with the mother church and the mother country and saw the growing tide of rebellion as improbable, unreasonable and sinful. However, Congregationalist and Presbyterian clergymen, guardians of the dissenting religious and moral spirit which had propelled the Pilgrims across the ocean fifteen decades earlier, were almost reflexive in their revolutionary commitment.

Not so the Quakers. Opposed to conflict as a matter of belief, they tended to lean toward the loyalist position because their pacifism favored the status quo. They also believed that British Americans had been blessed with peace and plenty. These were rewards from God which it was sacrilege to underrate or mock. Their leaders counseled them to fear God, honor the king and do good to all men, a prescription which rebels found both contradictory and dangerous. Some Quakers did sympathize with the Revolution. Some, like General Greene, who was read out of the Friends Meeting because of it, saw active service in the war. Others, like the Quaker elders of Philadelphia who were banished from that city, were treated with great suspicion and sometimes worse by rebel authorities.

Not a few rebels had their revolutionary commitment bolstered by deep-rooted anti-Catholic bigotry. Some Catholics were dedicated rebels. Charles Carroll, a member of Congress, was a signer of the Declaration of Independence. But John Adams reflected a common attitude in New England, the birthplace of the Revolution, when he reassuringly observed, "We have a few . . . Roman Catholics in this town [Braintree, Massachusetts], but they do not dare show themselves." "Pope's Day," November 5, was a raucous anti-Catholic festival, the New England version of Guy Fawkes Day in England, commemorating the abortive seventeenth-century plot by a group of Catholic conspirators to blow up Parliament.

When the British formally decreed toleration of Catholic worship among French Canadians who came under their rule, it convinced many devout New England Protestants that a papist plot to enslave the colonies was afoot, with British connivance. Warnings were issued that "we may live to see our churches converted into mass houses, and lands plundered of tythes for the support of a Popish clergy."*

Baptists too had reason to doubt rebel devotion to freedom. They also suffered discrimination which, in New England, savored, they said, "more of tyranny than any law of Great Britain." Baptists had been jailed in Massachusetts for refusing to pay taxes to support the Congregational Church.

There were few Jews in America at the time of the Revolution—no more than about twenty-five hundred scattered across most of the colonies, but situated mostly in the bigger towns. They were faced with a dilemma. Britain had treated Jews with far greater tolerance than almost all other Christian countries. At the same time, however, the principles of equality which were part of the rebel creed were appealing and exciting, and most Jews responded by being rebels as well.

Prominent among them were Rabbi Gershom Mendes Seixas, spiritual leader of Jewish communities in New York and Philadelphia, Colonel David S. Franks of the Continental Army, and Haym Salomon, who served first as a spy for the rebels and then as a broker for the congressional treasury. But Rabbi Isaac Truro of Newport was a confirmed loyalist, who ultimately went into exile in Jamaica, as was Isaac Hart, who died in combat defending a loyalist outpost on Long Island.

Refraining from openly espousing loyalty to the king was not always enough to protect loyalists from persecution. As the war

---

* When France joined the war on the rebel side, it was the turn of loyalists to exploit anti-Catholic sentiment. They warned that French aid was a prelude to the forcible conversion of American Protestants to Catholicism. They claimed that among the supplies the French were shipping across the Atlantic to help the rebels were instruments of torture for use in persuading recalcitrants to convert.

progressed and as fear of Tory subversion intensified, written loyalty oaths were required as proof of allegiance to Congress and to the cause of American liberty. The Rhode Island assembly ruled, for example, that any male over the age of sixteen could be asked to sign an oath of loyalty and could be fined and deprived of citizenship if he professed allegiance to the king instead.

Refusal to sign loyalty oaths left individuals exposed to all sorts of penalties. Peter Van Schaak, who declined to sign on principle, was ordered by a local committee to leave his home at Kinderhook, New York, and move to British-occupied Boston. His appeal against this order was successful, possibly because of his influential rebel friends and the respect he had long enjoyed in the community in which he lived. But when his wife later required medical attention in British-occupied New York City, loyalty commissioners refused permission for them to go there. She died soon afterward. When Van Schaak himself later needed medical attention in Britain for his failing eyesight, he was permitted to go but was sentenced to exile from the America he loved.

In some places, Americans were given a time limit by which to sign loyalty oaths or face the consequences. Communications being what they were at the time, there were cases where people found themselves threatened with punishment before they even learned of the oath requirement or had a chance to sign. Forty settlers living along the Monongahela in the wilds of western Pennsylvania protested against penalties decreed against them because they had been given no opportunity to give written affirmation of their loyalty to Congress.

Military officers and civil-government officials were also required to take oaths:

> I, ———, do acknowledge the United States of America to be free, independent and sovereign states, and declare that the people thereof owe no allegiance or obedience to George the 3d, King of Great Britain; and I renounce, refuse and abjure any allegiance or obedience to him; and I do swear that I will, to the utmost of my power, support, maintain, and defend the said United States of America against the said King George 3d and his heirs and successors.[13]

Junior officers in one regiment refused to sign the oath until cajoled into doing so by Washington himself. They considered it a slur on their honor and integrity. Bearing in mind the greater chances for promotion if they shifted over to state militias, they also feared that the oath would freeze them in the Continental Army and in their Continental Army ranks.

There is no indication that the loyalty oaths served any more of a purpose than the non-Communist oaths required of many Americans in the middle of the twentieth century, during the "McCarthy era." Benedict Arnold, who not only betrayed the Revolution but later also fought against it, had signed one. Thousands of civilians who swore allegiance on paper to the new America readily also swore allegiance to the king of England when British forces overran their districts and offered amnesties to those who would turn coat.

Liberty is always among the first casualities of war, even of wars fought to defend freedom. But its demise in revolutionary America, even before independence was proclaimed and before loyalists could be said to be lending aid and comfort to the enemy, showed liberty to be merely an empty catch phrase for many of the people aroused to action in its name. Not only was the liberty of individual dissidents suppressed with unseemly haste and unwarranted vigor, but freedom of the press, so proudly attained under British rule, quickly became a dead letter.

As the orators of the Revolution thundered on about individual rights, individuals who dared to publish sentiments opposing their condemnation of Britain and their call to arms were subjected to indignities, penalties and the forced closure of their journals. Newspapers which sought to remain impartial by publishing both rebel and loyalist articles soon were obliged to stop printing the latter. Newspapers which favored the loyalist position did so at great risk, except where under the protection of British forces. The editor of the *The New Hampshire Gazette* was censured by the rebel-controlled provincial congress for opposing independence and warned never again to print anything critical of the independence cause. Before the British arrived, the editor of the loyalist *Boston Chronicle* was forced to go into hiding and his paper was forced to suspend publication. *The Georgia Gazette* in Savannah suffered the same fate. The print shop of *Rivington's New-York Gazetteer* was ransacked, but, with British backing, Tory publisher James Rivington revived the paper and continued publishing until the end of the war. (He was later said to have been a spy for George Washington. A street on New York's Lower East Side is named after him.)

Not only newspapers were affected by the climate of crisis. Thomas Paine's *Common Sense* was an enormous success, but Charles Inglis, assistant rector of New York's Trinity Church, found that when he composed a rejoinder to Paine's attack on the British monarchy, a mob descended on the print shop and made certain the entire edition went up in flames.

Loyalists unwilling to switch or disguise their allegiances, incapable of enduring the abuse to which they were exposed, and not deterred by personal considerations from abandoning their homes and livelihoods, fled to parts of the colonies under British protection—to Boston, New York, Charleston and Savannah when those cities were occupied by the redcoats. There they could flaunt their Britishness and mount verbal barrages against rebel pretensions. In 1781, a "Declaration of Independence" of their own was issued in New York:

> We . . . Natives and Citizens of America . . . do renounce and disclaim all allegiance, duty or submission to the Congress or any government under [it], and declare that the United Colonies or States, so called, neither are, nor of right ought to be independent of the crown of Great Britain. . . .[14]

Though the rebels lumped them all together as contemptible Tories ("A loyalist is a thing whose head is in England, whose body is in America and whose neck needs stretching"), in British-occupied New York the refugees tried to retain their separate colonial identities. Pennsylvanians congregated at Birket's Tavern near Maiden Lane. Men from Massachusetts converged on Hick's Tavern to be with their friends and former neighbors. Virginians gathered at the Queen's Head.

Theirs was a fantasy world, erected around the conviction that the rebellion was a fleeting aberration, that they would soon be going home, and that home would be much as they had left it. Gradually, despite their undiminished belief in their own rectitude, they awakened to the bitter recognition that these were illusions.

For many of them, living conditions in New York were deplorable. The city's population more than doubled during the occupation. Housing was in extremely short supply. Rents were extortionate. Prices soared generally. The plight of those who crowded into the city for protection grew so severe that the British military command diverted some of its own supplies to help the most needy. Loyalist dignitaries organized charities for the same purpose.

There was also then, as there is now, a measure of antipathy toward New Yorkers among many Americans from other parts of the country, a conviction that the people of that city were unceasingly seized by a mindless, disagreeable frenzy. Having to live cheek by jowl with them discomforted many of the refugees. John Adams, who was of course not one of them, shared their feelings about New York City's residents at the end of the eighteenth century: ". . . there is no modesty, no attention to one another. They talk very loud, very fast, and all together. If they ask you a question, before you can utter three words of your answer they will break out upon you again, and talk away."

Loyalists who preferred not to live as refugees in their own land, whether in New York or anywhere else under British protection, did not have too many options. Those who sought to leave harassment behind by quietly beginning afresh in new American surroundings, where their disreputable convictions would not be common knowledge, found that this wasn't always easy to do. There were places where every stranger was required to show a certificate from his home Committee of Safety or equivalent body testifying to "his friendliness to the liberties of America" or face trial "as a person inimical thereto."

The convergence of thousands of loyalists on British-held regions placed a strain on British resources and strategy. The care and safety of Americans loyal to the crown added to the responsibilities of redcoat commanders. In Boston, for example, during the rebel siege of the city which prefaced the Revolution, the British commander had to concern himself with thousands of refugees at a time when a food shortage was already acute, a smallpox plague threatened and a shooting war was possible at any time.

For a while, the British toyed with the idea of converting part of virtually uninhabited Maine (officially attached to the Massachusetts colony) into a camp where loyalists would be safe and out of the way. According to George Sackville Germaine, British secretary of state for the American colonies, it was to be a place where "the King's loyal American subjects . . . driven from their habitations . . . by the rebels . . . may be enabled to support themselves and their families without being a continual burthern upon the revenue of Great Britain."

But it never happened. Instead, starting with the British evacuation of Boston on St. Patrick's Day 1776, loyalists who would not or could not come to terms with the reality of new America were evacuated abroad—to Canada, to England and to the British West Indies. Many went into exile confidently expecting to return soon to their American homeland—as soon as the Revolution was suppressed. Only a few would ever see their native land again.

An appalling number of people died in the fighting which marked the eight years of the War of Independence, but, compared to the French and Russian revolutions, few people paid with their lives specifically as a result of the American Revolution's civilian reign of terror. Nevertheless, many thousands were terrorized, impoverished and driven from their homes because of their political preferences.

Those responsible acted in the name of liberty, justice and equality; and, because liberty, justice and equality are good and proper, the tribulations of the loyalists have been minimized where at all remembered. Nevertheless, their plight constitutes a grim chapter in American history.

9

THE KING'S LOYAL AMERICAN FIGHTING MEN

I never had any idea of subduing the Americans. I meant to assist the good Americans to subdue the bad ones.

—GENERAL JAMES ROBERTSON, British military governor of New York

Benedict Arnold is an embarrassment. Had he not turned into the most despicable traitor America has ever produced, his patriotic exploits would have been among the most memorable in the War of Independence, perhaps even in all of American military history. Had he not thought himself undervalued by the rebel leadership and not been tempted by British rewards, American schoolboys today would be reciting tales of how he led men in the death-defying expedition through the winter wilds of Maine to join in the assault on Quebec; of his grudging retreat from Canada when he barred superior British forces from easy access to the route that would have split the rebel states; of his rush into battle against orders at Saratoga, where his audacity helped set the stage for the victory that was to make the ultimate triumph of the Revolution possible.

Arnold was a remarkable soldier, but it goes against the grain to think highly of turncoats. His defection to the British, when the rebel military position seemed on the verge of disintegration after so much blood had been spilled, was detestable, as some of his new comrades-in-arms were not slow to indicate. When he reached London, even loyalist refugees there turned away in the street rather than greet him. But Arnold was hardly alone among Americans who actively served the British in the war. Tens of thousands of his less notorious countrymen did so as well—for money, for the prospect of high office, because rebel efforts to intimidate them backfired, because British victories seemed to forecast a rebel defeat, most because they believed that the rebellion was wrong.

For a known loyalist to stay put without recanting publicly in the face of rebel persuasion was generally an invitation to trouble—to abuse, to fines, to jail sentences, to loss of property. It required either firm backbone or pigheaded recklessness. But even more determined opposition to the Revolution came from Americans prepared to go to war against it. At least thirty thousand men—more than George Washington had in his army at any one time—volunteered during the conflict to fight with the British to crush the rebellion of their compatriots. Some estimates put the total as high as fifty thousand. At times there were more Americans enrolled to fight against the Revolution than there were on active service with the Continental Army.

The bitterest fighting in the war was not between Americans and redcoats. It was between Americans and Americans. At the battle of Hanging Rock, South Carolina, not a single British soldier was present. The same was true at the slaughter at Ramsour's Mill, North Carolina, where neighbor fought neighbor. At King's Mountain, where loyalists were cut down by the rebels even after they had raised the white flag (in revenge for an earlier loyalist atrocity), the only redcoat to take part in the battle was the commander of the loyalist forces. Loyalist Americans struggled their way through two hundred miles of wilderness from Fort Niagara to perpetrate, with their Indian allies, the merciless massacre of rebels in the Wyoming Valley of Pennsylvania, where Wilkes-Barre is situated today.

The Wyoming Valley atrocity began as a response to rebel mistreatment of loyalists in the region and then accelerated into a murderous frenzy. Many other fratricidal encounters were similarly prompted by revenge, one party getting savagely even for the earlier misdeeds of the other. Skirmishes turned into vendettas. Battles produced enduring blood feuds, not unlike those for which the hills of Kentucky would later become famous.

Commenting on the bitterness which marked clashes between Americans of the rival political persuasions, Nathanael Greene noted, "They persecute each other with little less than savage fury. There is nothing but murder and devastation in every quarter."[1]

Another officer said, "Such scenes of devastation, bloodshed and deliberate murder I never was a witness to before. . . . The two opposite principles . . . have set the people of this country to cutting each other's throats." Nor did earlier ties and affinities calm the mutual malevolence between rebels and loyalists. A Connecticut man grieved that it was "neighbor . . . against neighbor, father against son and son against father, and he that would not thrust his own blade through his brother's heart was called an infamous villain."

At least fifty loyalist regiments and battalions, comprising more than three hundred companies of troops, joined with the British Army in the fight against the rebels. They came from all over what had been British America. Among them were the Queen's Loyal Virginians, Carolina King's Rangers, Georgia Light Dragoons, New Jersey Volunteers, Loyal New Englanders, Bucks County Light Dragoons from Pennsylvania, Nassau Blues and Westchester Refugees from New York, Detroit Volunteers, East Florida Rangers, American Legion, Maryland Loyalists, Roman Catholic Volunteers, and the Volunteers of Ireland, who, in 1779, held the first American St. Patrick's Day parade in British-occupied New York, an occasion commemorated with song:

Success to the shamrock, and all those who wear it;
Be honor their portion wherever they go.
May riches attend them, and stores of good claret,
For how to employ them sure none better know.
Every foe surveys them with terror,
But every silk petticoat wishes them nearer.
So Yankee keep off or you'll soon learn your error,
For Paddy shall prostrate lay every foe.
This day, but the year I can't rightly determine,
Saint Patrick the vipers did chase from the land.
Let's see if like him we can't sweep off the vermin,
Who dare 'gainst the sons of the shamrock to stand.
Hand in hand! Let's carol the chorus,

As long as the blessings of Ireland hang o'er us,
The crest of rebellion shall tremble before us,
Like brothers while thus we march hand in hand.[2]

To this day, when marching, the men of the Royal Greenjackets, a British infantry regiment, hold their rifles pioneer fashion, "at the trail" (at arm's length, muzzle forward). That was the way frontiersmen who were recruited into the Royal American Regiment of Foot during the Revolution carried their weapons, and the Greenjackets are partially descended from them.

In addition to the organized fighting units, there were thousands of loyalist irregulars, particularly in the South, where, like rebel irregulars, they came and went, depending on how the war was going. A major British success—at Charleston, for example—sent them into action across the countryside. A setback—as at King's Mountain—sent them drifting back to their farms and families.

Some of the officers of loyalist battalions were British. Others were British Americans of social standing and position, like Beverley Robinson, whose family had been well established in Virginia for generations and who founded the Loyal American Regiment, and Oliver De Lancey, who came from an equally distinguished New York family (a New York City street still bears its name). De Lancey's New York Volunteers fought with distinction alongside the British in the South.

Of more modest origins were men like David Fanning, who had been a sergeant of South Carolina militia but who later terrorized rebels and rebel sympathizers throughout the Carolinas. According to a contemporary account, "Always well mounted and accompanied by a band of kindred spirits, [Fanning] swept over the country like a Comanchee chief."

John Connolly, formerly a commander of Virginia rebel militia, recruited the nucleus of a regiment to fight to retake Virginia from the rebels. William Rankin, commander of a Pennsylvania militia unit, also left rebel ranks and recruited a corps of loyalist fighting men. Moses Kirkland, captain in the South Carolina militia, went over to the loyalists, too. Robert Rogers, famous for Indian-fighting exploits of his Rogers' Rangers, organized a detachment of rangers for the British.

As for the troops recruited by these loyalist commanders, they were of different sorts. There were refugees from rebel-controlled territory who flocked to British-conquered cities on the coast. There were newly arrived Highland Scots, Ulstermen and other Irishmen who chose to think of George III as still their king. There were rebel soldiers captured by the British and persuaded to change sides. There were men who deserted from the rebel forces because the British paid better and fed their troops more regularly. (Fed up with rigid discipline and much taken by their personal prospects in the New World, redcoats deserted the other way too.)

From time to time and from place to place, loyalists showed themselves to be, soldier for soldier, as good as and sometimes better than the best the rebels could field—at Brandywine, for example, and Charleston and Savannah. They were numerous. They were resourceful. They were usually well armed. They were often well led. Loyalists captured in battle were frequently shot as traitors by the rebels, which made even the least politicized of them inclined to fight to the end. They were unmoved by the rhetoric or principles of the Revolution. Volunteers one and all, these Americans—scattered though they were—were the makings of a dangerous element which had not featured in the plans or expectations of rebel leaders.

As well as fighting for the king, loyalist Americans also served the British in noncombatant roles. Some were administrators of occupied territory, like former congressman Joseph Galloway, who superintended civil government in Philadelphia during the British occupation of that city. Others served as spies, like Benjamin Franklin's friend Edward Bancroft, who kept the British posted on developments in the French-American alliance. (The British had a copy of the alliance treaty within two days of its signing.) There were no simple definitions for who was the traitor and who was not. The fact that all Americans had so recently been the king's loyal subjects made allegiances perplexing and strained for many people once the rebellion went past the speechifying stage.

The most distinguished of the Americans who spied for the British had been a member of the inner circle of radical leaders in Boston. A member of the Boston Committee of Correspondence, and ostensibly fanatically committed to the rebel cause, Dr. Benjamin Church had delivered moving memorial orations as tributes to the victims of the Boston Massacre. He had eloquently castigated the British for their tyrannical brutality. When the war began, Church proved his devotion to American liberties by becoming chief physician of the army besieging the British enemy in Boston. So prominent a rebel was he that he was named a member of the two-man delegation which officially received George Washington when he arrived in Massachusetts to take command of the Continental Army there. All the while, the good doctor was feeding the British a stream of information on rebel activities and positions.

His career in espionage was abruptly brought to a halt when a suspicious letter was found on a woman—Church's mistress—who had been trying to deliver it to the British in Boston. When decoded, the letter was found to contain, among other things, details of the strength and disposition of the rebel forces around the city. Under close questioning, the woman disclosed that it had been put in her care by Church. Despite his protests that the letter's contents had been misinterpreted and that his patriotic purity was untarnished, he was arrested and imprisoned, but later he was permitted to leave the country, on a ship which was lost at sea en route to the West Indies. Church's family later received a pension from the British, confirming that he had acted on their behalf.

William Demont was adjutant of a Pennsylvania rebel regiment, which did not prevent him in 1776 from passing on to the British the plans of Fort Washington, New York. He thus enabled them to capture the fort, plus a goodly number of rebels and large stores of their precious guns, without serious loss to themselves. Herman Zedwitz, a former Prussian officer who had become a lieutenant colonel in a New York regiment, offered his services to the British but was caught out before he could do any damage. John Vardill, an American who had gone to England in 1774 and who remained there thoughout the war, spied for the British on American sympathizers in London, of whom there were many. Countless Americans served as guides and informers for British forces on the move through the American countryside during the war—steering them past the rebel flank in Brooklyn, guiding them on the way to Philadelphia, alerting them to rebel movements and positions. And they offered them hospitality, which amounted to lending aid and comfort to the enemy. But to them the rebels were the enemy, not the British.

In Somerset County, Maryland, in September 1775, while the patriot army was laying siege to the British in Boston, half the local militiamen who turned up at assembly call wore red cockades in their hats to signify loyalty to the crown (which did not necessarily mean that all those who didn't were rebels). Farther south, Americans who were prepared to fight for the king were even more numerous. When the major British campaign in the South was launched three years into the Revolution, local loyalist units and irregulars lent strong support to the redcoats as they swept across the region, threatening there and then to smother the rebellion and restore the king's authority to America.

In the North, near the Canadian border, the British also had little trouble recruiting loyalist forces. Their popularity in that sparsely settled region was demonstrated in the troop buildup to the clash that ended in the rebel success at Saratoga, after which many Americans who had sided with the redcoats fled for sanctuary to Canada. So convoluted were allegiances in some places that peculiar anomalies resulted. There was, for example, the phenomenon of Ethan Allen, who had boldly seized Fort Ticonderoga from the British, the first rebel victory in the conflict. Before the war was over, that same patriotic hero was negotiating with the British over the possibility of bringing Vermont back into the British Empire, because of differences with Congress over recognizing it as a separate political entity.

Loyalists, near-loyalists and those who might have been persuaded to be loyalists were present in formidable numbers. But from beginning to end the British were remote from the realities of America. Their inability to fathom the mood of the colonies had led to the rebellion. Now they failed to gauge the value of the loyalist forces potentially at their disposal. They had little understanding of the American fighting men who rallied, or would have rallied, to the Union Jack or of the impulses which motivated them.

They could not grasp, until it was too late, that here was a force which could be transformed into a decisive instrument in the struggle for mastery in America. At first, they tended to dismiss

Americans, whether rebels or loyalists, as undisciplined and unmilitary, poor material for soldiering. Arrogant and shortsighted, they were incapable of the simple calculation that would have led them to conclude that Americans who swore allegiance to the king—and were willing to take the king's shilling—had more at stake in the war than they themselves had.

When it became clear that they actually had a fight on their hands, the British reversed themselves and developed inflated notions of the assistance that might be forthcoming from the loyalists they had neglected. Belatedly, King George himself urged his commanders to "call forth those who may have a sense of the duty they owe their mother country." In 1778, Sir Henry Clinton, who succeeded Howe as British commander in America, said, "The number and zeal of those colonists who still remained attached to the sovereignty of Great Britain undoubtedly formed the finest ground we could rest our hopes on for extinguishing rebellion."

Having come round to that conclusion, the British then proceeded to use it as an excuse for not dispatching adequate reinforcements of their own to America and for indulging in illusory estimates of local resources and how those resources could be employed.

Some British officers preferred to use loyalist volunteers only in noncombatant roles, freeing redcoats for battle. They were assigned to garrison and foraging duties and other menial jobs which demoralized those who had been prepared to risk their lives for their king. Their rebel countrymen mocked them for the little value placed on their services by the British:

Come, gentlemen Tories, firm, loyal and true,
Here are axes and shovels and something to do!
For the sake of our king,
Come labor and sing.

Loyalists who volunteered to fight also had other grievances against the British. They were offended when captured rebels were freed and permitted to join the British forces if they renounced rebellion, while loyalists taken prisoner by the rebels were sometimes executed. A British government minister concluded it was "poor encouragement for the friends of the government who have been suffering under the tyranny of the rebels to see their oppressors . . . put upon the same footing with themselves." Nor did loyalists who stood side by side with redcoats in battle take kindly to finding the British quartermaster neglecting to provision their units as adequately when the battle was over. This stepchild treatment hardly encouraged them to persist in the struggle.

Also contributing to loyalist disgruntlement was the way redcoats and Hessian mercenaries ignored the distinction between American civilians who were rebels and those who were not. They plundered the latter as readily as the former. Letters of protection supplied to loyalist civilians by British officers were ignored by soldiers of the king who couldn't read or didn't give a damn.

A Hempstead, Long Island, loyalist clergyman said that through such conduct the British Army hurt the king's cause far more than the rebels did. He might have added that loyalist marauders who engaged in brutal raids against civilians had the same effect. They alienated many Americans who had initially withheld their support from the Revolution. "Bloody Bill" Cunningham and his band of loyalist freebooters killed a lot of rebels in the South and frightened even more, but they pushed many uncommitted, law-abiding Southerners into the ranks of the rebellion. If professed loyalists could be responsible for indiscriminate killing, for plundering homes and for driving off cattle, where was the law and order they were supposed to be defending against the criminal anarchy of the enemies of the king?

In places, freebooters claiming to be patriots also indulged in cruel acts of banditry. A traveler through Westchester County, New York, was startled by what he saw of how people there reacted to raids first by one side, then by the other:

> They feared everybody they saw and loved nobody. . . . To every question they gave such an answer as would please the enquirer; or, if they despaired of pleasing, such an one as would not provoke him. Fear was, apparently, the only passion by which they were animated. . . . They were not civil, but obsequious; not obliging, but subservient. They yielded with a kind of apathy, and very quietly, what you asked and what they supposed it impossible for them to retain. If you treated them kindly, they received it coldly; not as a kindness, but as a compensation for injuries done them by others. . . . Both their countenances and their motions had

> lost every trace of animation and of feeling. Their features were smoothed not into serenity, but apathy; and instead of being settled in the attitude of quiet thinking, strongly indicated that all thought, beyond what was merely instinctive, had fled their minds forever. Their houses . . . were in great measure scenes of desolation. Their furniture was extensively plundered or broken to pieces. The walls, floors and windows were injured both by violence and decay; and were not repaired because they had not the means of repairing them and because they were exposed to the repetition of the same injuries. Their cattle was gone. Their enclosures were burnt. . . . Their fields were covered with a rank growth of weeds and wild grass.[3]

The failure of the rebel command to stop men who professed to be fighting for liberty from terrorizing civilians was a symptom of the overall fragility of rebel control. The inability of the British to harness the loyalists who were responsible for such outrages to more productive military tasks had a wider meaning. It was a symptom of their extraordinary failure fully to deploy Americans willing to fight under their command so that they might influence the course of the struggle.

Whether perpetrated by patriots or by Tories, those brutal bandit binges had no military significance whatsoever. All they accomplished was to make civilians, as well as soldiers, taste the horrors of war.

10

A MUFFLED BLACK DAWN

Blush ye pretended votaries for freedom! ye trifling patriots! who make a vain parade of being the advocates for liberties of mankind, who are thus making a mockery of your profession by trampling on the sacred natural rights and privileges of Africans; for while you are fasting, praying, non-importing, non-exporting, remonstrating, resolving, and pleading for a restoration of your charter rights, you at the same time are continuing this lawless, cruel, inhuman and abominable practice of enslaving your fellow creatures.

—ANONYMOUS NEW ENGLANDER, 1775[1]

After the British had been driven from their land, few white Americans could in all honesty say a yoke of tyranny had been lifted from their necks. Few had earlier realized the yoke had been there. But the ideals of liberty for which the rebels fought offered real hope to black slaves who enlisted to fight in the War of Independence.

Slaves signed up on both sides during the conflict, drawn into rebel or British ranks by the promise of freedom. Thousands did indeed gain their liberty as a result. But for most of the half-million blacks—about twenty percent of the population at the time—the situation remained dismally unchanged in the brave new nation founded on liberty and justice for all. The majority remained slaves till the day they died, while those who were freed were more likely than not to continue to suffer the humiliation, indignities and dangers of second-class citizenship.

Many rebels were keenly aware of the blatant contradiction between fighting for liberty and tolerating slavery. Many were not content to ignore the hypocrisy involved, especially when they were taunted about it, as they were by the English sage Samuel Johnson, who asked, "How is it that we hear the loudest yelps for liberty from the drivers of negroes?"

Samuel Webster of Salisbury, Massachusetts, said, "For God's sake, break every yoke and let these oppressed ones go free without delay—let them taste the sweets of that liberty which we so highly prize and are so earnestly supplicating God and man to grant us."[2] Thomas Jefferson wrote, "The whole commerce between master and slave is . . . the most unremitting despotism on the one part, and degrading submission on the other." Abigail Adams told her husband, "It always appeared a most iniquitous scheme to me to fight ourselves for what we are daily robbing and plundering from those who have as good a right to freedom as we have."

A British court decision four years before the Declaration of Independence exacerbated the chagrin of rebels opposed to slavery as they teamed up with unrepentant southern slave owners in the fight for freedom. That court decision, which was soon widely known in America, held that while living in England a slave owner could not exercise his property rights over a slave. Learning of the ruling, some slaves tried to find a way to escape across the Atlantic for the freedom they could not claim in America. Slave owners advertising for the recapture of runaways noted they might be trying to board a ship for England, "where they imagine they will be free—a notion now too prevalent among the Negroes, greatly to the vexation and prejudice of their masters."

Slavery, a stubborn reality in all the colonies, had deeply ingrained economic and social significance in the South, where the subjugation of blacks had become a central feature of the way of life. When James Madison suggested that regiments of black slaves be raised and offered their freedom to fight for the Revolution and American liberties, he was told it would drain off some of the best agricultural labor of the land, planters and farmers would be ruined, the South would be put in deep distress, and the war against the British might be lost because food production would be sharply reduced.

Instead of offering slaves their freedom, the rebel legislature of South Carolina and Virginia considered proposals to award slaves as bounties to men who enlisted in the revolutionary army. North Carolina passed a law authorizing the hunting, capture and sale of runaway slaves because "many Negroes are now going at large to the terror of the good people of the state." Benjamin Harrison of Virginia and Arthur Middleton of South Carolina, both signers of the Declaration of Independence, were among those much aggrieved at losing many of their best slaves who fled to freedom during the war and did not return. George Washington, who profoundly objected to slavery in principle, did what he could to get those of his own slaves who had absconded restored to him.

To ban slavery or brandish intentions to do so would immediately have driven the southern states out of the rebellion and doomed the revolutionary cause to defeat. But it is a mistake to assume from the outrage of Quakers and other abolitionists in the North that the northern parts of the country were spared their share of anxiety about the aspirations of black slaves. Unlike South Carolina, the New England colonies did not mount regular patrols to make certain that blacks did not acquire weapons, but when their militia marched off to Lexington to meet the redcoats and trigger the Revolution, people in Framingham, Massachusetts, terrified that their slaves would seize the opportunity to rise up and massacre them, armed themselves with axes and pitchforks and locked themselves in their homes till the militia returned. Though slavery served no central economic role in the North, relegation of blacks—slave or free—to subsidiary status was a fact throughout the colonies and was considered right and natural by most whites. The fight for liberty was a selective struggle.

But, for all its broken promises, the Revolution contained the roots of the black liberation movement. There had earlier been isolated slave revolts. In 1712, a group of black slaves attempted to seize New York City by violence, an inept plot which resulted in their slaughter. In 1720, there was a similar effort by slaves to seize the town of Charleston, South Carolina. In 1766, during the uproar over the Stamp Tax, a group of slaves, seduced by the calls for liberty which resounded through the colonies, sent the white citizens of Charleston scrambling home for their guns when they presumed to parade through the streets asking to be liberated as well. However, from the moment in 1619 when a Dutch "man-of-warre" sailed into port at Jamestown to sell the settlers there "twenty Negars," there had been no significant concerted campaign to gain freedom for America's blacks. Now that the slogans of the Revolution made the concept of slavery morally unacceptable, it was impossible to keep slaves from being infected by dreams of liberation. But it was the British oppressors who took the lead in doing something about it.

The evidence indicates that Crispus Attucks, the black who was shot down in the Boston Massacre, was, like the whites with him who provoked redcoat sentries into opening fire, a hoodlum bent on mischief rather than a patriot motivated by noble aspirations. The unwarranted attention accorded him as a national hero has served to rob blacks who genuinely participated in the struggle against the British of much of the recognition that is rightfully theirs. There were blacks among the Minutemen at Lexington and Concord and among the irregulars who laid siege to the British at Boston. Two blacks were with Washington when he made his famous crossing of the Delaware River. Many served in the rebel navy. Their presence in rebel ranks was observed by loyalists who mocked the unsoldierly appearance of the revolutionary troops:

The rebel clowns, oh! what a sight!
Too awkward was their figure.
'Twas yonder stood a pious wight,
And here and there a nigger.

Among the blacks defiantly manning the rebel defenses at Bunker Hill were Pomp Fisk and Titus Colburn, Caesar Weatherbee and Sampson Talbert. Peter Salem was in the thick of the fighting there, as was Salem Poor, of whom white commanders said he "behaved like an experienced officer as well as an excellent soldier."

The commendable performance of these men notwithstanding, the rebels had trouble coming to terms with the fact of black troops in their ranks. The image of a black man with a gun, regardless of which side he was on, was intolerable to southern rebels. They entertained horrific visions of slaves in South Carolina and Georgia, who outnumbered the whites in many places there, savagely rising up against their masters. As at Framingham, it was a fear which haunted many northern slave owners as well.

The Massachusetts Committee of Safety, as devoutly committed to the principles of liberty as any such body in insurrectionary America, decided in 1775 to ban slaves from the forces recruited to fight for liberty. To have slaves in the ranks, the committee resolved, would be "inconsistent with the principles that are to be supported." In New Jersey, the Shrewsbury Committee of Observation instructed all blacks with guns or other weapons to turn them in until "present troubles are settled."

Barely had the command structure of the Continental Army been established than a decision was made that the army could not be allowed to become a sanctuary for runaway slaves. Problems arose with regard to blacks who were not slaves and who, theoretically, enjoyed the same rights and privileges as whites. George Washington dealt with that difficulty in general orders which said, "Neither negroes, boys unable to bear arms, nor old men unfit to endure the fatigues of the campaign, are to be enlisted."[3] Blacks were blacks, slaves or otherwise. Recruiting officers had already been instructed not to sign up deserters, "nor any strollers, negro or vagabond."

Early in 1776, Congress ruled that blacks already serving could remain in the army but no others would be signed on. This was badly received by southern units expected to fight alongside northern regiments in which blacks were enrolled. So further consideration produced a decision that even serving blacks would not be permitted to remain after their enlistments expired. But it was a state of affairs that could not be long sustained. The enemy saw to that.

John Murray, the fourth Earl of Dunmore, a descendant of kings of England and the last royal governor of Virginia, was hardly a man of democratic inclinations. Nor did he have any great sympathy for the plight of the slaves. But he was convinced the Revolution could be nipped in the bud if he could quickly field enough fighting men to oppose it. To the horror of southern plantation owners, he set about gathering his forces indiscriminately. As the British laid siege to Boston farther north, Dunmore announced, "I do hereby declare all indentured servants, Negroes, or others free that are able and willing to bear arms, they joining His Majesty's troops."[4]

So anxious were Virginia blacks for freedom that, when premature word of the governor's intentions reached the plantations, a group of them made for the governor's residence to offer their services. Not yet ready for them, Dunmore had them dismissed without an audience. But once his formal declaration was issued, hundreds of blacks rushed to enroll in Lord Dunmore's Ethiopian Regiment before the week was out. Sashes tied across the uniforms they donned bore the inscription "Liberty to Slaves."

Still not sure of what it was up against in the war, the rebel leadership was rattled by this unexpected development. Washington was convinced that Dunmore could prove to be the most formidable enemy the rebels had. Joseph Reed urged that forces be dispatched so that Dunmore's men might be "instantly crushed, if it takes the force of the whole army to do it; otherwise, like a snowball in rolling, his army will get size."

There were reports of an unnerving restlessness among younger slaves on plantations throughout the South. A notice posted in Williamsburg, Virginia, urged blacks to stay true to their masters, "who would, were it in their power, or were they permitted, not only prevent any more negroes from losing their freedom, but restore it to such as have unhappily lost it." A report told of a black jostling whites in the streets of Philadelphia, mockingly urging them to wait until Lord Dunmore and his troops arrived.

As a military force, the Ethiopian Regiment proved useless. Its recruits, inadequately trained, were mauled in their first encounter with rebel units and never had a second chance. They were racked by a smallpox epidemic which, Lord Dunmore reported, "carried off a great many very fine fellows." Hundreds died. Little was left of the regiment. The survivors, perhaps three hundred in all, were shipped off to join the British forces farther north.

Dunmore set off for England by way of New York and later was named royal governor of the Bahamas. His counterrevolutionary activity had been futile. But during his brief adventure thousands of blacks identified his name, rather than those of George Washington and John Hancock, with their dream of freedom.

* * *

Blacks had no natural sympathies with the British. They had no ties with England, except that most of their forebears had been brought to America aboard British slave ships. They had little to lose if the American-British link was severed. But the English, for purposes of their own, had spoken of freedom for the slaves, while rebel slave masters shuddered at the prospect. Reverend Heinrich Melchior Mühlenberg of Pennsylvania, who had established the first Lutheran synod in America, believed that almost all slaves were convinced a British victory in the war would remove their shackles.

During every redcoat operation in slave regions, hundreds of blacks left with the British when they withdrew or followed hard upon their heels. When the British captured Charleston, so many slaves converged on the city seeking freedom that the redcoat commander had a hard time figuring out how to feed them all. Planters complained about raids in which the British made off with their "horses and slaves." Newspaper advertisements offering rewards for the return of runaway slaves suggested they might be heading for British lines (including one from Massachusetts who was said to be recognizable because he carried his violin with him although he played it very poorly). Warnings were issued that runaways would try to induce others to join them in trying to reach the enemy.

Special patrols were dispatched in the Chesapeake Bay area to block the escape of runaways trying to reach British ships which were offshore or which penetrated upriver. Hundreds of the runaways succeeded. Many of the slaves in the area knew every back road and every one of the tiny waterways which crisscrossed the region, and were not averse to building rafts or borrowing unguarded boats to make good their escape. When British ships anchored off St. Marys, Maryland, a rebel commander warned that most of the slaves in the region would try to reach them if given the opportunity. In Virginia, some planters complained that they "lost every slave they had in the world." The flow of slaves into British-controlled East Florida was so great that the authorities there grew concerned that the situation might get out of hand.

The flight of slaves to British lines and freedom, ironically, induced many southern Americans who had been neutral in the conflict to come out in support of the rebels. They were no more infatuated by the cause of liberty than they had been earlier, but the threat to their way of life and, often, to their livelihoods as well was too serious for them to quibble over fine points.

The work of many plantations ground to a halt. Many of the plantation and town craftsmen—blacksmiths, carpenters, wheelwrights, etc.—were black slaves, and their absence was sorely felt. Domestic tranquility in homes where slaves were valued servants was severely disrupted. Tales of hardship, some of which might not inspire much sympathy today, were widespread. People who had always been used to the comforts of life, their every convenience having been catered to by their slaves, suddenly had to fend for themselves. The unhappy story was told of an elderly couple who, after their other slaves had fled, had "but one little boy . . . left to wait on them within doors."[5] Congress, which had trouble recruiting enough troops to man the army, was urged to station thousands of soldiers in South Carolina only for the purpose of discouraging the "numerous black domestics who would undoubtedly flock in multitudes to the banners of the enemy whenever an opportunity arrived."

Recaptured slaves were supposed to be returned to their masters as expeditiously as possible, it being understood that Americans were fighting to safeguard their property as well as their liberty. Some runaways were, however, executed if caught serving with the British forces, and whipping was not uncommon. Some were sold, the proceeds going to their captors. South Carolina militia commander Andrew Pickens authorized his men to share out between them the spoils of war, including runaway slaves they caught.

Some masters who regained their runaways sold them off immediately as punishment. But most were pleased to have their property back and took greater care not to lose them again. They were not always successful.

There were cases in which masters crossed British lines in an effort to recover their slaves. Washington was none too pleased when he heard that his brother Lund had gone aboard a British ship with offerings of food to try to recover slaves who had fled to freedom from the Washington estate at Mount Vernon. Nevertheless, he wanted his escaped slaves back, and when peace came and the British evacuated New York he asked an officer superintending the British embarkation to keep an eye out for them:

> Some of my own slaves . . . may probably be in New York, but I am unable to give you their description—their names being so easily changed . . . If by chance, you should come at the knowledge of them, I will be much obliged by your securing them, so that I can obtain them again.[6]*

After the failure of Lord Dunmore's Ethiopian Regiment to make an impressive showing, efforts of the British to enroll slaves were largely designed to undermine rebel morale rather than to bolster their own forces. Though some blacks were armed and used in combat by the British, most were employed in menial military tasks—building fortifications, draining ditches, repairing roads, or serving as orderlies. According to Benjamin Quarles in *The Negro in the American Revolution*, at one point most of the teamsters in the quartermaster department of British-occupied New York were runaway slaves. Runaways proved excellent foragers, helping to provision British forces on the move, particularly through the South. Their success in liberating horses was an important factor in maintaining the mobility of the British cavalry during the southern campaign.

Blacks were also very useful to the British as spies reporting on rebel movements and positions, and as guides, many of them having unrivaled knowledge of little-known routes through marshes and rough terrain of the regions where they had been slaves. When the British took Savannah, a runaway slave led them through a swamp to the rear of rebel positions, sparing them what would have been a bloody frontal assault.

Generally, however, the British proved as reluctant as the rebels were at the beginning of the war to give guns to blacks. Sharing with southern loyalists a belief in the inherent unreliability of blacks, some British commanders specifically ordered that they be barred from their units. A number of blacks, reluctant to be so easily excluded, engaged in free-lance operations. One of them, a resourceful runaway called Tye, commanded a score of men of mixed races in guerrilla raids and plundering expeditions against rebels in New Jersey. For years after the war, a group of runaways who called themselves the King of England's Soldiers were marauders in the Georgia back country.

* While not prepared to do without his slaves, Washington made certain they would gain their freedom after he and his wife had died.

For many slaves, escaping to the British for freedom turned out to be a pointless escapade. Many of them were handed over to southern loyalist plantation owners to make up for the slaves they had lost in the upheaval. Many were sold by British officers, either in the South or to face an even less agreeable existence working the plantations of the West Indies.

On the rebel side, the ban on recruiting blacks into the army proved in time to be untenable. More fighting men were needed than were rallying to the flag. The turnout of volunteers and draftees should have been enough to satisfy requirements set by Congress and the army command—there were more than enough whites of appropriate ages to fill the ranks; but the rate of desertion, the failure of the states to meet their quotas, and the less than soldierly quality of many of the recruits meant that the color bar had to be broken, or at least significantly bent.

A precedent was set that was to be followed well into the twentieth century. Blacks were recruited, armed and sent into battle, but not until troop shortages made the situation desperate. Two years of fighting passed before any serious effort was made by the rebels to recruit blacks, and then only when the arguments for doing so became irrefutable, and when officers like Alexander Hamilton began to speak out forcefully: "The contempt we have been taught to entertain for blacks makes us fancy many things that are founded neither in reason nor experience . . . But it should be considered that, if we do not make use of them . . . the enemy probably will."

Other factors changed recruiting practices as well. Recruiting officers, who earned ten dollars or more for each man they enrolled, weren't above ignoring prevailing racial prejudice when money was to be made. The same was true for many officers whose promotions were geared to the number of troops they could recruit. Also, when efforts were made to enforce the draft of conscripts to fill the depleted ranks of the army, men who were reluctant to go off to war and who could pay to send substitutes found that blacks were readily available, and came cheap.

A Hessian officer reporting on the Continental Army noted, "The Negro can take the field instead of his master; and therefore no regiment is to be seen in which there are not Negroes in abundance; and among them there are able bodied, strong and brave fellows." A Connecticut man who sent his slave as a substitute for himself was dismayed to discover, when the enlistment period expired, that he couldn't send that slave again—and claim the bounty—because the man had reenlisted on his own account and the army wasn't prepared to concede that he hadn't the right to do so.

When Congress pressed the states to meet their obligations to supply troops, shortfalls among whites could readily be made up by sending blacks. Gradually, recruitment of blacks in the North became commonplace. Rhode Island decided to recruit a black fighting unit when it was unable to fulfill its quota obligations to the Continental Army any other way. Despite the persisting qualms of slave owners around Narragansett, the black Rhode Island battalion was formed and performed commendably whenever committed to battle.* Elsewhere, however, black troops were not segregated into separate units.

Runaway slaves who tried to join the army, like those caught on the run, were supposed to be sent back to their masters. Many were. However, it wasn't always possible to prove that a black was a runaway, and the man himself wasn't likely to admit it. In any case, northern recruiting sergeants weren't inclined to look too closely into a volunteer's origins, not when he was making money out of his willingness to rally to the colors. In several cases, senior rebel officers were asked to intercede to trace runaway slaves thought to have found refuge in the army. In one case, James McHenry (later secretary of war) appealed directly to George Washington for help in recovering from the army the slave of "one of the best old ladies in the world who was having trouble making do without him."

Even in parts of the South, the recruitment of blacks by the rebel forces became inevitable because of the shortage of white recruits. In Maryland, it was decreed that "any able-bodied slave between sixteen and forty years of age, who voluntarily enters into service, and is passed by the lieutenant, in the presence and with the consent and agreement of his master, may be accepted as a recruit." Enlistment bounties went, of course, to the master.

In 1779, with the British rampaging across the South and with

---

* A French officer at Yorktown, describing the Continental Army passing in review, commented, "Three quarters of the Rhode Island regiment consists of Negroes and that regiment is the most neatly dressed, the best under arms, and the most precise in its maneuvers."

few other rebel troops available to reinforce those trying to cope with the threat to the Revolution, South Carolina and Georgia were urged to recruit three thousand blacks to bolster rebel resistance. Congress offered slave owners compensation of up to a thousand dollars for each slave of "standard size" who was signed on for the duration of the war. The rebel assemblies of the two states were horrified at the suggestion. Christopher Gadsden, the South Carolina radical who had been so effective four years earlier in pressing for the break with Britain, declared, "We are much disgusted here at Congress recommending us to arm our slaves." Some leading South Carolina rebels were so outraged that they contemplated taking the state out of the war.

Colonel John Laurens of South Carolina, whose plan it had originally been and who was to command the proposed black southern forces (he was later killed in combat), had contended, "Men who have the habit of subordination indelibly impressed on them would have one very essential qualification of soldiers."[7] But southerners feared that other, less submissive attitudes might have been more subtly but just as indelibly impressed on the minds of their slaves, so the Deep South did without black rebel fighting men during the war. Shorthanded officers were, however, prepared to blink at the ban to the extent of employing slaves as military laborers. The slave owners were paid for their services.

In addition to serving as combat troops in rebel units of the northern and middle states and in more menial roles in the forces of all the states, blacks were employed by the rebels—as they were by the British—as guides, spies and informers. Blacks who had ties with some of the Indian tribes, having traded with them or lived among them, were at times able to warn rebel commanders of planned Indian raids.

When the war ended, the promise that slaves who had served as rebel soldiers would be freed was largely kept, though some had to appeal for government or court action to keep their former masters from reclaiming them. In northern states, the slaves of Tory exiles were granted their freedom, while those in the South were generally sold at auction, the proceeds going to the public treasury. But so many had left the Deep South that there was a sharp increase in the slave trade after the war to make good the losses. South Carolina was said to have lost at least 25,000 slaves. Thomas Jefferson said 30,000 slaves in Virginia fled bondage in

1778 alone. Fearing being reenslaved, thousands of blacks were evacuated when the British withdrew from their American garrisons at the end of the war. Most went to the West Indies or Canada. About one thousand ultimately made their way to Sierra Leone to found a colony of American blacks there.*

For all American blacks—those who fled to freedom and those who did not—the Revolution had important if not always immediate consequences. It stimulated wide-reaching debate on the position of slaves, and of blacks generally, in American society. Did freedom mean freedom for all, or was it something else from which certain people were excluded? In Massachusetts, William Gordon had called for voting rights as well as freedom for blacks. People might just as well be disenfranchised, he argued, for being "long-nosed, short-faced or higher or lower than five feet nine."

The efforts of Thomas Jefferson to insert antislavery sentiments into the Declaration of Independence had been thwarted by his fellow southerners. They insisted right through the war that slaves were, and should remain, the property of their masters. Though he considered the keeping of slaves both brutal and unworthy of free people, Jefferson seemed inclined to believe that blacks were intellectually inferior to whites. He made a point of questioning the abilities of celebrated blacks of his day—the poet Phillis Wheatley (whose poems were first published in London) and the mathematician Benjamin Banneker. Benjamin Rush argued, however, that the apparent inferiority of blacks was the product of their enslavement and that once they were free such inferiority would vanish in due time. "All the vices which are charged upon the Negroes . . . , such as idleness, treachery, theft and the like, are the genuine offspring of slavery, and serve as an argument to prove that they were not intended by providence for it."

In the northern and middle states, slavery was effectively abolished during the Revolution or soon afterward, and trafficking in slaves was banned in part of the South. It couldn't be otherwise.

---

* Washington considered the evacuation of runaway slaves by the British so serious that he stooped to a personal meeting with the British commanding officer to try to convince him it was wrong. He was, however, embarrassingly obliged to concede that the British, having offered freedom to slaves who joined their ranks, couldn't really be expected to go back on their word. "I have discovered enough," he regretfully reported, "to convince me that the slaves who have absconded from their masters never will be restored."

The principles of liberty and equality which had been so forcefully articulated by the rebels in fighting for American independence were articulated equally forcefully by growing numbers of abolitionists and an emerging corps of black spokesmen.

It may be that southern white attitudes, and the need for unity if the rebellion was to have a hope of success, ruled out congressional action to extend the inalienable rights of man to all Americans. Nevertheless, the great failure of the Revolution was its failure to pledge liberty to the only Americans who were denied it. That failure contributed to the slaughter of the Civil War eight decades later, to the long-term relegation of blacks to second-class citizenship, and to the absence still of an easy relationship between whites and blacks in the cities of the United States.

11

THE TOMAHAWK FACTOR

. . . most of the news from the frontier was bad news. Tories and Indians wiped out the flourishing settlements along the Susquehanna; ravaged the Mohawk and Schoharie valleys; and made New York borderlands an open wound all through the war. . . . The Indians ravaged Kentucky again and again, and carried the war to the smoking cabins on the Monongahela.

—HENRY STEELE COMMAGER AND RICHARD B. MORRIS, *The Spirit of 'Seventy-Six*

Whatever happened, the Indians would lose. They were already on the run. They stood no chance of stemming the white tide that was beginning to wash across the continent. They were, however, still far from being a spent force. Their inability to alter the course of events would neither soften nor diminish the terror they unleashed when drawn into action during the Revolution. For the people who lived along the frontier, it gave the War of Independence an additional dimension of anguish.

The Indians had always presented problems. They had always been a focus of special attention for the settlers who cut down their forests, claimed their land, drove them from their homes, and were the victims of their periodic frenzied retaliatory rampages. The Indians were mercurial. Sometimes they timidly accepted the destiny imposed on them by white men; sometimes they suddenly swooped down on a frontier settlement or farm to plunder or burn, kill and scalp.

There had been a few isolated incidents on the eve of the Revolution but no recent widespread outbursts of Indian violence. However, Pontiac's Conspiracy, an Indian uprising a few years earlier, had demonstrated that serious trouble could not be ruled out. It had shown that settlers along wide stretches of the frontier could be exposed to Indian paroxysms of rage if things turned nasty, and that rival tribes might join in concerted, bloody outbursts.

For the rebels who laid claim to the right to govern America and who were mounting a war to substantiate that claim, the Indian factor should have been a grave consideration from the start. However, though some thought was given to the problem, it was at first not easy for liberty-seeking revolutionaries from the safe, secure precincts of Boston and Philadelphia to appreciate exactly how grave a consideration it was.

During the war, the tribes proved to be a threat practically all along the frontier arching down from Maine to Florida. British troops could no longer be summoned to back up part-time militia when defensive forces were needed in the border regions and the militia itself was wanted elsewhere to do battle with the redcoats. If the Indian campaign against the settlers had been well organized, it would have conceled out any hopes of sustaining the war against the British. As it was, it took a dreadful toll among frontier people.

The rebels were inclined to encourage the Indians to stay completely out of the dispute. Once drawn into the conflict, even on their side, the tribes might not be easy to control. Expecting the war to be brief, the rebels were disinclined to introduce extraneous complications. In a message to the tribes in 1775, Congress urged the Indians to stay clear: "This is a family quarrel between us and old England. You Indians are not to take up the hatchet against the king's troops. We desire you to remain at home and not join on either side, but keep the hatchet buried deep."[1]

However, in trying to influence the attitude of the Indians, the rebels found their position ranging from awkward to impossible. Unlike the British, who came and went, American white men were the natural enemies of the tribes. They had, without qualms, claimed Indian territory as their own from the moment of their arrival on American soil. It was considered by them a totally respectable endeavor. In 1767, George Washington had asked a friend to seek out two thousand acres of good land in Indian territory in western Pennsylvania: "Could such a piece of land as this be found, you would do me a singular favor in falling upon some method to secure it immediately from the attempts of any other, as nothing is more certain than that the lands cannot remain ungranted once it is known that rights are to be had for them . . . "[2]

Not only property rights were involved as far as Indians were concerned. The white men were expelling them from fields, woods and hunting grounds to which their attachment was mystical and religious as well as geared to survival. What was more, the white men showed no sign of being content with what they had already expropriated. They continued to behave as though the land was up for grabs. Even those whose attitude toward the Indians was less than rapacious did not believe that the tribes had claims to any specific territory, "but only a general residency, like wild beasts in the forest."

It wasn't true. Their sense of property differed from that of the white man, but members of a tribe were perfectly aware of the boundaries of their lands and of those of neighboring tribes. Nevertheless, land speculators, surveyors and settlers continued to filter out from coastal regions which had long before been staked out by the white men as their own, to claim still more Indian territory, simply by taking it or through purchase and treaties which Indians subsequently felt they had been tricked into. Sometimes, in their ignorance (or indifference), whites acquired land belonging to one tribe by negotiating for it with another.

The British had pleased the Indians—and angered Americans—by banning further colonial settlement west of the Appalachians. Indications that land speculators and settlers had no intention of abiding by this prohibition made most Indians think even more kindly of the king over the water, who was at least trying to protect their interests, than they did of their American neighbors, who displayed few signs of concern over their well-being or fate.

Many American traders and trappers had established good personal relations with Indians with whom they met and dealt. In his prerevolutionary travels through the hinterland, Jonathan Carver observed, "Notwithstanding the inhabitants of Europe are apt to entertain horrid ideas of the ferocity of these savages, as they are termed, I received from every tribe of them in the interior parts, the most hospitable and courteous treatment."

White men who came in contact with them were sometimes adopted as honorary members of their tribes. But whichever side white men now were on in the war, they had usually made contact with the tribes ostensibly as servants of the great king far away—a concept which the Indians understood and respected. They weren't quite sure why the rebels were defying the king with such vehemence after always having spoken of him with great reverence. They had great difficulty in grasping why the British were quarreling among themselves. It was not easy for them to think of Americans as persecuted.

Like the rebels, the British initially had no wish to complicate the conflict by drawing Indians onto the war path. There was also another consideration for them. Despite the obstreperousness of so many of the king's American subjects, as guardians of the King's Peace the British authorities were obliged not to incite the "savages" against them. In London, the thought of the possibility of such incitement was viewed with horror.

Nevertheless, temptations were strong for the British to call the tribes to arms as the war progressed, and they were well placed to do so. The natural resentment of the Indians against the land-grabbing Americans was there to draw upon. In addition, as a matter of policy while administering His Majesty's dominions and subject peoples, the British had nurtured long-established ties with the various tribes on the fringes of the colonies.

As early as 1710, Indian chiefs had been brought to London to be received by Queen Anne with all the pomp and circumstance appropriate to their dignity and station. Links between the British and many of the tribes had been maintained by British American agents of the crown—men like Sir William Johnson, who lived for long periods among the Indians, took a succession of high-caste Indian maidens as his consorts and sired countless Indian children. Johnson's last "wife" was the granddaughter of an illustrious Mohawk chief. As a leading clan mother, she helped maintain an affection for the British among her people after Johnson died in 1774.

The inclination of Indian elders was to take Congress's advice and stay out of the dispute. They would thus avoid being linked with the defeated party, whichever that turned out to be. As a precaution, the Oneidas up north sent word to the rebel governor of Connecticut, "We love you both—old England and new." He said they would, therefore, decline to come to the aid of either party, even if their assistance was solicited.

There were, however, problems. While the elders counseled staying clear of the conflict, young braves bridled at the suggestion of neutrality. Battle was for them a sacred testing ground. Combat generally also meant plunder. Taking up the hatchet was an attractive prospect. In some cases, Indians, having repeatedly been victims of the white men's ability to have their own way, were convinced that no good would come to them from the fighting whether they participated or stayed aloof. It followed then that the best they could do would be to take whatever spoils came their way in the turmoil and hope the winning side wasn't overly offended by it.

Long-standing animosity between some tribes meant that if one chose to line up with the British, another felt disposed toward siding with the rebels or at least staying neutral. The rebels, however, did not have an easy time retaining what Indian support they could muster. Goodwill had to be nourished through trading and generous gift giving. That was an expensive process, especially when resources were in short supply.

During the early years of settlement, there had been a gesture toward parity in exchanges of goods and property between Indians and white men. It seems today as though the Indians were relentlessly defrauded. But, at the beginning, they valued the trinkets and goods they received from white men as much as they did the relatively small parcels of land they bartered away to unthreatening clusters of settlers. Later, however, as the white population expanded and became a threat to their lands and lives, the situation was transformed. The whites made no secret that they thought of the Indians as lesser mortals with neither rights nor privileges, and the Indians found themselves incapable of effectively challenging white superiority. Equality in status being lost, equality in gift giving and in trading was lost as well. The Indians came to expect more than they were prepared to give. To win their trust, traders, trappers and representatives of the king and the colonies were willing to oblige. Increasingly, some of the tribes came to expect gifts from white men without even a gesture toward reciprocating, and again the white man was willing to oblige.

Gift giving and receiving had always been a serious matter among Indians. Gifts had traditionally been used as peace offerings, tokens of friendship, tribute and reward. White men had latched onto the gift-giving ritual in their dealings with the tribes. They offered all sorts of things: food, weapons and ammunition, clothing, toys, jewelry, fabrics, trinkets, rum. In many cases, Indians grew spoiled by the gifts, neglected their own traditional wealth-creating practices, and came to depend on the goods bestowed on them by government agents, land speculators, traders and missionaries.

The British generally made certain their representatives came well supplied to keep their Indian clients and friends content. But, to their embarrassment and disadvantage, agents dispatched by Congress often arrived in Indian encampments with little more than good wishes and promises. This was self-defeating when, for example, Indians in Georgia knew that although they were getting only soothing words, the rebels had desirable goods teasingly warehoused in Savannah. If the rebels intended to replace the British, they would have to provide the services the British had provided. If they could not, their powers of persuasion among the Indians were undermined.

Even when supplies were duly shipped for distribution to the Indians, they did not always get through. Hard-pressed settlers frequently stopped and stripped supply trains of their goods before they could reach congressional agents trying to curry Indian favor. Regardless of what those agents said about the need to make friends with the Indians, people on the frontier had their own ideas and were particularly reluctant to let through powder for Indian guns, which was among the gifts most valued by the tribes. Settlers feared that whatever promises to the contrary might be made, Indian weapons would be used against them rather than for hunting. The tomahawk was a frightening enough weapon without providing potentially hostile tribal warriors with even more dangerous hardware, when every bark of a high-strung dog in an isolated farmhouse at night and every strange shadow behind a distant tree at midday was enough to make a frontier settler miss a heartbeat.

* * *

Despite the difficulties it encountered, Congress tried to cultivate Indian friendship once it came to appreciate the dangers of not doing so. Imitating the prewar British, it called a halt to further settlement on Indian territory (a ban that proved as full of holes as the British ban had been). The agents it dispatched into tribal lands were instructed to explain why Americans had taken up arms against soldiers of the king, and to make treaties with the tribes. "Brothers!" a congressional message said. "We live upon the same ground as you. . . . We desire to sit down under the same tree of peace with you. Let us water its roots and cherish its growth."[3]

But despite their advice to the Indians to stay out of the conflict, and their later accusations that the British were responsible for the Indian slaughter of innocent settlers, the rebels were the first to employ Indian warriors in the war. Braves of the Stockbridge tribe were among the men who laid siege to the British in Boston in 1775, and Massachusetts rebels sought the support of other tribes as well. The following May, Congress reversed its initial position and resolved, "It is highly expedient to engage Indians in the service of the United Colonies."[4] Washington was instructed to employ Indians to the extent he thought useful.

No matter how useful he might have thought they would be, most Indians had different ideas about where their interests lay. Warriors from the Mohawk, Onondaga, Cayuga, Seneca, Miami, Creek, Shawnee, Chippewa, Kickapoo and Chickamauga tribes were among those who were enlisted by the British to fight on their side or who took advantage of developments to harass settlers not benefiting from the king's protection, though they weren't always meticulous in checking the allegiances of their victims. General John Burgoyne, who called upon Indians to "strike at the common enemy of Great Britain and America," was, as he soon learned, far wide of the mark when he said the Indians served the British by spreading terror without barbarity.

The success of British cultivation of Indian allegiance was most powerfully personified by the Mohawk war chief Thayendanegea, better known as Joseph Brant. A man of great intelligence, Brant, an Anglican convert, translated Christian writings into the Mohawk language. Appointed a captain (later a colonel) in the British Army, he visited London in 1775 and was presented at court and feted by London society. He also conferred while in England with people sympathetic to the rebel cause, but became convinced that the rebels were determined to be undisputed rulers of America, depriving Indians of the protection of the crown.

Returning to America, Brant helped organize Indian backing for the British military effort. An able warrior, he took part in a series of campaigns against the rebels and is known personally to have killed many of them (once sparing the life of a rebel officer because he thought he was a fellow Freemason). It is likely, however, that atrocities against civilians with which Brant was charged were committed by other Indians and attributed to him because his name was widely known by people who rarely could tell one Indian from another. Few settlers believed that any Indians shared their aversion to senseless butchering, a conviction reinforced by reports of captured rebel soldiers being clubbed to death while "running the gauntlet" between rows of frenzied warriors and of others being tied to a stake and burned to death.

The British had warned the Indians against mistreating civilians and torturing captives. But those warnings had little effect. Clear across the frontier, settlements were terrified that they might be overrun and wiped out. No matter how far removed from military involvement or strategic importance, they were potential targets of Indian fury, particularly when warriors returned emptyhanded and disgruntled from battle setbacks. No frontier farmhouse could be considered safe. Farmers took to going about their chores in armed parties. Frontier folk abandoned remote holdings and converged for security on forts which punctuated the back country, sometimes having to race to get there before being overtaken by Indian marauders. Stories circulated about people savagely cut down within sight of safety.

The massacres in the Wyoming Valley of Pennsylvania and at Cherry Valley in New York horrified people of all political persuasions. In the House of Lords in London, Lord Chatham castigated the king's ministers for "letting loose . . . the savages of America." In America itself, visions of warpainted, snarling warriors wielding tomahawks, burning and mutilating, featured in many a nightmare. After the slaughter at Cherry Valley, the Indians claimed that their ferocity had been provoked by the sight of rebel soldiers who had been captured earlier and released on their promise to retire from the war, but who had then participated in destructive raids on Indian villages. Whatever the reasons, a loyalist officer who was unable to control Indian warriors in upstate New York observed "such acts of wanton cruelty committed by the bloodthirsty savages as humanity would shudder to mention."[5]

Whatever terror they unleashed along the frontier, and however serious their potential threat to the Revolution, the Indian warriors turned out in the last analysis to be of little use as fighting men in the white man's war. They had never fought as conventional army units and weren't about to start to suit a British (or rebel) commander. They did not believe in standing fast in the face of superior odds, regardless of orders or tactical considerations. Though they were effective in ambushes and forest skirmishes, signs of unexpected resistance or reports of enemy reinforcements nearby sent them disappearing into the woods, sometimes to be lost forever to the commander who had counted on their presence. Man-to-man combat was a test of courage and skill, but if that wasn't the form the battle took and there was no plunder either, it wasn't easy for Indians to grasp the point of it all.

Time and time again, British commanders came to realize that the support of Indian fighting men was a dubious advantage. They were useful when they weren't absolutely essential to an operation but unreliable in an emergency. At times, Indian warriors ignored instructions that they concentrate their attention on the main objective of an operation to attack and plunder nearby settlements and farms. Whether more meticulous planning and liaison by the British might have changed things is debatable, but, as one study of the situation has noted, "It is difficult to see how the Americans could have resisted a coordinated series of [British] attacks from the sea and a series of [Indian] attacks along the frontier."[6]

In the end, Indian assistance probably cost the British more than it contributed to their cause. One act of Indian savagery in the Hudson Valley helped produce the turning point in the war. It involved twenty-three-year-old Jane McCrae, a girl engaged to be married to David Jones, a young American who, ironically, was serving with the British Army. (Her brother was a rebel officer.) Jane was taken prisoner by Indians, who argued over which of them would claim the captive as his own. The dispute was settled when she was killed and scalped. Word of the girl's murder and mutilation horrified the British commander, General Burgoyne. He wanted the culprit caught and severely dealt with. But he was persuaded by one of his aides not to do anything about the incident. He was told that the Indians, who were part of Burgoyne's forces moving south to drive a wedge between the states, were already grumbling about the lack of plunder and would react badly. News of Jane McCrae's fate and of Burgoyne's failure to take action against the perpetrators quickly spread across the region. Settlers came scurrying to join the rebel forces. Seeking revenge and hoping to protect their own families from such savagery, they played a key role in the landmark defeat inflicted on Burgoyne at Saratoga.

Casualty figures for the war cannot accurately record the number of men, women and children who fell victim to Indian rampages. There was no record for the presence of many people who had settled on the frontier, much less for their disappearance. The casualty figures certainly also do not include the number of peaceful Indians slaughtered in revenge by the rebels.

Fearing the effects of Indian terror, the rebel command dispatched troops on retaliatory and preventive search-and-destroy missions. Indian villages were put to the torch. Indian crops were destroyed. Indians were expelled from ancestral homes or from homes they had newly established after having earlier been displaced elsewhere by white settlers.

Simply being an Indian was sometimes enough to be marked out for retribution. On the banks of the Muskingum River in what is now Ohio, militia units descended upon a settlement of peaceful, psalm-singing Christian Delaware Indians and tomahawked twenty-nine men, twenty-seven women and thirty-four children to get even for the savagery of other Indians.

Years after the war, an Indian chief told George Washington that "to this day" when the name Town Destroyer (by which Washington came to be known to some tribes) was mentioned, "our women . . . turn pale and our children cling to the necks of their mothers."[7] For the innocent victims, among both the whites and the Indians, the Revolution had a meaning remote from the ideals embodied in the Declaration of Independence.

12

SAD SANCTUARY

For my native country I feel a filial fondness; her follies I lament, her misfortunes I pity, her good I ardently wish, and to be restored to her embrace is the warmest of my desires.

—SAMUEL CURWEN, American loyalist refugee in England[1]

It is never very cold in London, and rarely very hot. Judging from temperature readings alone, it is an ideal retreat for people who favor a moderate climate. But, as anyone who has visited the British capital can testify, its weather is usually less than agreeable. It couldn't be otherwise in that comparatively small island nation caught between the meteorological whims of the Atlantic Ocean and the North Sea.

There is nothing comforting about British weather, except for those who are comforted by the possibility of changes from overcast to sunshine, from sunshine to downpour, from downpour to drizzle, from drizzle to sunset, all between dawn and dusk of a single day. It rains a lot in London. Sometimes it rains at least part of the day, every day, for weeks running. King Charles II observed wryly, "You can tell when summer comes to England. The rain gets warmer."

Despite this dreary picture, the British go about their affairs without being overly distressed by the fate the elements have imposed on them. Not so the Americans who fled their homeland and took refuge in London to escape the Revolution. To them it was an addendum to their misfortune. William Smith, formerly chief justice of New York, complained, "It is constantly raw and wet." It can be desperately cold in Massachusetts in the dead of winter and sweltering in Georgia in deepest summer, but for people accustomed to them such atmospheric perversities were no more, no less than natural; transplanted to the dampish precincts of London Town, they knew in their bones that something was amiss, and not only with the political situation. Dr. John Jeffries of Boston, who was one of their number and who attended many of them in their place of refuge, found that "from differences of climate, chagrin, and various circumstances" they were "very frequently disordered."

It wasn't too bad at first. Almost everything is tolerable in small doses, and they did not expect to stay long. Though they were British, and were convinced that all other Americans were British as well, they remained deeply attached to their American homeland. They had no doubt that there was where they belonged. Ancestors of some of them had settled in America several generations before, having arrived on the *Mayflower;* and those of others not far behind.

Most of those who fled to England (compared to most of those who made instead for Canada and the West Indies) had been—and believed they still were—people of rank and position in America. They were governors and judges, customs officials, Anglican clergymen and town dignitaries. Until the rebels had complicated their lives, until, as one of their number put it, they were "unable longer to bear [the] undeserved reproaches and menaces hourly denounced against myself and others," they had been pillars of their communities.

Among them were such dignitaries as Andrew Allen, who had been attorney general of Pennsylvania; Isaac Low, who had been a member of the First Continental Congress; Robert Alexander, who had been a member of the Second Continental Congress; Anthony Stokes, who had been chief justice of Georgia; John Randolph, who had been attorney general of Virginia; Josiah Martin, who had been governor of North Carolina; and Samuel Shoemaker, who had been mayor of Philadelphia.

They and their fathers had made and administered the laws of the colonies. They had founded schools and churches. They had been respected and revered. This was especially true of New

Englanders, who made up the largest contingent of those who sought sanctuary in England. A chronicler of the fate of the loyalists asserted, "To anyone at all familiar with the history of colonial New England, that list of men denounced to exile and loss of property on account of their opinions will read almost like the bead-roll of the oldest and noblest families concerned in the founding and upbuilding of New England civilization."[2]

Most of the loyalists who went as refugees to England arrived there at the beginning of the war, shortly after the redcoats had evacuated Boston in 1776. Though it was a great, costly inconvenience for them to leave their homes and homeland, it was not considered an absolute calamity. It was to be only a temporary interruption in their normal lives. They would return to America none the worse for wear as soon as the British Army had restored a sense of proportion, propriety, law and order to the colonies. Meantime, they would survive as comfortably as circumstances permitted. They would enjoy the splendors of the country to which they had remained heroically faithful and would keep as well informed as they could on developments in America, the better to plan their eventual return home.

Despite the weather, arriving in London was not at all unpleasant. The British capital was the hub of their universe, the center of culture and taste. It was to guard their British identity, as well as to sustain a rectitude in the affairs of men and government, that they had been loyalists in the first place rather than rebels. Though the sea crossing had been rough for some of them, and though they remained deeply distressed by recollections of their abuse at the hands of the rebels, many came as pilgrims might to the City of God.

Some were dazzled by the sight of the big city. They went to Hyde Park to sample the morning socialite fashion parade there. Like American visitors to London today, they devotedly made for Kew Gardens, the British Museum, Westminister Abbey and the Tower of London, which, at the time, housed a zoo where they found the monkeys to be enchantingly almost human. They attended public hangings at Tyburn, where Marble Arch stands today, and obligingly had their pockets picked there by reprobates who could have been hanged as well if caught. They went to exhibitions of acrobatic skills and to the theater, where they often were repelled by the way London audiences chucked fruit and hissed at performances found to be less than adequate. Back home in America, theatergoing was still largely a pastime of the genteel, and such disorderly practices would have been unthinkable.

They found wonder in the very streets of the British metropolis. Emerging from a building, Nellie Boucher told her husband they should wait till the crowd in front of them had passed and was astonished when informed that there was no more crowd there than usual. Boston and Philadelphia had never been like that. Reports of what they saw and experienced filled diaries and letters, like those of Samuel Curwen, an admiralty judge from Salem, whose ancestors had settled in America just a few years after the Pilgrims had done so and who was still a member of a club for the improvement of philosophy and literature in Massachusetts:

> Evening at Vauxhall Gardens; fine gravelled walks, shrubbery and covered alcoves lighted by lamps and rendered a most enchanted spot.
>
> At Covent Garden, obtained a very convenient place . . . when the oratorio called The Messiah was performed. The whole stage an orchestra; in the center a spacious organ, embellished by a portrait of Handel surrounded with . . . such rays as are placed around the heads of saints in the Romish calendar.
>
> The young chimney sweepers with their sooty and chalked faces are dressed with ribbons and gilt paper, a grotesque and merry-andrew appearance. . . . The milk maids appeared in fine and fantastic attire, and carried on their heads pyramids of three or four feet in height, finely decorated.[3]

After the unpleasantness they had experienced at home, the exiled Americans were pleased and intrigued to find the freedom about which they had been so righteously lectured by rebels to be a reality in England. Even the king could be, and was, subject to criticism and caricature, and the king's ministers were often as openly ridiculed on the streets of London as they had been in the taverns of Boston. It confirmed their belief that the Revolution was not at all about liberty, but was the work of cliques of power-seekers and demagogues.

The newcomers were, however, not overly charmed to hear pro-rebel sentiments lightly expressed by some people in London whose fighting men were at that moment tangling with the hated rebels. Also arousing their disquiet and disapproval were the realization that poverty on open display in the back streets of the British capital could be so widespread at the very heart of His Gracious Majesty's realm, and the appallingly great number of prostitutes and beggars to be encountered there.

To their English hosts, the refugees were a novelty and a curiosity at first. The most distinguished among them were received in high places and consulted on developments in America. Governor Thomas Hutchinson of Massachusetts, held to be the most senior among them, had an audience with the king (to whom he apologized for the somberness of his New England attire), met with leading members of the British government, and mercifully had the continuance of his salary while in exile confirmed.

But as their numbers multiplied and as the war dragged on, the English devoted less and less attention to their colonial guests and sometimes came to think of them perhaps as responsible as the rebels for "gnawing at the very entrails of Great Britain and spilling her best blood." They began to be objects of neglect and impatience, instead of the respect and gratitude they felt to be their due in recognition of the sacrifices they had made while trying to keep the Union Jack flying proudly over America. As is often true with refugees, they made their hosts feel queasy. In turn, they felt queasy themselves.

Little by little, it dawned on them that the Americans and the English were not one people separated only by three thousand miles of ocean. They came to realize that even senior British government figures had little understanding of the American situation and little desire to fathom more. Those among the refugees who volunteered their advice and insights were discreetly but unmistakably snubbed. Even Governor Hutchinson found that despite his rank at home and his loyalty to the crown his views were no longer sought. When he nevertheless conveyed them, modified to blunt the edge of his criticism of British methods, they carried little weight. He soon was reduced to self-pity: "We

Americans are plenty here and very cheap. Some of us at first coming are apt to think ourselves of importance but other people do not think so, and few if any of us are much consulted or enquired after."[4]

The treatment they were accorded lent the loyalists a greater sense of their American identity. Samuel Curwen grumbled, "It piques my pride . . . to hear us called 'our colonies, our plantations' in such terms and with such airs as if our property and persons were absolutely theirs." He was almost relieved when he ventured into the English countryside and found himself with "friends of American liberty" in a tavern, "talking treason and justifying American independence."

In fact, antiwar feeling was widespread in England. Though little revolutionary zeal intruded upon the English atmosphere, there was extensive sympathy for the principles of American liberty, so well articulated by rebel leaders and their British advocates. Merchants in London, Bristol and Liverpool were fed up with suspensions of trade with America, which had been so lucrative and could be again if the dismal war were ended. Many Englishmen wanted to know why, if loyalist sentiment was strong in America, the loyalists were unable to deal with the rebels themselves, without the need to squander British blood. The American refugees in their midst often found themselves to be the butt and target of accusations and insinuations.

Contrasts between personality characteristics of Britons and Americans also served to lessen the ardor of the fugitives for their place of refuge. After the first agreeable impressions of English dignity and gentility had worn thin, they found their hosts to be formal, reserved and aloof, or strangely lightweight. Proper Bostonians were offended by the triviality of court gossip, which seemed to occupy the attention of government ministers almost as much as did the war in the colonies.

After their purposeful existence in Massachusetts, those important enough to be entertained by the English upper classes at their country homes were dismayed by the aimlessness of life amidst unwarranted luxury. Governor Hutchinson said he would not have parted with his "humble cottage" at home for it.

> The first appearance of my Lord and Lady is in the breakfast room at 10. Breakfast is over at 11. Everyone then does

> what they please till 3:30 when all meet at dinner. Between 5 and 6 the ladies withdraw. The gentlemen go into the library, some chat. Others read. At 8 a call to one of the drawing rooms for tea or coffee, after that cards, conversation or reading. Exactly at 10 the sideboard is laid with a few light things if anyone is disposed to have supper, and exactly at 11 as many servants as there are gentlemen and ladies come in with, each of them, two wax candles and in procession we follow to the gallery at the head of the great staircase and file off to different rooms.

England was proving to be a strange land, as little a motherland to them as a woman might be a mother to a child who had never or rarely seen her before. Efforts by Americans, hungry for contact, to establish enduring relationships with English people proved fruitless more often than not. Though their circles back in America had also been bound by formalities and codes of behavior, they had not been as rigid or as exclusive as those the refugees encountered in London. Benjamin Marston, a merchant from Marblehead, said, "Americans used to call this country home, but it has become a very cold home to us. . . . The original connections and attachments are long since worn out and dissolved."[5]

The most serious problem facing the refugees in England was, however, more mundane. Few of them had sufficient resources at their disposal to maintain the lifestyles to which they had been accustomed in America. Though most of those who had fled to England were reasonably well-to-do, and some were very rich, none had expected to be separated from the sources of their incomes for very long. Even those who could have done so had neglected to arrange for a transfer of sufficient funds to make their exile a less trying experience. Though never before having had to scrimp or do without, they found England to be an exceedingly expensive place and soon learned to be very careful with their expenditures. They sought out cheaper lodgings than they would have liked and made other economies which they would have found unthinkable before.

For most, earning a living was out of the question. They didn't expect to be in England long enough to justify taking up a position suitable to their rank and status, and, anyway, there were few jobs available for men who had been senior judges in America or had subsisted comfortably on the proceeds of inherited property. Anglican ministers among the refugees expected the mother church to take care of them, but found themselves gathering only promises from bishops rather than positions in English parishes. Though few of the refugees were as desperate as Mrs. Elizabeth Dumaresq, who had not been poor in Boston but who was compelled to enter domestic service in London, the Americans were not amused by jokes about how there were enough of them about to guarantee against a shortage of haymakers at the next harvest time.

With no other recourse, and convinced that Britain owed them a debt of gratitude, the refugees turned to the British government for what they believed would be well-earned recompense for their sacrifices. What they received turned out to be no more than handouts, grudging favors rather than due reward. Those who were able to prevail upon people of influence, or who managed to impress officials responsible for the "pensions" with their need or merit, managed to be awarded tolerable sums. Many got less. Whatever it was, it was not as much as the recipient required to maintain his customary lifestyle.

Samuel Curwen, who was finally successful in soliciting a middling sum, had worried because "my little bark is in imminent hazard of being stranded unless the wind shifts quickly, or some friendly boat appears for its relief. In plain English, my purse is nearly empty." Another refugee boasted of learning to master the intricate trick of surviving on the "pittence" he had been awarded by an ungrateful British government.

Inevitably, some of the loyalists in England—particularly the more elderly among them—began to wonder if they had been wise to flee their homeland. Most still had friends and relatives at home with whom they were able to correspond from time to time. They received reports from them of how, for example, a Massachusetts loyalist did not "freely nor safely walk in the streets by reason of [the] malevolence and the uncontrolled rancour of some men." But many of those friends and relatives apparently managed to endure at home despite everything, keeping their opinions to themselves and doing what was required to avoid undue attention, making the best of a bad situation.

Not for them the prospect of prolonged exile. Not for them the infernal dampness of the London climate. Increasingly some of the refugees began to feel, as did Samuel Curwen, that they too might have done better to put up at home with "the comparative trifling conditions of insults, reproaches, and perhaps a dress of tar and feathers."

Deprived of comfortable living, unable to infiltrate London society, the refugees fell back on one another for companionship and sympathy. They had taken to living near one another in Little Americas in Soho, off the Strand, near Haymarket, and in Knightsbridge (near where Harrods department store stands today). Having little to do but contemplate their predicament, they spent much time calling on each other in their cramped, excessively costly rooms. Or they met at their favorite hangouts, including the St. Clemens Coffee House, the Crown and Anchor Tavern, the Jerusalem Tavern and the New England Coffee House, which became a rendezvous for New Englanders seeking to give or hear the latest news from home. As they did in British-occupied New York, people from Massachusetts tended to congregate in the same places, Virginians chose other venues, etc. Certain coffeehouses and taverns developed reputations as American retreats and were largely taken over by the refugees. Weather permitting, they also converged on St. James's Park to pass the time of day and hoping to encounter more well-connected compatriots who might help steer them toward a position or a pension.

Such isolation from involvement in British life was not without its internal frictions and altercations. There were moderates and extremists among the refugees: those who regretted having left home and those who despised them for their faintheartedness; those who were cheered by word of every rebel setback and those who reluctantly nurtured secret satisfaction at news of every rebel success. Some could not help being concerned about the devastation wreaked by the war. Others, like Governor Hutchinson, found themselves increasingly indifferent to what damage might be done and what grief might be inflicted: "Ten years ago, I should have felt for the poor inhabitants of Virginia if I had heard that the Creeks and Cherokee Indians had fallen upon them, but I have lost those feelings now and rather was pleased to read the account."

Disputes between refugees on developments at home could be

intense. Lloyd Dulany died of wounds administered by Reverend Bennet Allen in a duel over whether the Dulanys had shrewdly assigned some of their kin to stay put and stay quiet back in Maryland, in rebel country, to save their property from confiscation while other Dulanys had joined the loyalists in exile, so that the family property would not be forfeited no matter how the war turned out.

There were also Americans in England who were not refugees. Some, like Member of Parliament Henry Cruger and artist Benjamin West, had been resident there for many years but were still much troubled by developments in their native land. Among them also was Jonathan Carver, a remarkable New Englander who had moved to London in 1769. Carver was the first British American to venture deep into the American heartland, traveling alone and braving the dangers which such an expedition entailed. Well before Lewis and Clark set out on their famous expedition across America to the Pacific, Carver penetrated into the Midwest and made a perilous solo canoe voyage of discovery down the Mississippi. A captain in the British Army in America during the French and Indian War, he had gone to England to seek funds for a more extensive exploratory journey through the American wilderness. Failing to secure the backing he needed, he stayed on in London, where, to raise money for his projected expedition, he wrote a fascinating account of his earlier adventures. It was well received in Britain, but earned him little in the way of hard cash. Carver was later described as having been "forced for his livelihood to become a hack writer, and to bow himself down to such ill-paid tasks as the booksellers of London might choose to employ him in."

Carver gradually became impoverished, and his movements were confined. Having a deep love for his native land, of which he knew far more than most Americans, but having been a British officer, an experience untarnished because he was away from home during most of the prerevolutionary unpleasantness, he tried to avoid taking sides while he painfully monitored the course of events in the America he would never see again.

By 1778, the failure of the British command to produce the expected easy victory over the rebels raised questions in London about the advisability of continuing with what was beginning to seem an interminable struggle. Was it worth the effort and the expense? Under pressure from critics of the war, and of their handling of it, some ministers came to think that Britain should withdraw its troops and cast America adrift to sink in its own anarchy and confusion. Panicked by such musings, the refugees in Britain did what little they could to convince their hosts that the rebels were still only a rambunctious minority among Americans, that the colonies could still be saved, and that they were worth saving.

But the hapless loyalists also had to accept that the redcoats might finally prove incapable of administering the thorough thrashing which it once seemed certain the rebels would receive. Open criticism of the British military command was heard. The refugees told each other, and anyone else who would listen, that better-qualified generals "with half the force which has been employed . . . would have put an end to the rebellion." They referred mockingly to the days when British officials boasted that they would crush the rebel rabble in three months. Samuel Curwen noted the changed assessment of the situation:

> The dark aspect of affairs in America, on the side of the government, renders it likely that England or some foreign country will, for many months to come, be the residence of the wretched American fugitives. Our headquarter folk have, I learned, lowered their topsails and talk in a less positive strain; fear and apprehensions seem to have succeeded assurance.[6]

When news reached London of the British humiliation at Saratoga and of the French entry into the war on the side of the rebels, Curwen again reflected the ever-deepening gloom of the outcasts:

> God knows what is for the best, but I fear our perpetual banishment from America is written in the book of fate; nothing but the hopes of once more revisiting my native soil, enjoying my old friends within my own little domain, has hitherto supported my drooping courage; but that prop taken away leaves me in a condition too distressing to think of.

The recollection of the abuse which had driven them from their homes rankled too sharply for some of the refugees to contemplate a return, no matter what lay ahead for them in exile. Jonathan Sewall said, "The harsh conduct of my countrymen has given me a dose I shall never get over—God mend them and bless them—but let me never be cursed with a residence among them again."

For others, as the likelihood of a return home grew more remote, bouts of homesickness grew more frequent. The proud Hutchinson confessed, "I would rather die in a little country farm house in New England than in the best nobleman's seat in Old England." Charles Paxton, once a commissioner of customs in Massachusetts, offered a hundred guineas to be buried beside his parents in Boston, no matter how the war ended. (Samuel Curwen, on the other hand, made a point of instructing that he not be buried beside his wife—who, like many of the wives, had stayed behind in America—because he had no wish to have to see her first when Resurrection came on Judgment Day.)

Forebodings and gloom had prepared them, but the news of the British surrender at Yorktown, and the likelihood that Britain would soon sue for peace, sent a spasm of despair through the refugee community in England. That decisive failure of the British Army in the field finally and irrevocably proved that their faith in the British crown had been misplaced. The rebels, the archvillains, the vandals, had won.

To make matters worse, England did not seem overly distressed by this turn of events. The imminent end to the war loosed a wave of relief throughout Britain, despite the serious defeat it entailed and regardless of what it meant to Americans who had stayed true to the British motherland. There were resignations from the government in London and rumors that the king might abdicate, but English people generally did not share the end-of-the-world despondency which now settled like a shroud over the American loyalists. They certainly displayed little interest in the fate of the refugees. Anguished letters from some refugees to London newspapers told some of the story.

> The loyalists in this country are most shamefully and traitorously abandoned. Our fears at present surpass all description. Never was there upon the face of the earth a set of wretches in a more deplorable situation. Deprived of all the

> hope of future comfort or safety, either for themselves or their unhappy wives and children, many have lost their senses and now are in a state of perfect madness. Some have put a period to their miserable existence by drowning, shooting and hanging themselves, leaving their unfortunate wives and helpless infants destitute of bread to support them.[7]

Though such lamentations were exaggerated, the situation for most of the refugees was truly precarious, and some suicides were indeed reported. They now saw little hope of regaining the property they had left behind in America and of thereby reestablishing their financial independence. Some were shattered to learn, by reading Boston newspapers in their favorite London coffeehouses, that all their property at home had been sold, the proceeds going to finance the Revolution. Even Governor Hutchinson's family burial vault had been put up for sale, the remains of his ancestors removed and the name of the new owner engraved on the tomb. It was symbolic, as if even evidence of loyalist origins in America was being expunged. They were to find new places for their own graves and tombs.

It was time to start counting pennies in earnest. Refugees sought out less expensive accommodations, and then still less costly living quarters. Many fanned out across Britain—to Bristol, Birmingham, Glasgow, Cardiff and other parts of the country where living costs were substantially lower than in London and where they might start life anew, away from troubled memories of their frustrated hopes in the British capital. One loyalist sighed, "There will scarcely be a village in England without some American dust in it by the time we are all at rest."

13

THE WAY NORTH

Not drooping like poor fugitives they came,
In exodus to our Canadian wilds,
But full of heart and hope, with heads erect,
And fearless eyes, victorious in defeat.

—WILLIAM KIRBY

Being forced into exile can't ever be easy. But, for many Americans when home became unbearably hostile the escape route was relatively uncomplicated. Those in the northern states could slip into Canada without great difficulty. They tramped along trails through the woods with their children and chattel and made their way across the rivers and lakes that were comparatively simple to negotiate, or, if they lived by the coast, they went all the way by sea.

It wasn't far to go, though the sea journey from New York City could take up to twenty days. Sometimes they traveled in groups, clusters of refugees on the move. A former mayor of Albany, New York, led a party of three thousand loyalists to an uncertain sanctuary in the north. They sought out with trepidation a newer world than the New World they had known.

People farther from the border found their trek more trying. Some in southern states wandered like pilgrims through the Carolinas, seeking safe haven here and there, before taking to ships and heading past the farthest northern limits of rebel activity to Nova Scotia, that windswept slip of land tacked onto Canada's Atlantic coast like a geological afterthought.

Some drifted west till they reached the Mississippi, then north along the river, branching off from it to find the British outpost at Detroit, a stopping-off point on the road to exile. Some followed labyrinthine overland routes for long distances through the forests of the American hinterland, risking encounters with hostile Indians and living off the land as best they could as they made their way from the land of liberty to a different brand of freedom.

The exodus was in fits and starts. The flow depended on how the war was going, where the military activity was, and the intensity of rebel pressure. But this was no trifling, random population shift. It was the most concentrated internal migration North America had yet seen. Tens of thousands of Americans left their homes and their homeland to find a new life in the wilds of Canada, away from the strife and turbulence, the death and destruction, and the hard feelings which accompanied the birth and baptism of the United States of America.

Before their arrival, that part of British Canada populated by white people (only the southeastern corner of what Canada is today) was ruled and run by military officers, who made and implemented all decisions with little reference to, or concern with, the wishes of the inhabitants. That state of affairs would not long be tolerated by the new arrivals. Though not sharing the revolutionary yearnings of the rebels from whom they had fled, the refugees brought along the independence and obstinacy of the American character. Their start in Canada was marked by intense deprivation and hardship, but they laid the groundwork for a democratic, enterprising nation in the land they now called home. The American Revolution was as much a cradle for modern Canada as it was for the country the refugees had forsaken.

Some of the refugees to Canada had preferred to avoid active identification with either side in the war. All they sought was the safety and tranquility they had previously known, and which they felt they could no longer enjoy in what had suddenly become a field of battle. Most were unquestioning subjects of the king, anxious to start anew in a region where British law and order, and all the reassurances they provided, were still both cherished and operational. Among the refugees, as among those who had fled to England, were some of the most eminent people in American colonial society. Canadian historian Henry Smith Williams called the loyalists the makers of Canada:

> They were an army of leaders. The most influential judges, the most distinguished lawyers, the most capable and prominent physicians, the most highly educated clergy, the members of the councils of the various colonies, the crown officials, the people of culture and social distinction—these were the loyalists. Canada owes deep gratitude to her southern kinsmen who thus, from Maine to Georgia, picked out their choicest spirits, and sent them forth to people our northern wilds.[1]

These distinguished men with their well-bred wives and coddled children were in fact only a tiny fraction of the Americans who headed northward to escape the Revolution. Almost all were of less eminent and less insulated backgrounds—artisans, farmers, shopkeepers, laborers. Thousands had been soldiers in loyalist military units—the New Jersey Volunteers, the Queen's Rangers from Virginia, the Maryland Loyalists, the King's American Regiment from North Carolina, the New York Volunteers—who feared the consequences of remaining in America. Many arrived en masse as the war drew to a close. Some of the immigrants were deserters from the Continental Army who didn't wait that long.*

The Maritime Provinces of Canada, upon which the refugees converged, were very sparsely settled, mostly by people who, before the Revolution, had filtered north from the British American colonies in search of new frontiers and new opportunities. When the rebellion erupted, they had been torn by the same dilemma which afflicted so many Americans at home.

> We do all of us profess to be true friends and loyal subjects to George our King. We were almost all of us born in New England. We have fathers, brothers and sisters in that coun-

---

* Among the refugees was the man who, as a loyalist prisoner of the rebels, had hanged the much-admired British spy Major John André, who had been captured while plotting the surrender of West Point to the redcoats by its traitorous commander, Benedict Arnold. Upon arrival in Canada as a refugee, the hangman had received a grant of land. When his identity was discovered, he was driven off.

> try. Divided betwixt natural affection to our nearest relatives, and good faith and friendship to our King and Country, we want to know if we may be permitted at this time to live in a peaceable state.[2]

This claim to neutrality by the people of Yarmouth in Nova Scotia was shared by most British Canadians. They were so few in number that the handful of would-be rebels among them couldn't hope to exercise the kind of influence and control over the region that rebels farther south were able to wield. Without the active support of the people there, attempts by the American rebels to invade Canada and draw its inhabitants into the Revolution would have been doomed to failure even if invasion plans and attempts had been less haphazard.

The influx of the loyalists during and after the war, and the part they played in the development of Canada, helped frustrate the hopes of many a would-be American empire builder, then and later, for the emergence of a truly continental America, reaching as far north as north could be as well as from sea to shining sea. With the liberty of its people protected by law and practice, Canada would stay British for a long time to come. When it finally went its own way to complete independence in 1931, after having long been a self-governing British colony, it did so without bitterness, bloodshed or devastation.

The first band of Americans fleeing north came in 1776 when Boston was evacuated by the British. Loyalists who had sheltered there under redcoat protection during the rebel siege were loaded aboard 170 ships in Boston Harbor and carried away in convoy before the city was surrendered to the patriot forces. It was, Abigail Adams reported, "the largest fleet ever seen in America."

These refugees were shipped to Halifax, Nova Scotia, where they disembarked with great anxiety and not a little confusion. Some effort had been made to prepare for their arrival, but the British did not yet know what was required in such circumstances. After landing, some of these boat people were reported to be "sitting upon the rocks, crying, not knowing where to lay their heads." Better provision was later made for them, but it was an experience which many who followed would share.

At that stage, the refugees, like those who had made for

England, were convinced their exile would be temporary, lasting only until the British Army again made America safe for law-abiding subjects of the king. Reports of humiliating setbacks suffered by Washington's army lifted loyalists' spirits and confirmed their belief that their sojourn in Canada would be brief.

But as month followed month without news of a rebel collapse, and when word spread that perfidious France had formed an alliance with the American rebels, a longer stay on alien soil seemed inevitable. Nor were hopes of an early return home encouraged by the flow of Americans who continued to head north into Canada, abandoning regions caught up in the fighting.

The second major wave of refugees came from northern New York at the close of 1777, an exodus of people fearing retribution for having sided with the British just before the rebel victory at Saratoga, and of others in the region who just wanted to escape the sounds and the sights of war. Parts of the area were virtually depopulated. The luckier refugees reached British protection at Quebec, where barracks were built for them and provisions provided until they could fend for themselves. Others had to fend for themselves from the start.

The stream of immigrants dwindled when the focus of the fighting shifted to the southern states at the end of 1778. But after the redcoat surrender at Yorktown three years later, when the final British capitulation was seen to be only a matter of time, the British authorities realized that more detailed arrangements had to be made, especially for the thousands of loyalists still sheltering under the king's protection in New York, Charleston and Savannah. A party of loyalists was dispatched from New York to explore likely settlement sites in southeastern Canada. The glowing reports they sent back reassured people who hadn't yet decided to take to their heels but who were beginning to see permanent exile as both inevitable and imminent.

Here was a place where a person could confidently start anew. Cattle and poultry were cheaper there than in the American states. Sawmills could be set up to exploit the vast timber resources. And fish practically leaped out of the sea onto fishing boats. It was a place where communities could be established and professional people could prosper. The depressing experiences of earlier refugees would not be repeated. Emigrating to Nova Scotia suddenly became an agreeable prospect in loyalist circles.

America had become a land of affliction for them. Canada was the land of the future.

As the refugees, lured on by the pleasing accounts of what awaited them, reached the wild, lonely, barren shores of Nova Scotia, they were, however, deeply apprehensive. It was nothing like what they had been led to believe. Trees had to be felled and brush had to be cleared before they could even pitch tents to provide immediate shelter. Despite what had been reported, the means of sustenance were not apparent on that strange coast. At the landing site across the bay, where the city of St. John would grow, there was little but woods and swamp.

One woman said that as she watched the sails of the ship which had brought her to Canada disappear in the distance, "such a feeling of loneliness came over me that though I had not shed a tear through all the war, I sat down on the damp moss with my baby on my lap and cried bitterly." Few of the refugees possessed more than the clothes they wore and the fear that they had made a dreadful mistake.

Reports of the plight of their absconded compatriots filtered back to Boston, where rebels took some satisfaction in hearing that loyalist traitors had been suitably rewarded by hardship in "Nova Scarcity." The British did by then provide them with provisions, but the help offered made conditions only a little less trying. The British system was to distribute full rations to refugees the first year, diminishing to one-third rations the third and last year, after which the refugees were expected to provide for themselves.

It wasn't easy for those whose habits and practices had never before included physical labor and who expected more from the British than they received. Having trouble finding enough food on which to survive, Polly Diblee, formerly of Stamford , Connecticut, wrote to her brother, who had sought refuge in London instead, "O gracious God, that I should live to see such times under the protection of a British government for whose sake we have done and suffered everything but . . . dying."

Nova Scotia was said to be overstocked with starved lawyers. Edward Winslow, a Massachusetts man whose forebears had reached America on the *Mayflower,* wrote, "We are monstrous poor, I have not a spade, hoe, axe or any article of any kind."[3] Winslow was saved from penury by being given a senior position in the British administration, but not many refugees had the connections he had.

The weather was also demoralizing. Nine months of winter each year and the phenomenon of fog that bit right through to the bones were an unsettling novelty, particularly for people from the South. No effort was made by these immigrants to pretend that Canada was the New Jerusalem some had predicted it would be. Rebels back home couldn't help rubbing it in:

Of all the vile countries that ever were known,
In the frigid or torrid or temperate zone,
From accounts I had there is not such another,
It neither belongs to this world nor the other.

It was, however, very much of this world, offering earthly satisfactions as well as misery. When the weather softened, it was a pleasant place in which to be—not yet home but safe and secure from the perils of battle and rebel persecution. What had been a sleepy fishing village on the southeastern tip of Nova Scotia blossomed into Shelburne, the fourth most populous city in North America, outranked only by Philadelphia, New York and Boston. The city of St. John also took root—though it would never fulfill forecasts that it would one day dwarf New York as a port.

Concerned about population growth in the region, the British, with uncharacteristic prudence, took a close look at the situation and made changes in light of their disastrous American experiences. Small colonies had proved less likely to be rebellious and rambunctious than big ones. Rather than permit Nova Scotia to expand as an administrative unit large enough to develop ideas above its station, they established a new, adjoining colony, New Brunswick, to accommodate new arrivals and the overflow from Nova Scotia of dissatisfied refugees who had first settled there. It was a harbinger of things to come.

The initial concentration of the American refugees in that far-southeastern part of Canada was inevitable. The region was closest and most accessible to the American states. But people who had moved there had carried with them the wanderlust that was part of the national character, as was the hunger for new opportunities, new land and new challenges. People grew restless, particularly in towns which, by the standards of the time, had become congested and often disorderly. The miniature metropolis of Shelburne (where petty crime and drunkenness aroused concern) had really been only a product of British aid to refugees. Not required to do much to sustain themselves, they took what was on offer and settled down to subsist on it. When the handouts dried up, most Shelburnites moved on, as did many others who had first come to rest elsewhere in that corner of Canada. Just like their kith and kin back in the United States, they were lured westward. They abandoned makeshift homes and incipient farms to seek out more elbow room and find their own way to a Canadian future.

It was not an easy way. During the "starving time," a shattering famine in the late 1780s, many refugees thought longingly of the farms and towns they had forsaken in the American states years before. People survived by eating wild plants and stripping bark from trees to supplement their meager diets. After some had died from eating poisonous roots, those farmers fortunate enough still to own a pig watched to see which roots it ate to determine which were edible and which were not. Stories are still told of how beef bones were passed from home to home for soup and of dozens of acres offered for a bushel of potatoes or wheat. Indians who had fled into Canada to escape the army of the Revolution were a great help, showing these struggling pioneers how to survive, how to tap the forests and streams of their new habitat for sustenance, until the time of famine passed and crops could be won from the soil again.

As refugees drifted from the Maritime Provinces to seek new territory and new prospects, they encroached on the land which had long been, and still is, the home of descendants of the original French settlers. These were a people with a rich, distinct culture which had little in common with American ways and attitudes. Some of the newcomers moving in among them adapted to their ways, but most had trouble adjusting to the "rigorous rules, homages and reservations, and restrictions of the French laws and customs, which are so different from the mild tenures to which they had ever been accustomed." The British took steps to separate them before their quaint differences turned into something more volatile. Inland to the west, they set up the province of Upper Canada, later to be called Ontario, to accommodate the wayward Americans and preserve the integrity of French Canada.

In the process, they established a precedent for a less boisterous, less no-holds-barred westward migration than the one gathering steam farther south, across the border.

The American refugees were, nevertheless, never easily regimented by the British authorities. Those who tried to assume command over them were repeatedly frustrated. Few of the settlers were inclined to submit to instructions on the roles they were expected to play or the tasks they were expected to perform. Even their own leaders had only limited influence over them. A British report told of a "very dangerous jealousy and want of confidence between the majority of the settlers and their late officers." One loyalist leader who found difficulty retaining his prominent position among them recalled his experience in Boston before he had fled Massachusetts and moaned, "This cursed republican town meeting spirit has been the ruin of us already."

Unlike some of his more timorous countrymen, the first royally appointed chief administrative officer of Upper Canada, a British general named John Simcoe, an Eton and Oxford man, did not believe that enough Americans had emigrated northward. Simcoe had commanded loyalist troops in battle during the Revolution and included the capture of Richmond among his successes. Even after he assumed his office in Canada eight years after the end of the war, he nurtured an unshakable hatred for American rebels. He remained convinced that most Americans had been bullied into independence and really wished they were still British. He intended to persuade these secret loyalists to turn their backs on the United States and settle up north where the king was still the king. To strengthen their desire to be restored to the bosom of the empire, he offered two hundred acres of land (sometimes more) to anyone who would come.

Americans swarmed in, though not all who came were motivated by renewed allegiance to the crown. Two hundred acres was a princely gift. Such generosity by the authorities was not being duplicated at home. In addition to land, Simcoe had his officials make food available for the new arrivals, and building materials and tools: "nails, hammers, gimlets, plains, chizzels, gouges, hinges, iron rimmed locks, padlocks, handsaws, C cut saws, broad axes, adzes, rub stones, whipsaws, window glass, carpenters tools, blacksmith tools, carpenters squares and compasses, hoes, spades, pick axes, plow shares, twine." And if all that wasn't enough, it was promised that the children of the settlers would be given sizable stakes of land of their own as soon as they came of age. Simcoe was determined to populate Upper Canada with Americans.

Not all of those who came in response to the inducements dangled before them were prepared for what was expected of them. Land and tools were provided, but men who had been shopkeepers and clerks in Massachusetts and Pennsylvania had to chop down trees for timber with which to build their homes and had to saw and chisel wood for the furniture with which to fill them. Women who had always acquired what they needed from stores learned to clothe themselves. Sheep were introduced, as much for wool as mutton. People learned how to turn animal hides into garments for protection against Canada's fierce winters, though little could be done against the swarms of mosquitoes and black flies in summertime. Little by little, villages grew, and towns and cities which would not wither away as Shelburne had done, and the people who lived in them were no longer former Americans, but Canadians through and through.

Americans kept streaming north for a long time after the war ended. "Late loyalists" kept arriving for two decades after the independence of the United States had been won. The nation they and the earlier loyalist immigrants did so much to construct was and remains, for better or worse, a less exciting, a less tempestuous, a less interesting place. It soon acquired many of the features of the land the loyalists forsook, including basic freedoms for the individual, democracy and equality before the law, but Canada was deprived of (or spared) the revolutionary experience. Unlike the Founding Fathers of the United States in the Declaration of Independence, its leaders never suggested they acted in accordance with the "Laws of Nature and of Nature's God." Their country, a Canadian historian commented recently, "never burdened itself with the extravagant expectations which are part of the American ideology." They expected to build no utopias on earth.

14

GHOSTS OF THE PAST

"Alas! gentlemen," cried Rip . . . , "I am a poor quiet man, a native of the place, and a loyal subject of the king, God bless him!"

Here a general shout burst from the bystanders—

"A Tory! A Tory! A spy! A refugee! Hustle him! Away with him!"

—WASHINGTON IRVING, "Rip Van Winkle"

In dealings with people, bygones are rarely bygones. Ghosts of the past, and especially the recent past, always haunt us. The wrongs rebels and loyalists inflicted on one another had bitten hard and deep, spawning vindictiveness that persisted in America long after the signing of the peace treaty in 1783.

Loyalists could no longer be deemed a threat to American independence. Those who had not sought to undermine or desert the Revolution, or who had remained quietly neutral in the struggle, had nothing to fear at home any longer, except possibly the occasional taunts of their neighbors. Many doubters and dissidents who had stayed in America had by then been swept along by the tide of patriotism which invariably accompanies national triumph. Some had even discreetly joined the Continental Army or state militias after Yorktown when the rebel victory was assured. People who were suspected of having until then been closet loyalists were treated with disdain, but nothing worse.

However, many loyalists who had sought out British protection, either within America or abroad, or who had fought under the banners of the king, were made to pay for the error of their ways. They were warned not to try to return to the homes from which they had fled. If they did go back, they often were frightened off with threats, and even physically assaulted.

Arthur Stansbury returned from Canada to Philadelphia, where he was greeted with an anonymous letter suggesting that while it would be impossible for him to live there again, he might easily soon die there. He settled finally in New York. In Woodbridge, New Jersey, Cavalier Jouet was chased out of town by a band of vigilantes who saw him on his way with whips and sticks. Loyalist Prosper Brown was seized in New London, Connecticut, strung up, beaten and fitted out with a "New England jacket" (tar and feathers) before being shoved onto a boat for New York with the advice that he never return. At dawn one morning, a South Carolina loyalist found a mob of local people at his doorstep, advising him it would be wise to put thirty miles between himself and his home by sunset. It was a warning he took seriously, having already seen some of his fellow loyalists paraded through town on horseback, face to tail, their coats turned inside out, bringing "great joy and satisfaction to the spectators." A New York man who went to see his parents at the town of Wallkill was tarred and feathered after his head and eyebrows had been shaved. There were lynchings too, mostly in places where loyalist marauders had visited fearsome acts of murder and destruction on civilians.

Newspapers helped sustain wartime animosities. A Boston paper suggested that anyone counseling magnanimity toward loyalists should be sent to join them in exile. A New Jersey paper told loyalists that, having shown their country no mercy, they deserved none themselves. Overtaken by the formation of new local government bodies, revolutionary committees which had flourished during the war were shorn of their reason for existing, but many continued to exist nonetheless, giving ground reluctantly and finding vigilance against American traitors an appropriate function. Loyalist David Colden of New York saw the situation prevailing in 1783 as desperate:

> The spirit of persecution and violence against the unhappy loyalists does not appear to abate to any degree since the cessation of hostilities. They are not suffered to go into the country even to take a last farewell of their relations. Com-

> mittees are formed throughout the country who publish the most violent resolves against the loyalists. . . . We are told that these committees have allarm'd the people in power who wish to suppress them, but know not how.[1]

Many town councils were also little inclined to let the hatreds of the war slip away into history. In historic Lexington, Massachusetts, it was decided that the welfare of the United States required that loyalists be prevented from returning and that confiscated loyalist property not be restored to its owners. People prepared to bury their differences with the British now that independence was secure frequently felt that the prospect of reconciliation with their humbled fellow Americans was loathsome and offensive. An enemy could be forgiven; a traitor, never.

Resolving the loyalist conundrum proved to be the most harrowing part of negotiating a final peace agreement between Britain and its former colonies. Even before the treaty had been negotiated, the British, though still securely entrenched in a few American strongholds, conceded defeat. Parliament resolved that it would consider "as enemies of His Majesty . . . all those who shall endeavour . . . further prosecution of offensive war on the continent of North America, for the purpose of reducing the revolting colonies to obedience by force." But it was anxious for a formal conclusion to the war. Despite the virtual cessation of hostilities, redcoats still engaged in defensive operations, and their presence in the United States remained both a threat of renewed warfare and a drain on the exchequer. The British also wanted very badly to see an end to the alliance between America and their traditional French adversaries.

Americans, anxious to begin making good the enormous disruptions and damage of the war, were equally ready for the struggle to be brought to an official halt. Their economy was in tatters. Their army, unpaid and disgruntled, was mutinous and in disarray. They resented the continued presence of redcoats in America. And there were still the machinery and trappings of an independent nation to construct and the fruits of the fight for liberty to gather in. Besides, they feared that their French allies, who had other irons in the fire, might yet negotiate a deal with the

British that might not include recognition of full independence for His Majesty's American colonies.

Both parties were, therefore, ready to work out a quick settlement. However, sharp differences on how the loyalists should be dealt with in the peace treaty produced complications. The Americans would have preferred to ignore the loyalists and their problems altogether. Still bitter about what they considered the loyalists' wartime treachery, and convinced that their activities and attitudes had prolonged the conflict, they were reluctant to make concessions that might be interpreted as accepting that renegades were worthy of sympathy or consideration.

But the British could not ignore or neglect Americans who had remained faithful to the crown, risking and losing so much in the process. Aside from the moral implications of their obligations to the loyalists, if they ignored their plight they could not reasonably call on the loyalty of the king's subjects in other British colonies. The British negotiators were, therefore, instructed by their government to make recognition of American independence conditional on considerate treatment for the loyalists. Among other things, there would have to be a payoff by the United States to them for property that had been destroyed or seized by local authorities or individuals in the various states during the war.

The American negotiators needed no instructions from Congress to reject that demand. "After the harm they have done," Benjamin Franklin snorted, "it was imprudent to insist on our doing them good."[2] Franklin shrewdly suggested, however, that if Britain was willing to cede Canada to the United States, the proceeds might go to establishing a fund from which loyalist compensation might be derived. But, having lost so much of North America already, the British had no intention of losing the part of it they retained.

They pressed the American negotiators on the compensation question and received in reply the explanation that it was really a matter for the individual American states, while the negotiators could speak only for Congress. If the British insisted on something to show for their pleadings on behalf of the loyalist Americans, the best they could get—and they ultimately settled for it—was a commitment that Congress would "earnestly recommend" to the states that they "provide for the restitution of all estates, rights and properties which have been confiscated." In addition, there were to be no further confiscations, imprisoned loyalists were to be released, and loyalists were to be given an opportunity to reclaim money owed them in America before the war.

When word of these proposed treaty provisions reached the loyalists in British enclaves in America, it aroused nothing but contempt. They were convinced the assurances those provisions contained were no more than empty words. They saw them as a device which permitted the British to evade their responsibilities, leaving it to the triumphant rebels, who couldn't care less, to fulfill obligations solemnly agreed to. Whether Congress would or would not "earnestly recommend" that the states be kind to loyalists didn't really matter. To recommend was one thing; to make happen was another. The British still held New York, Charleston and Savannah as well as several western outposts. It gave them a strong bargaining hand, but still they failed to extract from the shrewd and obstinate American negotiators (Franklin, John Adams and Jay) binding guarantees for the loyalists, who were, as a result, deeply resentful:

'Tis an honour to serve the bravest of nations,
And be left to be hanged in their capitulations.

A New York loyalist newspaper indignantly noted that "even robbers, murderers and rebels are faithful to their fellows and never betray each other." Bitterness, irony and sarcasm earned the loyalists nothing. The peace treaty would soon be signed, the redcoats would soon depart, and loyalists ensconced in British-controlled sanctuaries in America had to decide what to do. The British offered to evacuate free of charge all loyalists who had sheltered in occupied areas for at least a year, but advertisements for passage to England and Canada began to appear in loyalist newspapers, as did announcements of sales of personal furniture and other belongings too cumbersome to carry abroad. Lawyers spread word that they were ready and able to look after the American interests of people who felt obliged to leave the country. New York tavern keepers who had extended credit to their loyalist regulars took to reminding them that it was getting to be time to settle up.

The departure of loyalists who chose to emigrate at war's end (mostly to Canada) was orderly. It was also a painful process. A British officer at the evacuation of Charleston in December 1782 wrote, "There are old, grey-headed men and women, husbands and wives with large families of little children, women with infants at their breasts, poor widows whose husbands had lost their lives in the service of their king and country, with a dozen half starved bantlings tugging at their skirts." No sooner had they been evacuated, he reported, than the rebels

> like so many furies . . . entered the town . . . The loyalists [who had not departed] were seized, hove into dungeons, prisons and provosts. Some were tied up and whipped, others were tarred and feathered. Some were dragged to horse-ponds and drenched till near dead . . . All of the loyalists were turned out of their houses and obliged to sleep in the streets and fields . . . and twenty-four reputable loyalists were hanged.

Loyalists were quickly proved right in supposing that the individual states would not feel bound by the terms of the peace agreement. Even where voices were raised for magnanimity and charity, the residue of wartime bile was great. In Virginia it was pointed out that, peace agreement or no peace agreement, all debts to loyalists, for which the treaty said they might claim post-war payment, had been canceled by law during the conflict and could not be revived. As for restitution for seized or destroyed loyalist property, Virginians said it would have to wait until the British or the loyalists made restitution for the great number of slaves who had been stolen or induced to flee from their rightful masters during the war.

In New Jersey, loyalist property was still up for sale at public auction for years after the peace treaty had been ratified. Such confiscations and sales continued in other places as well. The excuse was sometimes offered that their owners had been indicted for treason during the war and had not returned to stand trial.

New York's assembly passed a law holding loyalist and British occupiers of rebel property during the war responsible for back rent and the cost of damage repair. Some states drew up blacklists of loyalists charged with high treason, virtually daring them to return to reclaim property. Pennsylvania's blacklist contained the names of more than four hundred men, many of whom had been owners of large estates in the colony. Few of them returned to risk the consequences. Ultimately the British accepted responsibility for loyalist losses, reviewed the claims made by loyalists, and gradually made at least partial resititution. America's refusal to do so was considered a violation of the peace agreement and gave the British an excuse for holding on to western outposts they had been obliged by the treaty to surrender. The question of restitution caused friction and diplomatic squabbling between America and Britain for several years after the Revolution.

The passion for revenge was not unanimously shared among Americans. Many felt that refusal to put aside past rancor, hatred and vindictiveness only marred the beginnings of the American nation. It only complicated the grave problems with which the new nation had to cope. It was pointed out that among the loyalists were many who could make important contributions to rebuilding the damage done in the war and to helping the nation expand into the welcoming western wilderness. Patrick Henry sought to use reason to convince those of his countrymen who were bent on vengeance:

> We have . . . an extensive country, without population. What can be a more obvious policy than that this country ought to be peopled . . . ? Let us have magnanimity . . . to lay aside our antipathies and prejudices, and consider the subject in a political light. Those are enterprising, moneyed people.[3]

General Benjamin Lincoln warned, "We are not only driving from us many men who might be very useful but we are obliging them [the loyalists who had fled to Canada] to people Nova Scotia,"[4] which was British and which could prove a future threat to the new nation. General Greene said, "It would be the excess of intolerance to persecute men for opinions which, but twenty years before, had been the universal belief of every class of society."[5]

Others also tried to coax Americans to turn their backs on wartime memories and forgive and forget. They pointed out that it was especially important to lure back to their cities and states merchants who had fled to British enclaves or to England and who would be useful in restoring shattered local economies. Reviewing the loyalist problem generally, Alexander Hamilton declared, "We have already lost too large a number of valuable citizens."

* * *

Some loyalists did return to America to find they were neither persecuted nor prosecuted. Peter Van Schaak returned from England and vowed to be as "good a subject of the new government as I ever was of the old." Loyalist newspaper publisher James Humphreys returned without trouble to Pennsylvania. Philip Key, uncle of Francis Scott Key who wrote the national anthem, not only returned to Maryland without difficulty, though he had served as an officer in a loyalist fighting unit, but later was elected to Congress by his home district. Although some returnees to Massachusetts had less agreeable experiences and the town authorities of other communities had at first been urged to join with Boston in banning loyalists, William Paine returned without fuss to that city and later founded the American Antiquarian Society there. Other Bostonian loyalists also discovered they could, sooner or later, return and come to terms without serious difficulty with the city and country from which they had fled.

Gradually the hatreds of the war years diminished across the country and antiloyalist laws were permitted to lapse, though some returnees did not easily adjust to the changes which had occurred. He was not molested, but Samuel Curwen, who had longed for his native land while in England, found his hometown of Salem no longer to his liking: "By plunder and rapine some few have accumulated wealth, but many more are greatly injured in their circumstances; some have to lament over the wreck of their departed wealth and estates, of which pitiable number I am; my affairs having sunk into irretrievable ruin." Curwen was also unhappy because some among those who had been "meaner people" earlier had now become "almost the only men of power, riches and influence." Among the upstarts, he named the Cabots, of whom, some time later, it would be suggested that they were so exalted in society that they spoke only to God.

Other loyalist Americans who could have returned from exile, if not immediately, then soon afterward, chose not to. A lucky few took up royal appointments in British imperial outposts to earn their keep. Such a man was Samuel Quincy, one of the distinguished Boston Quincys, amongst whom were numbered prominent rebels. As a crown counsel in Boston in 1773, Quincy had prosecuted the British soldiers involved in the Boston Massacre. He went on to the British colony of Antigua from London, to serve in the customs service there. He could not face returning to Massachusetts to occupy a less honored place in society than the one that had once been his. "I am too proud," he confessed, "to live despised where I was once respected."

Exiles who remained in England subsisted on pensions or on British compensation for their lost American property. Their children grew up, were absorbed into British life and culture, and shared none of the ties their parents had once had with America. Some became distinguished Englishmen. The son of Boston artist John Singleton Copley, though born in Massachusetts three years before his family went off with him to Britain, became lord chancellor of England. It was not difficult for the children to adjust to their new identities. But many of the adults remained refugees in thought and spirit, pining the rest of their lives for the homes they had forsaken an ocean away.

For loyalists who had fled to Canada, so close to the United States, the situation was different. Few of the tens of thousands who had gone there had either pensions or valuable property in America for which they could claim compensation from the British. Some of them found the going too tough. They grew homesick and pined after families they had left behind. In time, a small but significant trickle back across the border developed. To this day, descendants of some Americans who had made for Canada during or shortly after the Revolution but who later filtered back can be found with roots now firmly planted in the northeastern tier of American states, within an hour or two of the sanctuary to which their ancestors had briefly fled.

But, for many decades, loyalists who remained in Canada continued to think of their native land, and of the rebels who had driven them from it, with great bitterness. During the War of 1812, when a Canadian regiment composed of loyalists met an American regiment in battle, a Canadian transplanted from Connecticut discovered that an American he had just shot dead was his brother. He showed no regret. "Served him right," he said, "for fighting for the rebels when all the rest of his family fought for King George."[6]

15

WHAT PRICE GLORY?

I asked him if he fought because of the oppression of the British government. He said he had never noticed it. Whether it was because of the stamp tax? He had never seen a stamp. Whether it was because of tea? He said he had never drunk a cup of tea in his life. Whether it was because of the doctrines of Sidney and of Locke? He said he had never heard of them. Then why had he fought at Lexington? Because, he said, we had always governed ourselves. We always meant to. They didn't mean we should.

—Conversation with a minuteman who had faced the British at Lexington in 1775, from *New York in the American Revolution*, by Wilbur C. Abbott.

The Declaration of Independence catalogues a long list of grievances against the king of England—his suppression of the legal and natural rights of Americans, his obstruction of the administration of justice in America, his clamp-down on American commerce. But if it had been only a question of the actual impact of Britain's misdeeds—the taxes, trade restrictions and other high-handed acts of the king and his ministers—there would have been no Revolution.

Much that was set down in the Declaration of Independence was highly inflated legalistic backup, designed to justify a course of action based on principle rather than on fact. As has been noted elsewhere, in drafting that monumental document Thomas Jefferson was not writing history; he was making it.

British transgressions against the liberties of the king's American subjects had been undeniable. But they had been no greater, and often less troubling, than those that would occur when America was independent and Americans appointed their own officials, came before their own courts, and contended with their own lawmen. Britain's attempt to control America's economy for its own profit and advantage was presumptuous and unacceptable. But, for all the fury it aroused, the damage done was insignificant.

People in the colonies cried out in genuine anguish about the suppression of their rights and the restraint of their trade. But despite the reputation Americans have for being the only people in the western world resistant to doctrine and dogma, who demand proof before they believe anything, it was blind belief rather than fact which brought them onto the field of battle and kept some of them there for years. Despite their personal experience to the contrary, at a time when they were freer than the people of any other nation on earth, they had been convinced they were being enslaved. They were sufficiently outraged by this illusion to go to war, and to pay the price the war extracted.

Casualty figures for the War of Independence can only be rough estimates. Accurate counts could not always be taken, though figures were quoted for many of the battlefield encounters. Two hundred Americans were killed in the battle of Long Island; two hundred more at Brandywine; two hundred and fifty at Camden. But those who died in actual combat consitituted only a fraction of the fatalities of the war. Far more troops died from wounds, disease and exposure in their encampments or on the move. Continental Army surgeon James Thacher said it was estimated that seventy thousand American servicemen died in the conflict, but that seems to be a great exaggeration, perhaps credible to Thacher because of his own horrific experiences in the struggle.

It is more likely that the war claimed the lives of about 25,000 troops* of the Continental Army and rebel militias—one in every eight who served in the patriotic forces in the war, and one in

* That figure is quoted by Howard H. Peckham in *The Toll of Independence*, a detailed study of American casualties in the war.

every hundred Americans. That includes those who died while prisoners of the British, many of whom were viciously mistreated. It does not, however, include Americans who died fighting for the British. It is estimated that the loyalists lost more than three hundred dead at the battle of King's Mountain, North Carolina, alone. In view of the rate of desertion before, during and after military operations, it is pointless to try to calculate how many men went missing in action. Calculations of how many civilians were killed, mostly in raids by loyalist or rebel guerrillas and in Indian attacks, can also be little more than guesses.

The losses in the war were sorely felt for long years afterward. They were reflected in the great number of widows and fatherless children in many parts of the country. Populations of some regions were decimated. In Tryon County, New York, thousands of farms were left uncultivated (many of them abandoned by fleeing loyalists).

There were countless places where every house, every barn had been burned to the ground. New Jersey was ravaged by Hessian mercenaries. Norfolk was set ablaze. So was Charleston. So were New London and Norwalk, Connecticut, and dozens of smaller towns and villages. Much of the Rhode Island coast was ravaged. Georgia would have to wait until the Civil War before it would again be as devastated as it was by the British and by rival American forces during the war.

Nor were the benefits of victory immediately recognizable. The financial cost of the war had been immense. For years afterward, people who had complained about British taxes had to pay taxes for postwar reconstruction, settling of war debts and growth of independent government vastly in excess of those they had known before. To satisfy tax requirements, some Americans had to watch their homes and property disposed of at forced sales for fractions of their value.* In 1787, a Boston man lamented that taxes were robbing the people of "the fruits of liberty." A leader of tax resisters in Virginia vowed that rather than permit tax laws to be enforced, he would take up his musket and fight. To be a tax collector was a hazardous profession, particularly in the back country, where people believed that townsfolk, who had greater

* During the war, George Washington had been forced to sell some of his property in Virginia to pay the taxes on the property he retained.[1]

say in devising tax laws, were making things easier for themselves.

The economy of the country lapsed into deep and demoralizing doldrums. Three years after the war, exports from the enterprising New England states were one quarter of what they had been a year before the war. Offshore fishing slumped to such an extent that some Massachusetts fishermen emigrated to England in order to pursue their trade more profitably. In the South, the departure of thousands of slaves did not end slavery, but it severely disrupted the plantation economy. Everywhere, people who had borrowed inflated money were required to pay it back in disinflated currency worth many times the original sum.

It also seemed as though democracy wasn't the grand and glorious thing it was supposed to be. A Connecticut newspaper grumbled, "Every man wants to be a judge, a justice, a sheriff, a deputy, or something else which will bring him a little money, or what is better, a little authority." People who thought "equality" meant that the rich would not retain privileged status were disappointed to see that they did nevertheless. At the same time, fears were aroused that "democracy" meant that the politics of the mob would undermine ordered society. Even old radical conspirator Samuel Adams warned "there may be danger of errors on the side of the people."[2] Militia and federal troops had to be called out in 1786 when armed rebellion in Massachusetts, led by a former Continental Army captain, Daniel Shays, showed that some people believed the Revolution had morally justified armed insurrection against the authorities whenever grievances had to be redressed—in this case, against property foreclosures and the requirement that debts be paid in hard money.

The American nation might well have had a less spectacular genesis. The ability of the recalcitrant colonies to force the British to withdraw the most far-reaching tax it had imposed on Americans, and the growing popular objections within Britain to its America policies, showed how shaky was that country's resolve to keep a tight grip on the colonies. The financial strains on the British Treasury, even before it was called upon to finance a full-scale war three thousand miles away, would have made the prospect of extensive operations to keep the colonies under control unpalatable to the British government had American radicals not forced the pace.

The prewar dispatch of British troops to occupy disobedient Boston was considered pointless by many British politicians. "A great many redcoats will never govern America," Edmund Burke told Parliament. The taxes the British extracted from Americans were hardly worth the cost of collecting them. The belated willingness of the British, at the height of the war, to offer Americans all they had originally wanted, self-rule under the crown, showed how flimsy British resistance would have been to sustained nonviolent pressure by Americans to take charge of their own domestic affairs (as they had already begun to do) and shape their own destiny. A "revolution" in the relationship with the mother country was inevitable—but war, slaughter and devastation (and glory) were not.

If, instead of holding out for full independence, Americans had been prepared to settle for the status of self-governing colonies, how long would they have been willing to tolerate even such a limited subservient position? The experience of Canada and Australia might provide a clue. Both these countries, which still retain close links with Britain but which developed distinctive national identities, were content to pledge allegiance to the British crown till well into the twentieth century. The liberties of Canadians and Australians were not restricted by their colonial status, nor were they, as individuals, denied the protection of the law or equality under the law. They both developed democratic forms of government early on.

Victory in the War of Independence was an exhilarating moment far beyond America's own shores. Details were considered irrelevant. It was the bigger picture which mattered. In the last analysis, youthful exuberance, fighting the good fight in the name of liberty, had outlasted and vanquished superannuated despotism. Daring imagination had swept away the cobwebs of dreary, unfeeling tradition. A cluster of ordinary men had routed a bevy of noble lords. "I will!" had ousted "May I?" Never before had freedom and the personal worth of each and every person been so widely broadcast that even tyrants and rogues felt obliged to borrow the vocabularies associated with those admirable concepts.

In Germany, the poet Goethe, deeply moved, said, "America, you are more fortunate than our continent." In France, whose own revolution would be launched six years after American independence was won, Mirabeau called the Declaration of Independence a "sublime manifesto." In England, a parliamentary committee urged the curtailment of the authority of the king, pointing the way toward eventual relegation of the monarchy to mostly figurehead status. In other places too, the words and sentiments which inspired American independence captured the imagination and stirred the hopes of people.

In many ways, America and the world would be poorer and drearier if Americans had recognized in 1775 that they already enjoyed much of what the rebel leaders believed they were striving for. America would be a less bouyant, less dynamic land if the patriotic forces pressing for independence in 1776 had been thwarted. Had America, its right to govern itself largely conceded, remained within the British Empire, its development would have proceeded along much different lines, and not simply because the Royal American Dragoons rather than the United States Cavalry would have galloped to the rescue when needed.

The impact of the libertarian convictions of people like Thomas Jefferson, Patrick Henry, John Adams and Benjamin Rush would have been strongly felt. They represented the principles and views of an energetic, forceful, imaginative minority. But the residue of British administrative practices, and the influence of loyalists who would not have felt impelled to go into foreign exile, would have had a moderating influence on the character and on the peopling of the American hinterland, making it a less headstrong, less turbulent experience, with momentous implications for the development of American attitudes.

The country's historic sense of destiny, reflected in Tom Paine's pronouncement that the cause of America is "in great measure the cause of all mankind," would not have been so sharply honed. No reason would have been found to formulate the constitutional right for Americans to keep and bear arms so that, like the Minutemen in the Revolution, they could rise quickly to the defense of their country, and the gun culture would not be as deeply ingrained in the American experience as it is today.

Having less of a tradition of making their rules as they went along, Americans might have developed less spontaneous, less impulsive response mechanisms in dealing with problems that arise. From the dismal confusions and heroic exploits of the Revolution, from the lofty ideals and wretched disappointments, from the protracted agony and ultimate victory, there emerged in the American character a spirit of *can do,* a confidence in the capacity to overcome the most formidable of obstacles and emerge from the challenge untarnished and unbowed. From the realities and myths which attended the beginnings of the United States of America there sprang a persisting dream of triumph and glory just around the corner.

A peaceful resolution of differences with Britain might have had even more far-reaching historical consequences. Some years before the Revolution, Benjamin Franklin said he had "long been of the opinion that the foundation of the future grandeur and stability of the British empire lie [*sic*] in America."[3] He was not alone in that belief. Daniel Leonard, a Boston loyalist who later fled to England, had a similar vision:

> After many more centuries shall have rolled away, long after we, who are now bustling on the stage of life have been received to the bosom of mother earth, and our names are forgotten, the colonies may be so far increased as to have the balance of wealth, numbers and power in their favor. The good of the empire may make it necessary to fix the seat of government here, and some future George, equally a friend of mankind with him that now sways the British sceptre, may cross the Atlantic and rule Great Britain by an American Parliament.[4]

It is hard to imagine a transplanted British monarch long retaining his crown in the New World. But what a remarkable America that would have been, encompassing Canada as well as the United States and numbering the English, the Scotch, the Welsh and possibly the Irish among its far-flung peoples, unless, of course, they chose to rebel against real or imagined American tyranny and succeeded in doing so.

NOTES

Chapter 1
LESS THAN GLORY

1. Huntington, *Letters,* 87.
2. Burnett, *Continental Congress,* 317.
3. Sabine, *The American Loyalists,* 33.
4. Miller, *Origins,* 265. See also Mary Augustina, *American Opinion of Roman Catholicism.*
5. Brown, *The King's Friends,* 124.
6. Royster, *A Revolutionary People at War,* 365.

Chapter 2
THE ROOTS OF REBELLION

1. Burnett, *Letters,* I, 98.
2. Sabine, *The American Loyalists,* 67.
3. Jensen, *The Founding of a Nation,* 33.
4. Shy, *A People Numerous and Armed,* 16.
5. Miller, *This New Man, The American,* 450.

Chapter 3
THE ROAD TO WAR

1. Speech by Senator Hoar in Boston, March 18, 1901, when dedicating a monument commemorating the British evacuation of the city in 1776.
2. Nelson, *The American Tory,* 116.
3. Schlesinger, *Birth of a Nation,* 228.
4. Miller, *Origins,* 207.
5. Granger, *Political Satire,* 42.
6. Jensen, *The Founding of a Nation,* 145.
7. For newspaper sensationalism see Schlesinger, *Prelude to In-*

dependence, and Davidson, *Propaganda and the American Revolution.*

8. Adams, *Works,* II, 507.

Chapter 4
CONCLAVE OF PATRIOTS

1. Burnett, *Continental Congress,* 45.
2. Commager and Morris, *The Spirit of 'Seventy-Six,* I, 55.
3. Mitchell, *The Price of Independence,* 42.
4. Burnett, *Continental Congress,* 317.
5. Montross, *Reluctant Rebels,* 10.
6. Burnett, *Continental Congress,* 36.
7. *Ibid.,* 52.
8. Adams, *Works,* II, 327.
9. Burnett, *Continental Congress,* 25.
10. Adams, *Works,* I, 154.
11. Jensen, *Founding of a Nation,* 490.
12. Tyler, *Literary History of the American Revolution,* I, 482.
13. Burnett, *Continental Congress,* 138.
14. Adams, *Works,* I, 209.
15. Montross, *Reluctant Rebels,* 145.
16. Rakove, *The Beginnings of National Politics,* 114.
17. Mitchell, *The Price of Independence,* 43.
18. Montross, *Reluctant Rebels,* 291.
19. Hart, *American History Told by Contemporaries,* II, 544.
20. Rakove, 158.
21. Montross, *Reluctant Rebels,* 213.
22. *Ibid.,* 195.
23. Burnett, *Letters,* II, 147.
24. Montross, *Reluctant Rebels,* 222.
25. Burnett, *Continental Congress,* 317.
26. Hart, II, 591.
27. Montross, *Reluctant Rebels,* 257.
28. Rakove, 205.

Chapter 5
AMERICA'S FIRST ARMY

1. Montross, *Rag, Tag and Bobtail,* 466.
2. Commager and Morris, *The Spirit of 'Seventy-Six,* I, 61.

3. Trevelyan, *The American Revolution,* II, 39.
4. Huntington, *Letters,* 78.
5. Barck and Lefler, *Colonial America,* 604.
6. Bowman, *The Morale of the American Revolutionary Army,* 19.
7. Cumming and Rankin, *Fate of the Nation,* 228.
8. Miller, *The Triumph of Freedom,* 237.
9. Bowman, *The Morale of the American Revolutionary Army,* 68.
10. Van Tyne, *England and America,* 136.
11. Bowman, 14.
12. Royster, *A Revolutionary People at War,* 85.
13. Commager and Morris, I, 152.
14. Montross, *Reluctant Rebels,* 203.
15. Freeman, *George Washington,* III, 570.
16. Van Tyne, *England and America,* 133.
17. Freeman, IV, 7.
18. Bowman, 41.
19. Trevelyan, III, 516.
20. Shy, 188.
21. Freeman, IV, 570.
22. *Ibid.,* IV, 576.
23. Lecky, *The American Revolution,* 401.
24. Mackesy, *The War for America,* 350.
25. Miller, *Triumph of Freedom,* 330.
26. Jefferson, *Papers,* IV, 700.

Chapter 6
THE COMMANDER UNDER FIRE

1. Fitzpatrick, *George Washington Himself,* XI.
2. Freeman, *George Washington,* IV, 586.
3. Royster, *A Revolutionary People at War,* 179.
4. Fitzpatrick, 173.
5. Roche, *Joseph Reed,* 98.
6. Fitzpatrick, 276.
7. Miller, *Triumph of Freedom,* 256.
8. Burnett, *Continental Congress,* 284.
9. Fitzpatrick, 339.
10. Davidson, *Propaganda and the American Revolution,* 318.

Chapter 7
LIFE, LIBERTY AND THE PURSUIT OF SOMETHING ELSE

1. Miller, *Triumph of Freedom,* 447.
2. Burnett, *Continental Congress,* 410.
3. *Ibid.,* 420.
4. Becker, *Revolution, Reform and the Politics of American Taxation,* 164.
5. Brown, *Good Americans,* 89.
6. Thacher, *A Military Journal,* 236.
7. Bezanson, *Prices and Inflation During the American Revolution,* 54.
8. Montross, *Reluctant Rebels,* 354.
9. Harrell, *Loyalism in Virginia,* 26.
10. Royster, *A Revolutionary People at War,* 272.
11. Miller, *Triumph,* 477.

Chapter 8
THE SILENCED MAJORITY

1. Brown, *The King's Friends,* 131.
2. Van Tyne, *The Loyalists in the American Revolution,* 17.
3. Shy, *A People Numerous and Armed,* 13.
4. Van Tyne, *Loyalists,* 65.
5. Norton, *The British-Americans,* 21.
6. *Ibid.,* 21.
7. Montross, *Reluctant Rebels,* 215.
8. Eddis, *Letters from America,* 110.
9. Tyler, *Literary History of the American Revolution,* II, 54.
10. *Pennsylvania Journal,* March 1, 1775.
11. Hart, *American History Told by Contemporaries,* II, 471.
12. Norton, 25.
13. Hyman, *To Try Men's Souls,* 82.
14. Van Tyne, *Loyalists,* 317.

Chapter 9
THE KING'S LOYAL AMERICAN FIGHTING MEN

1. Callahan, *Royal Raiders,* 225.
2. Moore, *Diary of the American Revolution,* II, 261.
3. Dwight, *Travels,* III, 491.

Chapter 10
A MUFFLED BLACK DAWN

1. Foner, *Blacks in the American Revolution,* 33.
2. Locke, *Anti-Slavery in America,* 50.
3. Quarles, *The Negro in the American Revolution,* 15.
4. *Ibid.,* 19.
5. *Ibid.,* 119.
6. Mazyck, *George Washington and the Negro,* 84.
7. Miller, *The Triumph of Freedom,* 510.

Chapter 11
THE TOMAHAWK FACTOR

1. Graymont, *The Iroquois in the American Revolution,* 72.
2. Washington, *Writings,* II, 219.
3. Burnett, *Continental Congress,* 97.
4. Lecky, *The American Revolution,* 264.
5. Graymont, 190.
6. Commager and Morris, *The Spirit of 'Seventy-Six,* II, 998
7. Graymont, 192.

Chapter 12
SAD SANCTUARY

1. Brown, *The King's Friends,* 271.
2. Howard, *Preliminaries of the Revolution,* 319.
3. Curwen, *Journals and Letters,* 49–54.
4. Nelson, *The American Tory,* 159.
5. Callahan, *Flight from the Republic,* 111.
6. Curwen, 151.
7. Callahan, *Flight,* 106.

Chapter 13
THE WAY NORTH

1. Boatner, *Encyclopedia of the American Revolution,* 662.
2. Brebner, *Neutral Yankees of Nova Scotia,* 291.
3. Wrong, *Canada and the American Revolution,* 418.

Chapter 14
GHOSTS OF THE PAST

1. *American Historical Review* XXV, October 1919.
2. Einstein, *Divided Loyalties,* 232.
3. Meade, *Patrick Henry,* 263.
4. Brown, *Good Americans,* 176.
5. *Ibid.,* 177.
6. *Ibid.,* 212.

Chapter 15
WHAT PRICE GLORY?

1. Robert A. Becker, *Revolution, Reform and the Politics of American Taxation,* 122.
2. Wood, *The Creation of the American Republic,* 67.
3. Simmons, *The American Colonies,* 319.
4. Van Tyne, *The War of Independence,* II, 32.

BIBLIOGRAPHY

There are countless books on the American Revolution, covering all aspects of that momentous event. A selected bibliography of works consulted during research for *Less Than Glory* follows. But for those who believe, as does the author, that such bibliographies can sometimes prove to be quicksand for readers who wish to pursue specific points that have been raised in a study of this kind, here is a shortened list of works, extracted from that bibliography, which proved particularly instructive.

For a general overview of the Revolution: Commager and Morris's excellent selection of source materials in *The Spirit of 'Seventy-Six,* Tyler's *The Literary History of the American Revolution,* Jensen's *The Founding of a Nation,* Miller's *The Triumph of Freedom,* Shy's *A People Numerous and Armed* and Rakove's *The Beginnings of National Politics.* The studies by Lecky and Trevelyan are classic British interpretations of the Revolution.

On the origins and causes of the Revolution: Schlesinger's *Prelude to Independence,* Miller's *The Origins of the American Revolution* and Maier's *From Resistance to Revolution.*

On the workings of the Contintental Congress: Burnett's *The Continental Congress* and *Letters,* Montross's *Reluctant Rebels* and Meigs's *The Violent Men.*

On the revolutionary army: Bowman's *The Morale of the American Revolutionary Army,* Bolton's *The Private Soldier*

Under Washington, Royster's *A Revolutionary People at War,* as well as the writings of Washington and Freeman's monumental biography of the commander in chief.

On Washington under attack: again Washington's writings and Freeman's biography, Fitzpatrick's *George Washington Himself,* Knollenberg's *Washington and the Revolution,* and the chapter "The Conway Cabal" in Miller's *The Triumph of Freedom.*

On the revolutionary economy of the United States: Bezanson's *Prices and Inflation,* Ferguson's *The Power of the Purse* and Becker's *Revolution, Reform and the Politics of American Taxation.* Also Schlesinger's *The Colonial Merchants and the American Revolution.*

On the loyalists: The study which first restored those Americans who opposed the Revolution to a measure of dignity was Van Tyne's *The Loyalists in the American Revolution.* Other rewarding studies are Brown's *The Good Americans* and *The King's Friends* and Sabine's *The American Loyalists.* For the attitudes and activities of loyalists in specific regions of the fledgling American nation, see the books of Harrell, De Mond, Coleman, Flick and Stark.

On loyalists who fought actively against the Revolution: The article by Raymond is an excellent introduction. Other works offering details on King George's loyal American fighting men are Callahan's *Royal Raiders* and Smith's *Loyalists and Redcoats.*

On blacks in the Revolution: Quarles's *The Negro in the American Revolution,* Foner's *Blacks in the American Revolution* and Locke's *Anti-Slavery in America.*

On Indians and the Revolution: Graymont's *The Iroquois in the American Revolution* and O'Donnell's *Southern Indians in the American Revolution.*

On the loyalist refugees in England: Samuel Curwen's *Journals* provide particularly moving insight into their experiences and feelings. Also Norton's *The British-Americans* and Nelson's *The American Tory.*

On loyalists in Canada: Wrong's *Canada and the American Revolution* and Bradley's *United Empire Loyalists.*

On the price Americans paid for the Revolution: Peckham's *The Toll of Independence* is dryly statistical but tells a harrowing tale. See also the books by Ferguson and Robert Becker.

* * *

Abbott, Wilbur C. *New York in the American Revolution.* New York: Scribner's, 1929.

Abernethy, Thomas P. *Western Lands and the American Revolution.* New York: Appleton-Century, 1937.

Adams, Charles Francis (ed.). *Familiar Letters of John Adams and His Wife, Abigail Adams, During the Revolution.* New York: Hurd & Houghton, 1876.

Adams, John. *A Biography in His Own Words,* ed. J. B. Peabody. New York: Newsweek, 1973.

———. *Papers,* ed. R. J. Taylor, 4 vols. Cambridge, Mass.; Belknap Press, 1977–79.

———. *The Works of John Adams,* ed. Charles Francis Adams, 10 vols. Boston: Little, Brown, 1851–56.

Alden, John Richard. *A History of the American Revolution.* London: Macdonald, 1969.

———. *The South in the Revolution.* Baton Rouge: Louisiana State University Press, 1957.

Andrews, Charles M. *The Colonial Background of the Revolution.* New Haven: Yale University Press, 1924.

Aptheker, Herbert. *The Negro in the American Revolution.* New York: International Publishers, 1940.

Bailyn, Bernard. *The Ideological Origins of the American Revolution.* Cambridge, Mass.: Belknap Press, 1967.

Bakeless, John. *Turncoats, Traitors and Heroes.* Philadelphia: Lippincott, 1960.

Barck, O. T., and H. T. Lefler. *Colonial America.* New York: Macmillan, 1958.

Becker, Carl. *The Declaration of Independence.* New York: Harcourt, Brace, 1922.

Becker, Robert A. *Revolution, Reform and the Politics of American Taxation.* Baton Rouge: Louisiana State University Press, 1980.

Beloff, Max. *Debate on the American Revolution.* London: Nicholas Kage, 1949.

Bezanson, Anne. *Prices and Inflation During the American Revolution.* Philadelphia: University of Pennsylvania Press, 1951.

Billias, George Athan (ed.). *George Washington's Generals.* New York: Morrow, 1964.

Boatner, Mark Mayo III. *Encyclopedia of the American Revolution.* New York: David McKay, 1976.

Bolton, Charles K. *The Private Soldier Under Washington.* New York: Scribner's, 1902.

Booth, Sally S. *Seeds of Anger.* New York: Hastings House, 1977.

Bowman, Allen. *The Morale of the American Revolutionary Army.* Washington: American Council on Public Affairs, 1943.

Bradley, Arthur G. *United Empire Loyalists.* London: Thornton, Butterworth, 1932.

Brebner, J. B. *Neutral Yankees of Nova Scotia.* Toronto: McClelland & Stewart, 1969.

Bridenbaugh, Carl. *Rebels and Gentlemen.* New York: Reynal & Hitchcock, 1942.

Brown, Wallace. *The Good Americans.* New York: Morrow, 1969.

———. *The King's Friends.* Providence: Brown University Press, 1966.

Buel, Richard. *Dear Liberty.* Middletown, Conn.: Wesleyan University Press, 1941.

Burnett, Edmund Cody. *The Continental Congress.* New York: Macmillan, 1941.

———. *Letters of Members of the Continental Congress,* 8 vols. Washington: Carnegie Institute, 1921–36.

Callahan, North. *Flight from the Republic.* Indianapolis and New York: Bobbs-Merrill, 1967.

———. *Royal Raiders.* Indianapolis and New York: Bobbs-Merrill, 1963.

Coburn, Frank W. *The Battle of April 19, 1775.* Port Washington, N.Y.: Kennikat Press, 1970.

Coleman, Kenneth. *The American Revolution in Georgia.* Athens, Ga.: University of Georgia Press, 1955.

Commager, Henry Steele, and Richard B. Morris. *The Spirit of 'Seventy-Six,* 2 vols. Indianapolis and New York: Bobbs-Merrill, 1958.

Craig, G. M. *Upper Canada.* Toronto: McClelland & Stewart, 1963.

Cumming, William P., and Hugh F. Rankin. *The Fate of the Nation.* London: Phaidon, 1975.

Cunliffe, Marcus. *George Washington.* London: Collins, 1959.

Curwen, Samuel. *The Journals and Letters of Samuel Curwen.* New York: C. S. Francis and Co., 1842.

Davidson, Philip. *Propaganda and the American Revolution.* Chapel Hill: University of North Carolina Press, 1941.

De Mond, Robert. *Loyalists in North Carolina.* Durham, N.C.: Duke University Press, 1940.

Dorfman, Joseph. *The Economic Mind in American Civilization.* New York: Viking, 1946.

Douglass, Elisha. *Rebels and Democrats.* Chapel Hill: University of North Carolina Press, 1955.

Dwight, Timothy. *Travels in New England and New York,* 3 vols. New Haven, 1821–22.

East, Robert. *Loyalist Americans.* Tarrytown, N.Y.: Sleepy Hollow Publications, 1975.

Eddis, William. *Letters from America.* Cambridge, Mass.: Belknap Press, 1969.

Einstein, Lewis. *Divided Loyalties.* Boston: Houghton Mifflin, 1916.

Ferguson, E. James. *The Power of the Purse.* Chapel Hill: University of North Carolina Press, 1961.

Fitzpatrick, John C. *George Washington Himself.* Indianapolis: Bobbs-Merrill, 1933.

Flexner, James Thomas. *George Washington.* Boston: Little, Brown, 1965.

Flick, Alexander Clarence. *Loyalism in New York During the American Revolution.* New York: Columbia University Press, 1901.

Foner, Philip S. *Blacks in the American Revolution.* Westport, Conn.: Greenwood Press, 1975.

Force, Peter (ed.). *American Archives,* Fifth Series. Washington: M. St. Clair Clarke and Peter Force, 1848–53.

Franklin, J. H. *From Slavery to Freedom.* New York: Knopf, 1964.

Freeman, Douglas Southall. *George Washington,* 6 vols. New York: Scribner's, 1948–54.

Fulton, Richard M. *The Revolution That Wasn't.* Port Washington, N.Y.: Kennikat Press, 1981.

Gipson, L. H. *The Coming of the Revolution.* New York: Harper, 1954.

Granger, Bruce. *Political Satire in the American Revolution.* Ithaca, N.Y.: Cornell University Press, 1960.

Graymont, Barbara. *The Iroquois in the American Revolution.* Syracuse, N.Y.: Syracuse University Press, 1972.

Greene, Evarts Boutell. *The Revolutionary Generation.* New York: Macmillan, 1943.

Haight, Canniff. *Before the Coming of the Loyalists.* Toronto: Haight and Co., 1897.

Hancock, Harold. *Loyalists in Revolutionary Delaware.* Newark, Del.: University of Delaware Press, 1977.

Hansen, Marcus Lee. *The Mingling of the Canadian and American Peoples.* New Haven: Yale University Press, 1940.

Harrell, Isaac S. *Loyalism in Virginia.* Durham, N.C.: Duke University Press, 1926.

Hart, Albert B. *American History Told by Contemporaries,* 5 vols. New York: Macmillan, 1897–1929.

Higginbotham, Don. *The War of American Independence.* New York: Macmillan, 1971.

Howard, George Elliott. *Preliminaries of the Revolution.* New York: Harper, 1904.

Huntington, Ebenezer. *Letters Written During the American Revolution.* New York: privately printed, 1914.

Hyman, Harold. *To Try Men's Souls.* Berkeley: University of California Press, 1959.

Jameson, John F. *The American Revolution Considered as a Social Movement.* Princeton: Princeton University Press, 1926.

Jefferson, Thomas. *The Papers of Thomas Jefferson,* ed. Julian P. Boyd, 20 vols. Princeton: Princeton University Press, 1950–82.

Jensen, Merrill. *The Founding of a Nation.* New York: Oxford University Press, 1968.

Jones, Thomas. *The History of New York During the Revolutionary War.* New York: New-York Historical Society, 1879.

Jordan, Winthrop. *White Over Black.* Chapel Hill: University of North Carolina Press, 1968.

Ketchum, Richard M. *The Winter Soldiers.* New York: Doubleday, 1973.

Knollenberg, Bernhard. *Washington and the Revolution.* New York: Macmillan, 1940.

Labaree, Leonard. *Conservatism in Early America.* Ithaca, N.Y.: Great Seal Books, 1948.

Lecky, William Edward. *The American Revolution.* New York: Appleton and Co., 1932.

Livermore, George. *An Historical Research Respecting the Opinions of the Founders of the Republic on Negroes as Slaves, as Citizens, as Soldiers.* Boston, 1862.

Locke, Mary. *Anti-Slavery in America.* Cambridge, Mass.: Radcliffe College, 1894.

Mackesy, Piers. *The War for America.* London: Longmans, 1964.

Maier, Pauline. *From Resistance to Revolution.* New York: Knopf, 1972.

Main, Jackson T. *The Social Structure of Revolutionary America.* Princeton: Princeton University Press, 1965.

Mary Augustina, Sister. *American Opinion of Roman Catholicism.* New York: Columbia University Press, 1936.

Mazyck, Walter H. *George Washington and the Negro.* Washington: Associated Publishers, 1932.

Meade, R. D. *Patrick Henry.* Philadelphia and New York: Lippincott, 1957.

Meigs, Cornelia. *The Violent Men.* New York: Macmillan, 1949.

Middlekauff, Robert. *The Glorious Cause.* New York: Oxford University Press, 1982.

Miller, John C. *The Origins of the American Revolution.* London: Faber and Faber, 1945.

———. *This New Man, The American.* New York: McGraw-Hill, 1974.

———. *The Triumph of Freedom.* Boston: Little, Brown, 1948.

Mitchell, Broadus. *The Price of Independence.* New York: Oxford University Press, 1974.

Montross, Lynn. *Rag, Tag and Bobtail.* New York: Harper, 1952.

———. *The Reluctant Rebels.* New York: Harper, 1950.

Moore, Frank. *Diary of the American Revolution,* 2 vols. New York: The Zenger Club, 1861.

Moore, George H. *Notes on the History of Slavery in Massachusetts.* New York, 1866.

Morgan, Edmund S. and Helen. *The Stamp Act Crisis.* Chapel Hill: University of North Carolina Press, 1953.

Nelson, William H. *The American Tory.* Oxford, Eng.: Oxford University Press, 1961.

Nevins, Allan. *The American States During and After the Revolution.* New York: Macmillan, 1924.

Norton, Mary Beth. *The British-Americans.* London: Constable, 1974.

O'Donnell, James. *Southern Indians in the American Revolution.* Knoxville, University of Tennessee Press, 1973.

Peckham, Howard H. *The Toll of Independence.* Chicago: University of Chicago Press, 1974.

Quarles, Benjamin. *The Negro in the American Revolution.* Chapel Hill: University of North Carolina Press, 1961.

Rakove, Jack N. *The Beginnings of National Politics.* New York: Knopf, 1979.

Rankin, Hugh F. *The American Revolution.* London: Secker and Warburg, 1964.

Raymond, W. O. *Loyalists in Arms.* New Brunswick Historical Society Collections, No. 5, 1904.

Rezneck, Samuel. *Unrecognized Patriots.* Westport, Conn.: Greenwood Press, 1975.

Roche, John F. *Joseph Reed.* New York: Columbia University Press, 1957.

Royster, Charles. *A Revolutionary People at War.* Chapel Hill: University of North Carolina Press, 1979.

Sabine, Lorenzo. *The American Loyalists.* Boston, 1847.

Sachse, William L. *The Colonial Americans in Britain.* Madison: University of Wisconsin Press, 1956.

Schachner, Nathan. *Thomas Jefferson.* New York: Appleton-Century-Crofts, 1951.

Scheer, George F., and Hugh F. Rankin. *Rebels and Redcoats.* New York: New American Library, 1971.

Schlesinger, Arthur Meier. *The Birth of the Nation.* New York: Knopf, 1969.

———. *The Colonial Merchants and the American Revolution.* New York: Columbia University Press, 1918.

———. *Prelude to Independence.* New York: Knopf, 1966.

Shy, John W. *A People Numerous and Armed.* New York: Oxford University Press, 1976.

Simmons, R. C. *The American Colonies.* London: Longmans, 1976.

Smith, Paul H. *Loyalists and Redcoats.* Chapel Hill: University of North Carolina Press, 1964.

Sosin, Jack M. *The Revolutionary Frontier.* New York: Holt, Rinehart & Winston, 1967.

Stark, James. *The Loyalists of Massachusetts.* Boston: J. H. Stark, 1910.

Thacher, James. *A Military Journal.* Boston: Cottons and Barnard, 1827.

Trevelyan, George Otto. *The American Revolution.*, 3 vols. London: Longmans, 1899–1907.

Tyler, Moses Coit. *The Literary History of the American Revolution,* 2 vols. New York: G. P. Putnam's Sons, 1897.

Van Doren, Carl. *Secret History of the American Revolution.* New York: Viking, 1941.

Van Tyne, Claude Halstead. *England and America.* Cambridge, Eng.: Cambridge University Press, 1927.

———. *The Loyalists in the American Revolution.* New York: Macmillan, 1902.

———. *The War of Independence.* Boston: Houghton Mifflin, 1922.

Wallace, Willard. *Appeal to Arms.* New York: Harper, 1951.

Ward, Christopher. *The War of the Revolution,* ed. John Richard Alden, 2 vols. New York: Macmillan, 1952.

Washington, George. *The Writings of George Washington,* ed. Worthington Chauncey Ford, 14 vols. New York: G. P. Putnam's Sons, 1889–93.

Wood, Gordon S. *The Creation of the American Republic.* Chapel Hill: University of North Carolina Press, 1969.

Wrong, George M. *Canada and the American Revolution.* London: Macmillan, 1928.

INDEX